America Discovers C. S. Lewis

America Discovers C. S. Lewis

His Profound Impact

K. Alan Snyder

WIPF & STOCK · Eugene, Oregon

AMERICA DISCOVERS C. S. LEWIS
His Profound Impact

Copyright © 2016 K. Alan Snyder. All rights reserved. Except for brief quotations in critical publications or reviews, no part of this book may be reproduced in any manner without prior written permission from the publisher. Write: Permissions, Wipf and Stock Publishers, 199 W. 8th Ave., Suite 3, Eugene, OR 97401.

Wipf & Stock
An Imprint of Wipf and Stock Publishers
199 W. 8th Ave., Suite 3
Eugene, OR 97401

www.wipfandstock.com

PAPERBACK ISBN: 978-1-4982-9820-9
HARDCOVER ISBN: 978-1-4982-4771-9
EBOOK ISBN: 978-1-4982-9821-6

Manufactured in the U.S.A.   JULY 27, 2016

Quotations from the letters, books, and essays of C. S. Lewis are by the permission of the Lewis Company.

Quotations from Walter Hooper's documents, "Personal Testimony" (originally titled "Rockingham CC"), "Editing Lewis," and an e-mail from Hooper to K. Alan Snyder are by the permission of Walter Hooper.

This book is dedicated to someone I don't remember: that person who first either mentioned the name C. S. Lewis to me or who first recommended one of his books. Although I don't remember you, God does, and I hope we shall meet again when we dwell in His presence.

"It was a very deep friendship on my part: no man ever did so much to shape my mind, quite aside from Christianity, which of course shaped my whole life. I have never loved a man more. And I must believe, from things he said and wrote to me, that he felt both friendship and affection for me. . . . After this severe and splendid letter, I loved Lewis like a brother. A brother and father combined."

Sheldon Vanauken, *A Severe Mercy*

Table of Contents

Preface | *ix*
Acknowledgments | *xiii*
Introduction | *xv*
Chapter 1—C. S. Lewis and America | 1
Chapter 2—Chad Walsh: A Baptized Imagination | 16
Chapter 3—A Story of Joy . . . and Grief | 26
Chapter 4—Walter Hooper: Keeper of the Flame | 48
Chapter 5—The Academy and the Ministry | 64
Chapter 6—Writing to Americans | 108
Chapter 7—The C. S. Lewis Societies | 138
Chapter 8—The Surveys | 151
Chapter 9—Conclusion: The C. S. Lewis Impact on America | 173

Bibliography | 189
Index | 193

Preface

ON THE MORNING OF 27 March 1951, Clive Staples Lewis wrote letters to two Americans. This was becoming a near-daily routine ever since his popular works began to be published across the Atlantic in the mid-1940s. The number of letters he received from Americans started as a trickle, but by 1951, they were escalating into a steady stream. Yet, despite the pressures he already faced as an Oxford tutor, and from the publishing deadline for his long-promised volume for the series *The Oxford History of English Literature*, he felt an obligation to respond to each one. His letters on this day were for Americans with whom he had already established a regular correspondence.

Vera Mathews of Beverly Hills, California, in her last letter, had informed Lewis of the death of her father. He offered sympathy, of course, but he seemed to have caught a whiff of an illusion in her comments. He was direct and sympathetic simultaneously, noting that she had to be careful not to act as if it hadn't happened. It matters when people close to us die, he counseled, and he hoped she would not pretend otherwise.[1]

The other letter was addressed to Warfield M. Firor, a rather famous surgeon and faculty member at Johns Hopkins in Baltimore. Firor can legitimately be called the first of Lewis's regular American correspondents, having written to him since 1945. Lewis considered Firor a heavenly gift to himself and to his fellow Inklings at Oxford for his continued assistance in sending food packages—especially hams—during postwar rationing. Firor kept inviting Lewis to America, but Lewis always begged off, citing his multiple duties. But they did meet. Firor made a trip to Britain in 1949 and spent an evening and a morning with his Oxford friend. Letters between

---

1. Letter from Lewis to Vera Mathews, 27 March 1951, Hooper, *Collected Letters*, Vol. III, 103–4.

them after that meeting had become more substantial, with Lewis often reflecting on life, old age, and the nature of true worship.

On this day, though, 27 March 1951, the letter was more mundane, with comments on the weather. Yet, as with the letter to Vera Mathews, death was one of the topics. Lewis had taken care of an elderly woman, Mrs. Janie King Moore, for a couple of decades. She was particularly feisty in her old age, and her insistent demands had practically worn him down over the previous years. She went into a nursing home in 1950, and then died early in 1951. Lewis's comments on her death to Firor in the letter of the 27th seemed to indicate he was relieved of a great burden. His attitude may seem a little harsh to the uninitiated reader, but it reflects a realistic outlook on life and can be taken out of context, forgetting how he willingly submitted to serving her every need for all those years. Lewis didn't want to be a hypocrite and express a deep grief that he didn't really feel.[2] He could now relax and concentrate on other matters.

Lewis went about his routine the rest of that day, unaware that in a small town in northern Indiana—a place he would never even know existed—a child was born on that same 27 March 1951. That, in itself, is not an essential part of the C. S. Lewis story, but since I was that child, it has some importance to me.

I grew up in Bremen, Indiana, population roughly four thousand, surrounded by corn fields and a significant Amish community, half a world away from Oxford and in an entirely different environment. My parents had never read any of Lewis's works; there was nothing in my background to lead me in that direction. By the end of the decade of the 1950s, I could ride a bike and fill my bike's basket with books from our local public library, a feat I accomplished consistently. Already, before the age of ten, I was a voracious reader. Yet I never borrowed anything in the library by C. S. Lewis. All of his Narnia books had been published by then, but if they were in that library, they never crossed my path, and my affinity for fantasy/science fiction reading surely would have aroused my interest if I had seen them.

Since I knew nothing of Lewis in 1960, I was unaware that his wife, Joy, had died that July. It would have had no meaning in my young life. When Lewis himself died on 22 November 1963, again I took no notice. But I wasn't alone—the whole world was startled and anxious over the death of another man that the world deemed more consequential. As the president of the United States, John F. Kennedy, was placed in his grave shortly afterward, so was C. S. Lewis. Today, which of those two is of greater

---

2. Letter from Lewis to Warfield M. Firor, 27 March 1951, ibid., 104–6.

significance? I would argue that Lewis has influenced more American lives since his death than has the former president.

So when did I first make an acquaintance with Lewis? It might have been in high school, but if so, the memory is dim. Sometime during my college years, though, he entered my world, and in a big way. I don't recall which of Lewis's books I read first. Was it *The Screwtape Letters*? That's possible. Or perhaps it was *Out of the Silent Planet*, followed by *Perelandra* and *That Hideous Strength*, the so-called Space Trilogy that would have appealed to my science fiction bent. Then there was *The Great Divorce*, which fascinated me as I followed Lewis's fantasy bus trip from hell to heaven. I also recall, although faintly, that I delved into some of his more substantive treatises to help bolster my burgeoning Christian faith. I think *The Problem of Pain*, *Miracles*, and *The Abolition of Man* were added to my reading list during those years at Purdue University.

My degree program at the time was radio, television, and film production. For my final project in my television directing course, I chose a scene from *The Great Divorce*. My staging for the scene was simple: two spotlights—one on the inhabitant of heaven, the other on the visitor from hell—and dialogue straight from the book as the heavenly man tries to convince the "Episcopal Ghost" to join him in the joys of God's presence. The Ghost puts him off, remembering that he has to be back the next Friday to deliver a paper to his little Theological Society in hell (which he doesn't recognize as hell, so deceived he has become). I enjoyed the project, and as an evangelical, I also intended it as a witness to the truth, hoping it would make my fellow students contemplate their own relationship with God. Lewis became one of my mentors in the faith.

The years have passed quickly (as people my age invariably say) and my respect for Lewis has only increased over time. Pushed to the back burner of my thoughts—due to so many other obligations as a professor of history—was the idea of a book of some kind that I could write about Lewis. The desire was present, but I just wasn't sure what it could be.

While on a cruise ship in March of 2013, I was reading Alister McGrath's recent biography of Lewis. Near the end, he made a statement about Lewis and Americans that stuck in my mind: "Lewis has always been appreciated more in the United States than in England."[3] That one sentence sparked a thought: Why hasn't anyone written a book specifically focused on the impact Lewis made on Americans? I tucked that thought away for a more opportune time.

---

3. McGrath, *C. S. Lewis, A Life*, 369.

Opportunity opened its arms when my university granted a sabbatical for research and writing for the academic year 2014–2015. I had more than one project on the table for that year, but the Lewis possibility loomed larger as that year approached. When I traveled to Wheaton College to research at the Billy Graham Center for a collaborative venture with a colleague, I also took the opportunity to experience what the Marion E. Wade Center might have to offer. I knew it was the repository for Lewis's papers and all things Lewis (as well as six other British authors), so I spent three of my days burrowing into whatever the Wade had on Lewis's influence on Americans. They were three glorious days, as I found excellent material and confirmation that a book on this topic remained to be written.

The Wade Center then worked with me to collect testimonies from Americans on how they first encountered Lewis, which of his books were most influential on their lives and thinking, and their analysis of the value of his many writings. In addition, the Center put me in touch with Walter Hooper, one of the few people still alive who knew Lewis personally and who worked closely with him during the last months of his life. A chapter on Hooper is included in this volume, so I won't spend time here expanding on his lifelong labor of joy to ensure Lewis's works would never be forgotten. I'll simply say that his willingness to communicate with me on this project, and his sharing of personal insights, was tremendously helpful.

Why another book on C. S. Lewis? When a scholar finds a niche that has not yet been fully explored, it is a worthwhile enterprise to begin that exploration. This book contains the testimonies of many Americans who have found Lewis to be a faithful guide for their Christian life. May this volume provide greater light on the man who has shown so many the light of Christ and the path His followers must take.

Acknowledgments

My thanks to the Marion E. Wade Center at Wheaton College, and, in particular, archivist Laura Schmidt, who not only helped me find the resources I needed in Wade's collections, but who also actively promoted my survey of how Lewis has impacted Americans. She ensured the survey got the maximum exposure on the Wade website and through its Facebook page. That survey proved invaluable for gauging Lewis's influence in the lives of those who responded to the survey.

I also was blessed to have the generous help of Walter Hooper, who was Lewis's close companion/secretary for those summer months in 1963 prior to Lewis's heavenly promotion. Mr. Hooper sent me information and encouraged my quest for tracing Lewis's reception in the United States. His painstaking collection of Lewis's correspondence, running into three large volumes, proved invaluable, as I could sit in the comfort of my own study and pore through those letters daily. Truly, Walter Hooper has been the keeper of the flame.

The reason I had the time to spend scouring Lewis's correspondence was due to the sabbatical I received from Southeastern University in 2014–2015. After twenty-five years of devoted teaching at Christian colleges and universities—usually with a teaching load of four-plus courses per semester—the sabbatical was a welcome relief. It also was a time of reflection on how God has used the life of one man—C. S. Lewis—to affect so many others over many decades. Studying Lewis only added to my devotional life as each day brought new thoughts and meditations on God's truths.

My introduction into the world of Lewis followers, via the C. S. Lewis Foundation, has provided me with a clearer understanding of this community. When I was invited to present a paper at the Academic Roundtable at one of the Foundation's retreats, it marked my entry into this particular Lewis community. I seek to know my fellow pilgrims on the Lewis path better over the next few years.

I appreciate Wipf & Stock Publishers for recognizing the value of a scholarly work that would attract a certain audience, and that audience consists in a burgeoning number of people, not all scholars by any means, who love what Lewis has to offer. Even though I have called my book a scholarly work, I trust it is written in a way that will appeal to a more general readership as well.

Finally, I have the distinct privilege of being married to a woman who not only has put up with my dreams and visions—both fulfilled and unfulfilled—for forty-four years, but who, as a professional editor herself, put that skill into practice by combing through this manuscript with a fine eye for anything that seemed awry. It is a better product because of her diligence. So, Jan Snyder, thank you for a lifetime of helping and encouraging.

I have always wanted to write about Lewis. That is now one of those fulfilled visions. I hope that after reading this book, my readers will be glad that vision found its fulfillment.

Introduction

NEW C. S. LEWIS books are published regularly. Yet, even with all the new books on this favorite Christian author, some aspects of his life and writings have received scant attention. Among those is the enduring influence of Lewis on the American public generally and the evangelical subculture specifically. There is no way to quantify that influence, but we can amass as much evidence as possible in the way of letters written by Lewis to Americans, reviews of his works, both apologetic and fiction, by his American audience, and testimonies from Americans whose lives have been touched by his words. That is what this study purports to do.

Chapter one looks at the relationship between Lewis and America. What was his attitude toward Americans and their country? Did it change over time? What did he like about the land he never got around to visiting and what did he critique about it? What conclusions can we reach about his views on Mother England's former colony?

The second chapter introduces Chad Walsh, an English professor at Beloit College in Wisconsin, the first American to write a book-length treatment of Lewis's thought. In fact, Walsh was the first person, American or not, to do so. We discover that he not only met Lewis but became good friends with him.

Joy Davidman Gresham Lewis enters the story in chapter three. An American Jewish woman who rejected religion entirely, she committed herself to the communist vision for the future in her younger days, only to become disillusioned with that false worldview over time. C. S. Lewis filled the vacuum, showing her the way to the true faith. That relationship, which began in letters, blossomed eventually into marriage with Lewis, transforming his bachelor existence in his later years. The joy of that journey together was tested by the pain of cancer and her death, but their marriage is a testament to the essence of a love inspired by God.

How can one know Lewis personally for only a few months yet feel as if one has known him for many years? Walter Hooper experienced that as a young American who arrived in Oxford to meet with Lewis for only one afternoon but ended up being a close friend and companion who went on to edit Lewis's works and ensure he would not be forgotten by future generations. His story is the subject of chapter four.

Lewis became friends as well with a number of other academics on the other side of the Atlantic. Some he met in person, others only by letter. He helped fashion their Biblical worldviews, and they returned the favor by publicizing his works in America. Clyde Kilby of Wheaton College is a prime example; Sheldon Vanauken, who met Lewis at Oxford University and then returned to teach in an American college, is another. There is a second generation that knew not Lewis, but that owes him a great intellectual and spiritual debt. That generation is also examined in chapter five, along with representatives from American evangelicals who have depended a great deal on Lewis for their respective ministries. Charles Colson, caught in the Watergate net as a high-ranking member of the Nixon administration, read *Mere Christianity* and committed his life to the Lord, resulting in the worldwide ministry of Prison Fellowship. Colson's journey to faith is recounted in this chapter.

Chapter six delves into the letters Lewis wrote to a number of regular American correspondents over the years. Most of these correspondents are not well known, but Lewis's patient commitment to helping them understand better the essentials for living a victorious Christian life is central to his responses. He met those correspondents wherever they were along the Christian path and sought to lead them further. This sixth chapter also includes some of his most poignant letters to American children, most of whom contacted him after reading The Chronicles of Narnia books.

Chapter seven details three organizations in America that were established as a result of their appreciation for Lewis's works: the New York C. S. Lewis Society; the C. S. Lewis Institute; and the C. S. Lewis Foundation. Their ongoing ministries testify to the impact that Lewis's legacy continues to have on Americans. The Foundation even bought Lewis's Oxford home, the Kilns, and has made it a study center for visiting Americans.

Surveys of Americans to deduce how Lewis has influenced their lives form the substance of chapter eight. Two of those surveys, conducted in 1986 and 1996, simply asked for testimonies. The final survey, taken in 2014, expands the questions answered by the respondents and provides an even greater insight into how contemporary Americans view their C. S. Lewis experience.

The ninth, and concluding, chapter offers some analyses by Lewis experts on the extent of his impact on America and reasons for his popularity.

After reviewing what the experts say, I close with my own personal evaluation of their insights.

C. S. Lewis's popularity, primarily among evangelicals, but also into other segments of American society, is a topic that has been broached only occasionally and not at length. This study corrects that oversight and, hopefully, provides some new perspectives not only on the history of his contact with Americans, but also on his continuing impact on a country he never had the opportunity to see in person.

1

C. S. Lewis and America

ON THE VERY FIRST page of *The Narnian: The Life and Imagination of C. S. Lewis*, author Alan Jacobs tells the story of a precocious "Jack" Lewis, probably no more than eight years old at the time, entering his father's study to make this following pronouncement: "I have a prejudice against the French." Naturally, his father, Albert, wanted to know why his younger son would have such a definite opinion. The answer he received is perhaps an indication of the astute reasoning that would continue to be a hallmark throughout C. S. Lewis's life: "If I knew *why*," he calmly asserted, "it would not be a prejudice."[1] Early on, then, it appears that Lewis had a clear understanding of the unreasonable nature of coming to conclusions about people without evidence.

James T. Como, editor of a volume now renamed *Remembering C. S. Lewis: Recollections of Those Who Knew Him*, remarks that stories have always circulated about Lewis being antagonistic toward Americans. One story Como mentions in particular has Lewis turning down an invitation to speak to an American audience, and adding a rather spiteful twist to the refusal by writing his response on a piece of toilet paper. The only problem with the story, Como notes, is that it never happened; there is no evidence for it. Como then comments, "Lewis is not on record as possessed of an antagonism toward Americans."[2]

One perhaps might be excused for thinking Lewis had a dislike for America—and Americans—if all one had to go on were early statements prior to his conversion. Firsthand contact with Americans was minimal

1. Jacobs, *The Narnian*, 1.
2. Como, *Remembering C. S. Lewis*, 11.

in his life until he became famous in America, during World War II. After that, though, as his correspondence with Americans became nearly a flood, one sees instead a man who treats people as individuals, and not as stereotypes. It is instructive to witness this metamorphosis over time and trace not only Lewis's changing attitude toward America but also his impact on individual Americans.

Early Comments

As one studies Lewis's voluminous correspondence, one notices the first mention of America appears in a letter just prior to his eighteenth birthday to lifelong friend and Belfast neighbor Arthur Greeves. As might be expected, given his later career as a professor of literature, Lewis indicates to Greeves that he is beginning to read some American authors, singling out Nathaniel Hawthorne, whom he admires. Yet he thought it a shame that someone of Hawthorne's genius had to be an American.[3] His seeming distaste for America surfaced again less than two months later when writing to his brother, Warnie, who had apparently made a negative comment about Woodrow Wilson. He agreed with Warnie's analysis of the American president.[4] A year and a half later, as World War I was winding down, Lewis complained to his father that America now was taking the lead internationally, putting Britain in a seemingly secondary role.[5]

When Lewis returned to Oxford after the war to resume his studies, he commented on the increasing number of Americans on campus, calling it an invasion.[6] He related a story to his father about a professor who read a paper at a literary meeting and who acknowledged his effort wasn't all that good; he thought he needed to apologize for even offering it. He had meant to publish it, he told the group, but felt it was so bad that he sent it to an American magazine instead. Lewis found that appropriately amusing.[7]

In a 1927 letter to Warnie, Lewis offers another complaint about Americans. He attempts to convince Warnie to read Charles Dickens's *Martin Chuzzlewit*, and notes that Dickens and Warnie have a lot in common in their mutual disdain for America.[8] In another letter to Warnie, three

---

3. Letter from Lewis to Arthur Greeves, 19 November 1916, Hooper, *Collected Letters, Vol. 1*, 259.
4. Letter from Lewis to Warren Lewis, 8 January 1917, ibid., 266.
5. Letter from Lewis to Albert Lewis, 10 October 1918, ibid., 405.
6. Letter from Lewis to Albert Lewis, 27 May 1923, ibid., 608.
7. Letter from Lewis to Albert Lewis, 21 January 1921, ibid., 517.
8. Letter from Lewis to Warren Lewis, 3 September 1927, ibid., 727.

months later, he praises James Russell Lowell, the American Romantic poet. One of the features he likes about Lowell is that he appears to hate his own fellow citizens.[9]

All of these comments emanate from a pre-Christian Lewis. This doesn't mean that his conversion necessarily changed all of his thinking about Americans, but slowly, over time, he got to know more Americans on a personal basis, and those views were tempered accordingly. There is at least one discordant commentary, though, about the later Lewis, from his former student and good friend George Sayer. In his biography of Lewis, which is largely praised as one of the best, if not the very best, Sayer includes an account of Lewis's first meeting with Joy Davidman Gresham, later to become, of course, Joy Lewis. What stands out, in Sayer's testimony, is his reference to a continuing anti-American attitude in Lewis. Sayer says Lewis was "delighted by her bluntness and her anti-American views." He goes on to say that Lewis liked this exchange with Joy about America because it fit well "with his own anti-American prejudice." Sayer adds, "I remember his saying to me when I was his pupil, 'What are you doing, going around with the Americans?'"[10] Sayer was a student of Lewis's in the 1930s. Did he conflate an earlier Lewis with the later one? What evidence exists to show that Lewis, by the time he met Joy for the first time, had changed his views about Americans? A review of his attitude toward America through an examination of his correspondence with Americans, in particular, may help resolve any quandary about this.

Getting to Know Americans

C. S. Lewis was already a middle-aged man of forty-five before he became known to many Americans, and before he began a constant correspondence with them. In fact, that steady stream of correspondence didn't start until he was nearly fifty. His Christian writings began in 1933 with *The Pilgrim's Regress*, which was largely unknown in America at that time. Neither did many Americans get acquainted with *Out of the Silent Planet*, the first installment of his Space Trilogy, which appeared in 1938. A few American scholars critiqued his *The Allegory of Love*, a highly regarded study of love in the Middle Ages that was published in 1936, which was not meant for a general audience. Neither did his first apologetic work, *The Problem of Pain*, have an American edition in 1940, at its first publication. It wasn't until the American edition of *The Screwtape Letters* appeared in 1943 that his fame

9. Letter from Lewis to Warren Lewis, 12 December 1927, ibid., 743.
10. Sayer, *Jack*, 214–15.

leapt over the Atlantic. That introduction to the writings of C. S. Lewis then triggered a spate of American editions of all of his works by the late 1940s.

Probably the first real American scholar Lewis ever sat down and talked seriously with was Paul Elmer More, a critic and philosopher who had taught at both Harvard and Bryn Mawr College and had then devoted himself to journalism and to the writing of books. More came to Oxford in 1933, where he and Lewis talked philosophy. Lewis wasn't able to develop a long-term relationship with More, as he died in 1937. Yet, more than two decades later, reflecting back on More, he recalled a wonderful time of conversation with him; he considered More to be quite wise and humorous.[11]

Early knowledge of Lewis in America misidentified him as a Catholic. In *The Pilgrim's Regress*, he had allegorically called the representative of Christianity "Mother Kirk." That language led to the misidentification. When the *Presbyterian Guardian* reviewed the book in 1936, the reviewer, Henry Welbon, while praising Lewis's exposure of false philosophies, incorrectly called him a Catholic. Welbon sent Lewis his review and asked for more information about him; his reply set the record straight as to his Anglican affiliation. There was not another Protestant and/or evangelical review of any of Lewis's writings for another seven years.

When Lewis engaged E. M. W. Tillyard in a debate on poetry, which was published in 1939 as *The Personal Heresy*, the American Catholic writer Thomas Merton reviewed the book in the *New York Times*. Historian Mark Noll considers this review the most "intriguing" of American responses to Lewis's early literary work. Merton, says Noll, recognized the theological message in Lewis that others were slower to realize.[12]

Then came *The Screwtape Letters*. Chad Walsh, an English professor at Beloit College in Wisconsin, who became the first American to write a book about Lewis, described the impact that slim volume had in America:

> In America . . . Lewis's wide reputation began all at once in 1943 when the American edition of *The Screwtape Letters* was published. The combination of urbanity, wit, imagination and uncompromising orthodoxy caught the imagination of many reviewers and a large reading public. . . . It had been a long time . . . since this combination of passionate faith and wit had been available. And it contrasted mightily with the dull or heavily strident works of most religious writers. A certain snob quality may have entered into the appeal of *The Screwtape Letters*. Here at last was a religious book, indeed a specifically Christian book,

---

11. Letter from Lewis to Corbin Scott Carnell, 10 December 1958, Hooper, *Collected Letters, Vol. III*, 994.

12. Noll, "C. S. Lewis in America, 1932–1945."

written with such sophistication and elegance that one need not apologize for leaving it out on the coffee table.[13]

In April 1944, *Saturday Review* did a cover story on him, and soon after reviewed *The Great Divorce*. *His* magazine, produced by InterVarsity Christian Fellowship, began to include abridgements of some of Lewis's writings and offered positive notices. The *Westminster Theological Journal*, organ for the conservative Presbyterians, also showed interest. In both cases, they concentrated on his expositional works, not *Screwtape* or the Space Trilogy.

Letters started arriving from America. One of the earliest, and most amusing, came from Walnut Creek, California, from a group calling itself The Society for the Prevention of Progress. The letter was an invitation for Lewis to become a member, and asking him to send his credentials so they might determine if he would be qualified for membership. In the same spirit as the original letter, he responded that he felt he probably was a member of any society so-named just by the fact of his birth. He hoped that his "unremitting practice of Reaction, Obstruction, and Stagnation" and his *The Abolition of Man* would suffice to make him a member in good standing.[14]

More serious letters also arrived. One came from Charles A. Brady, professor of English at Canisius College, a Catholic institution in Buffalo, New York. Brady sent Lewis two articles he had written in the Jesuit periodical *America*: "Introduction to Lewis" and "C. S. Lewis II." Both articles were laudatory, and Lewis responded not only with gratitude but with a compliment of his own when he told Brady that he was the only reviewer thus far who fully grasped what he was trying to communicate in his books. Brady, Lewis felt, had become an authority on his writings; he invited him to come visit, promising Brady he would be well received not only by Lewis himself, but also by his colleagues, a reference to the circle known as the Inklings.[15]

Lewis's rising popularity in America, which started with *Screwtape*, reached a new height when *Time* magazine did a cover story on him in its 8 September 1947 issue. With his face staring out at the reader and a devil with a pitchfork in the background, Lewis was now in the mainstream of American culture. The article itself wasn't all that pleasing to him, he confided to one of his new American correspondents, because it insinuated he didn't like women, which was a baseless accusation.[16] Complaints about the journalistic profession show up constantly in his letters. He rarely read

13. Walsh, "Impact on America," 109.
14. Letter from Lewis to The Society for the Prevention of Progress, May 1944, Hooper, *Collected Letters, Vol. II*, 613–14.
15. Letter from Lewis to Charles A. Brady, 29 October 1944, ibid., 629, 631.
16. Letter from Lewis to Margaret Fuller, 8 April 1948, ibid., 849.

newspapers because he didn't trust they were providing truthful accounts. This experience with *Time* certainly didn't change his low opinion. But the article was a watershed; the volume of letters from Americans increased noticeably in 1948. In fact, Lewis was beginning to feel overwhelmed. Yet the onslaught was only beginning. Once his BBC broadcast talks were combined into *Mere Christianity* and The Chronicles of Narnia began to appear year after year, he found himself inundated with letters from Americans for the remainder of his life.

Invitations from Americans

Lewis received many invitations to come to America to speak. The first invitation may have been the one he received from a nun, Sister Madeleva, who traveled to Oxford in 1934 to sit in on his lectures on medieval poetry. She met Lewis personally, and they exchanged letters after she returned to America to take up the presidency of St. Mary's College, a sister school to Notre Dame. In that capacity, she asked if he would come speak at St. Mary's. He graciously declined, as he did with every invitation; he never did make it to America.

Karl Young, a professor of English at Yale, instigated a formal invitation from his department in 1943 for Lewis to come lecture. He was tempted, but begged off due to his constant strain of work. He had met Young before and truly wanted to see him again, and added that he did have a desire to see America as well. He was also enamored with the idea of traveling across the ocean and having the unusual sensation (for him) of getting away from his normal routine.[17] This certainly doesn't come across as someone who has any particular antipathy toward America at this point in his life.

By 1945, Lewis was concerned that his constant refusals to accept invitations might give people the wrong impression. One major reason he wouldn't consider a trip overseas was his living arrangement, having bought a house back in 1930 with Mrs. Janie Moore, the mother of a friend who died in World War I. He had come to refer to her as *his* mother, even though they were not related. She was in poor health and, truth be told, made incessant demands on his time as she moved ever closer to senility. His brother, Warnie, also lived with them, but was not always reliable—his fondness for alcohol sometimes landed him in a hospital for drying out. Consequently, Lewis felt a heavy responsibility to take care of Mrs. Moore. One of his letters to an American

---

17. Letter from Lewis to Karl Young, 7 April 1943, ibid., 567–68.

man was an appeal to spread the word as to why he was unable to accept any invitations, citing the need to look after Mrs. Moore.[18]

Mrs. Moore died in early 1951, but Lewis, although released from that responsibility, still had others to fulfill. He had pledged for many years to write his contribution to *The Oxford History of English Literature*, and the time was coming due for its publication. Although he was given a year's sabbatical to finish it, the project was all-encompassing. So when another of his correspondents, Dr. Warfield M. Firor, a well-known American surgeon Lewis had met and deeply appreciated, inquired whether he might make a visit to the States, Lewis wrote that he had to turn down the invitation because of the deadline for that volume.[19]

Clyde S. Kilby, the English professor at Wheaton College who was largely responsible for starting Wheaton's massive archival collection of Lewis's papers and works (which has now expanded to seven distinguished British authors), wrote in 1958, requesting that Lewis come to Wheaton. By then, Lewis had accepted a professorship at Cambridge designed especially for him, which lightened his load somewhat, but he still felt too tied down to accept Kilby's offer. His duties, he regretted, made it impossible for him to come.[20] One wonders, though, if the circumstances of his recent marriage to Joy, along with the health concerns they both experienced at that time, might also have been a significant factor in his decision not to accept the offer.

Joy died in July 1960. Two months later, Father Frederick Joseph Adelmann, a Jesuit priest who chaired the philosophy department at Boston College, sought to bring Lewis there to lecture. Lewis, still grieving perhaps, and aware of the new responsibility of raising his two stepsons alone, felt the timing was not appropriate.[21] Lewis's health deteriorated throughout 1962 and into his final year. Another Catholic priest, Father George A. Restrepo, wanted to know if he could speak with the theologians at Woodstock College in Maryland. Lewis wrote back that he had hoped to accompany his American wife to the States sometime, but with her death and his current ill health, he thought it unlikely he would be making any more temporal journeys prior to what he called "the Great Journey!"[22] He knew his time

---

18. Letter from Lewis to Mr. McClain, 7 March 1945, ibid., 641.

19. Letter from Lewis to Warfield M. Firor, 23 April 1951, Hooper, *Collected Letters, Vol. III*, 112.

20. Letter from Lewis to Clyde S. Kilby, 6 June 1958, ibid., 951.

21. Letter from Lewis to Father Frederick Joseph Adelmann, 21 September 1960, ibid., 1185–86.

22. Letter from Lewis to Father George A. Restrepo, 1 December 1962, ibid., 1386–87.

was limited and that there would now never be any hope of visiting the country that had received him with such enthusiasm.

Interest in Seeing America

Although Lewis declined all invitations to visit America due to his personal circumstances, that did not mean he wasn't attracted to some of what the New World had to offer. Sprinkled throughout his letters to Americans, one finds comments that reveal the longing of his heart to make the journey. He was developing a new appreciation for the literary tastes of the American public, confessing to Firor that he would love to visit the country where his own favorite book at the time—*Perelandra*—had been more enthusiastically received than in his native land.[23] Lewis stated more than once that he was not drawn to the cities of America, but instead he hoped for the opportunity to experience what nature had to offer in the New World. In having to reject Firor's offer of a stay in a cabin in the woods, Lewis lamented his lost opportunity, as he would have loved to have witnessed American wildlife and the mountainous landscape.[24]

Lewis never shied away from acknowledging his preferences for places to see in America. He wrote to a Beverly Hills resident that he didn't think he would like that kind of climate on a permanent basis. He needed to have snow, he confided to her.[25] To another who had sent pictures of California, he admitted it looked attractive, but that he would prefer New England.[26] Why? He confessed to another correspondent that in temperament and habit, he was actually more like a Polar Bear.[27]

One letter, in particular, pretty much summarized what he would do if he ever did take the opportunity to travel through the United States, and how he would handle the entire trip: his focus would be on meeting the friends he had made through his American correspondence, seeing the natural wonders—the Rockies and Yellowstone Park—and just taking his time to enjoy the entire getaway. The only way he would ever consider arriving in

---

23. Letter from Lewis to Warfield M. Firor, 23 April 1945, Hooper, *Collected Letters*, Vol. II, 645.

24. Letter from Lewis to Warfield M. Firor, 22 January 1949, ibid., 908.

25. Letter from Lewis to Vera Mathews, 25 November 1950, Hooper, *Collected Letters*, Vol. III, 63.

26. Letter from Lewis to Mrs. Frank L. Jones, 21 December 1950, ibid., 73.

27. Letter from Lewis to Mary Van Deusen, 8 October 1956, ibid., 794–95.

America, he confessed, was by a slow boat so he could enjoy the maritime voyage.[28]

Gratitude for Americans' Selfless Giving

Post-World War II Britain was fast becoming a socialist haven, albeit a haven without some of the basic features of life to which most Brits had become accustomed. Government rationing of food and other commodities continued for years after the war until Winston Churchill won back the prime minister's position and reversed the socialist drift. Those lean years saw Lewis on the receiving end of American largesse. Numerous American Christians who loved his writings and who heard of the shortages in his country, opened up their wallets and showered him with gifts—food, stationery, and assorted luxuries. Lewis was overwhelmed by their spirit of giving. As Trevor Hart, professor of divinity at the University of St. Andrews in Scotland, commented at a Wheaton College seminar on Lewis, he wrote so many thank-you letters that he had to become quite imaginative in how he communicated his thanks.[29] The stream of gifts, for a number of years, was constant.

Edward A. Allen sent not only food, but even suits for the Lewis brothers to wear. His flow of gifts over many years astounded Lewis, and he admitted to Allen that he was amazed by the generosity of Americans. Lewis contemplated how Britain's hard situation had one great silver lining for his own understanding. While he didn't like the current situation in his homeland, he was grateful that the hard times allowed him to see that Americans could be quite kind.[30] To Vera Mathews (later Vera Gebbert), he expressed the utter futility of figuring out how to say thank you in any way that he had not already done and acknowledged that it was the goodness of Americans that was helping his nation get through the crisis.[31] Two years later, he was still thanking her, while finding another unique way of conveying his appreciation for her gifts, noting that he was receiving parcels from her almost as regularly as from British income tax officials; the former, however, always met with a much more appreciative reception.[32]

28. Letter from Lewis to Vera Gebbert, 7 November 1953, ibid., 376–77.

29. Hart, "Other Side of the Pond."

30. Letter from Lewis to Edward A. Allen, 20 July 1948, Hooper, *Collected Letters*, Vol. II, 862.

31. Letter from Lewis to Vera Mathews, 3 June 1948, ibid., 856.

32. Letter from Lewis to Vera Mathews, 12 June 1950, Hooper, *Collected Letters*, Vol. III, 35–36.

What irritated Lewis considerably was the reluctance of the British government to publicly acknowledge the help flowing from American citizens. In one of his few comments during his lifetime that praised the press, he informed Edward Allen that reports from the press were showing the British just how much they had the Americans to thank for their better standard of living. If Lewis had harbored any lingering prejudices against Americans, this flood tide of giving after World War II gave him the basis for changing his earlier views. And by the way he communicated his gratitude, one may say with a great degree of certitude that his views definitely did change.

Appreciation for American Literature

As noted previously, Lewis, beginning in the mid-1930s, started to have contacts with a few American academics—Sister Madeleva, Paul Elmer More, Charles Brady, Karl Young—and seemed to interact well with them. Even in his earlier years, when he would sometimes write of his disdain for Americans, he had fancied some of the early American writers like Hawthorne and Lowell. Another of America's authors he began to appreciate was Mark Twain. To Warfield Firor he wrote of his fascination with two of Twain's most famous works, *Tom Sawyer* and *Huckleberry Finn*, and expressed wonder why Twain never wrote anything else of that high caliber.[33] This link to the American academic sphere in general, and the literature field in particular, helped develop an even stronger tie to America through writers that he admired.

Two of Lewis's main interests were science fiction and poetry. His own science fiction works—the Space Trilogy of *Out of the Silent Planet*, *Perelandra*, and *That Hideous Strength*—had a good following in the 1940s, which continues today. Lewis's first attempts at publishing were poems—*Spirits in Bondage* (1919) and *Dymer* (1926). Neither had found a popular reception, thereby dashing his hopes of becoming a recognized poet. Lack of enthusiasm for his poetry and his new teaching appointment at Oxford pushed him in other directions, but he never lost his love for the art.

He stayed abreast of developments in both fields. To an American English professor, Nathan Comfort Starr, he enthused over some books he had recently read by author Ray Bradbury. He was impressed by Bradbury's inventiveness and fine prose.[34] Lewis also was in touch with American writer William Anthony Parker White, who wrote science fiction under the pen name of Anthony Boucher, and who published, from 1949 to 1958, *The*

---

33. Letter from Lewis to Warfield M. Firor, 6 December 1950, ibid., 66–67.
34. Letter from Lewis to Nathan Comfort Starr, 3 February 1953, ibid., 287–88.

Magazine of Fantasy and Science Fiction. Two of Lewis's short stories, "The Shoddy Lands" and "Ministering Angels," appeared in the magazine.[35]

On the poetry side, Lewis made some rather startling pronouncements comparing what American and British poets were publishing in his day. After reading Stephen Vincent Benét's *Western Star*, which he considered to be even better than *John Brown's Body*, he opined to Warfield Firor that American poetry was far better than anything currently being produced in Britain.[36] To his former student, Dom Bede Griffiths, he said much the same; a number of American poets, he felt, really had "something to *say* and some real art."[37]

Concerns about America

Lewis always claimed not to be interested in politics. To be sure, it was not a primary interest. Yet he often engaged in commentary and/or questions with his American correspondents over the state of American politics and government. After the surprise choice of Harry Truman in the 1948 presidential election, Lewis turned to Edward Allen for enlightenment on what had just occurred. Socialists and Conservatives in Britain disagreed over whether the Truman victory was good for socialism or for traditional British freedoms. He sought Allen's insight on which side was closer to the truth.[38] As the 1952 presidential election approached, Lewis turned to Vera Gebbert for her opinion on what was transpiring, asking her if even Americans really understood what was happening on their political scene. He told her about another American correspondent who had sent him eight pages of political analysis "so hot that they nearly burnt my fingers." That correspondent had concluded that the Democrats should really be known as the "Dumbocrats" and were "a sort of mixture of Hitler, the Russian secret police, and the inmates of the village lunatic asylum."[39]

Besides the political scene, Lewis expressed interest in the culture as well, although his views of that might have been somewhat colored by the tales of woe he received from some of his correspondents, especially in letters from women who would unburden themselves of their family troubles. Mary

---

35. Letter from Lewis to Anthony Boucher, 5 February 1953, ibid., 289.

36. Letter from Lewis to Warfield M. Firor, 27 June 1953, ibid., 340–42.

37. Letter from Lewis to Dom Bede Griffiths, 22 April 1954, ibid., 461.

38. Letter from Lewis to Edward A. Allen, 20 November 1948, Hooper, *Collected Letters, Vol. II*, 892.

39. Letter from Lewis to Vera Gebbert, 28 July 1952, Hooper, *Collected Letters, Vol. III*, 218–20.

Willis Shelburne, one of his most constant and, one might say, insistent, correspondents, usually had some bad news to share about her daughter and son-in-law. The stories she related, along with what other correspondents were telling him, led to some rather stark conclusions about marriage in America. After one particularly detailed letter, Lewis concluded that America suffered from a type of male tyranny unknown in Britain.[40] His comments about that presumed tyranny were even more pointed in another response to Shelburne when he asked if the Statue of Liberty might actually be facing away from America rather than looking out over New York.[41] One might excuse him for having a skewed view of the American domestic scene.

Critiques of Britain

One cannot truly evaluate a person's views of another nation in a vacuum. Comparisons are necessary. What better way to evaluate Lewis's views on America than to look also at his views on the Britain of his day? If he entertained a low opinion of British government and culture, would we say he was anti-British? Or would he merely be pointing out the problems that needed to be corrected? In fact, Lewis's comments on his native country appear to be far harsher than anything he said about America.

When Nathan Comfort Starr sought to bring Lewis to America and Lewis had to decline, he did invite Starr to Britain, but not with a sterling recommendation, referring to Britain as "this luckless country."[42] In offering the same invitation to Warfield Firor, the image of Britain he used in the letter was "this bleak island," and he wondered why Firor would even want to visit it.[43] Why the bleak state of affairs? For Lewis, the blame fell on the Labour government and its socialist policies, which not only ruined the nation economically but was siphoning off its liberties and making Britain a less-than-stellar partner for the United States. As he explained to Firor, the government always seemed to be thinking of ways to take more liberties from the people. "Try not to judge us by our rulers," he pleaded.[44]

By 1954, rationing in Britain finally came to an end, thanks to the new Conservative government. He informed Vera Gebbert he wouldn't be

---

40. Letter from Lewis to Mary Willis Shelburne, 22 June 1953, ibid., 338–40.
41. Letter from Lewis to Mary Willis Shelburne, 12 June 1955, ibid., 621–22.
42. Letter from Lewis to Nathan Comfort Starr, 3 November 1947, Hooper, *Collected Letters, Vol. II*, 809.
43. Letter from Lewis to Warfield M. Firor, 11 February 1949, ibid., 916.
44. Letter from Lewis to Warfield M. Firor, 26 July 1950, Hooper, *Collected Letters, Vol. III*, 43–45.

needing her gifts anymore, but there was a possibility, if she really missed sending him all those items, that she might be able to begin anew, noting that if the Socialists ever regained the majority, she could once again show her kindness "by supplying us, not with little luxuries, but with the necessities of life!"[45] He continued to sound the warning, such as when Gebbert was thinking of moving permanently to Britain. While they would be glad to welcome her, she needed to know the truth: there would always be the threat of a revival of a government ruled by the Socialists, "which would finish us off completely."[46]

Dealing with National Stereotypes

Lewis did not see Americans as only one type; he could clearly differentiate, as he did in a letter to Edward Allen in 1951, describing the influx of Americans visiting Oxford in the summer. His first concern was that they would get the wrong impression of English summers, since the weather was especially awful that year. As he looked at the Americans arriving, though, he marked a difference in the kinds of Americans who were now showing up: they were no longer the wealthy ones but the nicer, more middle-class type.[47] He said much the same to Allen's mother, Belle, a year later, rejoicing that Oxford was getting the Americans of more modest means because he believed "the *rich* of any country are usually the least attractive specimens of the nation." But then he added an asterisk to that sentence and picked up the thought again further down, saying that, overall, he didn't view people by nationality; he preferred to see them as unique individuals, regardless of their country of origin.[48]

He made the same point with Mary Van Deusen when she wrote to ask him what he thought of the concept of loving one's own country. His reply indicates a man striving to find the balance between nations and individuals. Love of country, he theorized, was primarily love for those with whom one had a lot in common. He cautioned, "Mind you, I'm in considerable doubt about the whole thing. My mind tends to move in a world of individuals not of societies."[49] That tendency in Lewis's mind to "move in a world of individuals" and "not of societies," would also lend itself to a tendency not to wed oneself to stereotypes, whether of good traits in a people group

---

45. Letter from Lewis to Vera Gebbert, 25 September 1954, ibid., 508–9.
46. Letter from Lewis to Vera Gebbert, 8 May 1959, ibid., 1046–47.
47. Letter from Lewis to Edward A. Allen, 4 June 1951, ibid., 121–23.
48. Letter from Lewis to Belle Allen, 9 December 1952, ibid., 259–61.
49. Letter from Lewis to Mary Van Deusen, 25 May 1951, ibid., 118–19.

or less-admirable ones. Whatever prejudices he may have had at the outset were set aside as he came to know more Americans.

Perhaps the most fitting conclusion to this specific question of Lewis's attitude toward Americans comes from Walter Hooper, who met Lewis in the last year of his life, and for a few months served as his private secretary. Hooper will be the subject of another chapter in this book, but it is appropriate at this point to offer thanks for his insights into Lewis's thinking from the conversations he had with him. In an e-mail exchange I had with Hooper, he offered these thoughts:

> Let us suppose that when you were two years old your father slapped your hand to prevent you putting it in the fire, and you said to your mother, "Don't like Daddy!" Would you, or would you not, be a fool to allow that statement to stand for your settled belief about your father? Well, there was a man who used to write a lot about Lewis who used a chance, ignorant comment Lewis made as an 18-year-old student about Oxford dons to stand for—as this man did—for "Lewis's Belief About Oxford Dons." [A "don" is a university fellow or tutor.] To accept that as Lewis's opinion on Oxford would be as ignorant and foolish for someone to regard "Don't like Daddy!" to be regarded as your settled opinion about your father.
>
> Lewis himself drew my attention to another illustration of ignorance that needs unmasking. I forget where it is, but Jonathan Swift, the Irish writer, when asked if he liked or disliked the Irish, the English, the Japanese, etc. etc, pointed out that he didn't know *all* the Irish people, so how could he possibly know where he liked or loathed them. Of course, like nearly everyone else, some Irish he liked, some he didn't.
>
> And so to Lewis, who I think must have liked many, many Americans considering that roughly three-quarters of his letters were to them. One of them to whom he wrote to for years, Mary Willis Shelburne . . . he provided with a pension, paid for by his American publishers. And as we all know, he married an American, and—hardly of similar importance—he made another his secretary.[50]

---

50. E-mail from Walter Hooper to K. Alan Snyder, 24 October 2014.

Lewis's Ongoing Influence

Billy Graham, who may have been, to some degree, America's Pastor for many decades, held a crusade in England in 1955. He and C. S. Lewis met and talked. In a 1963 interview conducted by Sherwood Wirt, editor of Graham's *Decision* magazine, Lewis talked about that meeting. "I had the pleasure of meeting Billy Graham once. We had dinner together during his visit to Cambridge University in 1955, while he was conducting a mission to students. I thought he was a very modest and a very sensible man, and I liked him very much indeed."[51] Graham's own enterprise, *Christianity Today*, which began at about the same time as that meeting, continually tried to draw Lewis into its orbit. Carl Henry, the editor, attempted to get him to write some original pieces for the magazine, but Lewis declined, saying he had nothing new to offer in the way of apologetics; he already had made his views clear in his books. Yet, from that point on, Lewis's stature among evangelicals was on the rise, as he was given the stamp of approval from Graham and those associated with him. Historian George Marsden has commented that many evangelicals were now beginning to appreciate more Lewis's "freshness" in explaining the faith, which was counter to the way they had been raised.[52] One of the keys to this new attention to Lewis by evangelicals was the increasing popularity of *Mere Christianity*, once it had been made into just one book in 1952. It was there, in those pages, that many evangelicals embraced the "freshness" of Lewis's approach.

Large-scale popularity for Lewis among evangelicals, though, had to wait until the 1960s, and, ironically, after his death. Lewis had famously predicted that he would be forgotten once he had passed from the scene, but there were a number of Americans who wanted to be sure that never happened. One was Clyde Kilby, professor of English at Wheaton College, who published, in 1964, *The Christian World of C. S. Lewis*. Wheaton, of course, is now the American repository of the Lewis Papers. *Christianity Today*, at the turn of the new century, ranked *Mere Christianity* as the most influential Christian book of the twentieth century. C. S. Lewis's influence remains strong, especially in America, where his hold on the minds of Christians seems to be pervasive. The rest of this book will document the lives of individual Americans who have been impacted by his writings.

---

51. Wacker, *America's Pastor*, 366, n. 59.
52. Marsden, "*Mere Christianity* and American Culture."

2

Chad Walsh: A Baptized Imagination

"Chad Walsh, a longtime English professor, poet and writer, died on Jan. 17 at The Arbors, a nursing home in Shelburne, Vt. He was 76 years old and lived in South Burlington, Vt." Those were the opening words of a 1991 obituary in the *New York Times*. Walsh earned a *Times* obituary because he had contributed, over his lifetime, a number of poems and book reviews for that newspaper. The obituary, as it chronicled Walsh's career as an English professor at Beloit College in Wisconsin, and as an author of some repute of both children's books and treatises on Christian faith for adults, did not fail to mention the direct influence of C. S. Lewis on his life and work, and that Walsh chose Lewis as the subject for two of his books. As the obituary notes, "It was probably inevitable that Mr. Walsh should write about Mr. Lewis, whose own books helped convert Mr. Walsh from agnosticism to Christianity."[1]

"In my case there was no childhood faith," Walsh wrote in an account of how he eventually found the Christian path. "If I ever believed in God as a small child, no memory of the time remains with me. I regarded myself as an atheist from the moment I learned to read—and, indeed, pamphlet editions of Ingersoll, et cetera, were part of my earliest reading." Why would a young boy be so attracted to a non-Christian worldview? Walsh, although ultimately placing the blame on his own stubbornness and pride, also pointed to a reaction he had to the community in which he was raised: "Undoubtedly my atheism was in part a revolt against the Fundamentalism of my home town—Marion, Virginia. . . . It was not a winsome faith, and I was

---

1. Obituary, "Chad Walsh."

in full agreement with H. L. Mencken about the superstitious backwardness of the 'Bible Belt.'"[2]

His attitude was so unique in the town that many came alongside to try to convince him of the truth of Christianity. The hardline approach of some only increased his intransigence. He eventually escaped what he considered the confines of that small town and found the atmosphere of the University of Virginia more to his liking. There he didn't have to worry about people shoving religion at him. He was free, he felt, but the freedom did not settle the bigger questions that began to crowd upon his mind. While he claimed to be a self-satisfied atheist, doubts crept in. "Is there such a thing as good or evil?" he often wondered. "Is there any meaning in life and the universe?" World events in the 1930s helped crystallize the answers.

The rise of Hitler in Germany, and the growing awareness of the actions of that regime, forced him to confront the problem of evil in the world. Walsh's companions in atheism and/or agnosticism, when challenged by Walsh to come up with a response to what Hitler was doing, would provide excuses, albeit excuses that were actually consistent with their worldview. Walsh recounts, "They agreed with me that the world was a senseless jungle. Very well, they reasoned, if the world is a jungle, it's absurd to speak of right and wrong. Everything is relative. Hitler thinks he's doing right to invade Poland and murder the Jews. Very well, it *is* right *for him*. It's all in the way you look at it."[3] That response shook him. He knew he had to come to grips with the reality of evil.

> I began to see that concepts of good and evil are deeply ingrained in each of us. If we throw them out the window, they sneak in through the back door. And the state of the world at that time made it more and more difficult to believe . . . that education and science would rather easily bring about a utopia in which people would be nice to each other because there was nothing to quarrel about. I began dimly to perceive the cruel and irrational depths of human nature. I was not yet ready to see such unsightly depths in myself, but I could see them in Hitler and his kind.[4]

Walsh's second question, about the meaning of life and the universe, intruded more on his thoughts once he was forced to recognize that real goodness and real evil existed, and that there was a decided difference between the two. "My own life was exciting and meaningful *to me*," he realized.

2. Walsh, "Several Roads," 119–20.
3. Ibid., 123.
4. Ibid.

"But in time I began to wonder whether there could really be any meaning in the individual's life if the universe as a whole was haphazard. Everything—from the spiral nebulae to human life—seemed sheer accident. Would it not logically follow that the meaning I thought I saw in my own life was an illusion?"[5] His atheism was crumbling. He lived in a transition from atheist to Christian for a few years, trying to figure out what he should believe. It all came down to the person of Jesus Christ. Walsh began reading the New Testament. What he found surprised him. He had preconceived ideas of Jesus as some weak character—the words "meek and mild" were stuck in his mind from childhood. What he saw in the pages of the Gospels was something different: "The man I encountered in the Gospels was a towering figure of strength; even his death was that of a man strong enough to accept death voluntarily. So I was up against the final question: What or who was Jesus?" Eventually, reason led to faith:

> I finally got over this last and greatest hurdle—the divinity of Christ—because of several factors. For one thing, my reading of the New Testament (coupled with some of C. S. Lewis' books) confronted me with Augustine's dilemma, that Christ is "either God or not a good man." I could not believe that the central figure of the Gospels was a madman or an impostor—his obvious sanity and integrity made me feel utterly inadequate—yet he obviously believed that he was divine, and acted accordingly.[6]

The Lewis Factor

Walsh's account of his spiritual birth offers only a brief mention of Lewis as one of the reasons. In another essay, however, Walsh went into more detail as to how he initially encountered a Lewis book and what it did for him while he was in his "transition" period. It was in either 1944 or 1945, he recalls, on a short vacation to Vermont, that a friend enthusiastically lent him a book she had just finished reading; she just knew he would love it. That book was *Perelandra*, the second in Lewis's Space Trilogy in which the protagonist, Elwin Ransom, is transported to Venus to save an innocent world from falling into sin. Walsh was transported as well: "I quickly consumed it from cover to cover. I was struck first of all by the sheer beauty of the book. It transported me into a kind of Elysian Fields—or better yet, an unspoiled Eden, inhabited by the innocent and unfallen." A second revelation was

---

5. Ibid., 124.
6. Ibid., 127.

that, even though he had always been a science fiction fan, he had never read any science fiction like this, where it could be used as a "vehicle of great philosophic and psychological myth." The third revelation, though, was the greatest of all:

> Finally, and most importantly, in *Perelandra* I found my imagination being baptized. At the time I was slowly thinking, feeling, and fumbling my way towards the Christian faith and had reached the point where I was more than half convinced that it was true. This conviction, however, was a thing more of the mind than of the imagination and heart. In *Perelandra* I got the taste and smell of Christian truth. My senses as well as my soul were baptized. It was as though an intellectual abstraction or speculation had become flesh and dwelt in its solid bodily glory among us.[7]

As Walsh looked back on this event years later, he came to the realization that the way he found Lewis was quite typical. A person reads something by Lewis, becomes so enthused that he/she lends the book to a friend, who in turn catches that enthusiasm and passes it on to others. For Walsh, "The result was that I began buying everything else by him that was available in America and also passed along word of the discovery to other friends. It was as though I had discovered a new ingredient in my intellectual, emotional, and spiritual diet that I had unconsciously desired but had not previously found. I think many others, coming on Lewis for the first time, felt the same way."[8]

Not long after the *Perelandra* revelation, Walsh wrote his first letter to Lewis, seeking to know if another science fiction work was to be expected. Lewis's response pointed to *That Hideous Strength*, third and last in the series, but he let Walsh know it would be the final installment; he felt he had run out of available planets.[9] Thus began a friendship that would last until Lewis's death in 1963.

Apostle to the Skeptics

Walsh published an article on Lewis in *The Atlantic Monthly* in September 1946. He entitled it "C. S. Lewis, Apostle to the Skeptics." It was his first foray into trying to explain Lewis to an American audience, but it spurred

---

7. Walsh, "Impact on America," 107.
8. Ibid., 108.
9. Letter from Lewis to Chad Walsh, 18 December 1945, Hooper, *Collected Letters*, Vol. II, 686.

him on to turn those first thoughts into a book with the same title. This called for a trip to Oxford to interview his subject, which occurred in June 1948. Lewis, at first, had not encouraged Walsh's effort, feeling he was not a proper subject for scrutiny at that time. "He had urged me to desist and devote my time to better subjects (such as some safely dead writer)," Walsh relates in the book, "but once he became convinced that I considered the study worth doing he wholeheartedly cooperated with me. He answered innumerable questions without evasion, and his friendliness did much to make my stay in England enjoyable."[10] Writing to his wife, Eva, he told the story of his "first encounter":

> I went out after breakfast to shop. Came back at 10, and there was a note, asking me to call CSL at Magdalen. I called, and a deep, very English voice, said, "Is that you, Walsh?" He told me to come over to the college.
>
> I did so, and by asking a succession of people found my way thru the maze of vault-like passages. Reached his sanctum—a two-room affair—and at last laid my eyes on CSL.
>
> He greeted me warmly. He looks much like his pictures. A little more slender than I had imagined. A wrinkled gray suit, brown tie messily tied, scruffed black shoes. We chatted a while, then in about an hour's time I got most of the info I need from him. He was very cooperative, as well as marvelous entertaining. . . .
>
> He said, "I think you did a good job with those three chapters you sent me. But *what* are you going to write about in the other 17?"[11]

They had a number of meetings, as Walsh questioned him thoroughly on his views. Almost from the start, they hit it off, and the relationship became more than interviewer with interviewee. As Walsh happily recounted to his wife, "Reached CSL's rooms at Magdalen a little after 10, & was warmly received. I soon finished with questions, so . . . we adjourned to the King's Arms. . . . We talked of everything under the sun—when I parted I felt that we were hovering on the edge of really knowing each other. I think he takes a genuine interest in me, and really likes me—half as one colleague to another, half as father to son."[12] Writing to Eva again the next day, he added, "Lewis is definitely old-fashioned in many ways. Nostalgia about the 19th c. Can't see

---

10. Walsh, *Apostle*, x.

11. Letter from Chad Walsh to Eva Walsh, 14 June 1948, Chad Walsh Papers, Folder 1—Letters from Chad to Eva Walsh.

12. Letter from Chad Walsh to Eva Walsh, 23 June 1948, ibid.

the possibilities in surrealist art that I think I see. Loathes the present British gov't—'those swine,' as he frequently calls them."[13]

Further reflections on Lewis's character and manner are found in Walsh's finished book, particularly in chapter two, "The Man." Before meeting Lewis for the first time, Walsh couldn't figure out why the pictures of him on the book dust-jackets—"sad-eyed, world-weary"—didn't seem to match the "wit and grace" he experienced in the books. "Only after I met Lewis did I see that the solution to the enigma was simpler than the theories I had been busy devising. He consented to pose for a couple of snapshots and I perceived that—like half of humanity—he stands stiffly at attention and freezes into impersonality when a camera is pointed his way. The picture on the dust-jackets resembles him about as much as a mummy resembles a living man."[14]

Walsh was most taken by what he called "the aliveness of his face," both when he was talking and when listening. His "quick smile," Walsh noted, could have been called "sweet" except for the feminine connotation of that word. It did not ring true for Lewis, who was "one of the most masculine persons I have ever known." It became obvious to the interviewer that his subject had very little regard for making carefully guarded statements. Concern for public relations was not part of his internal makeup. "I never detected him pausing to phrase a reply carefully for fear it might be used against him. If I mentioned prominent names he commented on them with matter-of-fact candor (whether favorably or no) and did not add that this was 'off the record.'" Neither did Lewis try to paint himself as an expert on every subject. Walsh witnessed genuine humility: "When I inquired his opinions on a vast variety of matters he answered with equal directness—though sometimes his response was simply, 'I don't know enough to have an opinion.'" Walsh's conclusion? "It adds up to plain unselfconsciousness. . . . To the world outside of Oxford he is a famous figure. To himself he is an Oxford don who writes an occasional book in odd moments."[15]

Apostle to the Skeptics begins with a quote from a Lewis detractor in America: "'C. S. Lewis, the Oxford don, the pious paradox-monger and audacious word-juggler, will surely meet his match one of these days and be subjected to a severe debunking operation,' wrote Victor S. Yarros recently in *The American Freeman*. 'He is asking for it. Oh, for a Huxley, or a Heine, or an Ingersoll, to expose his tricks and call his bluffs!'" Walsh then provides an example of a positive view that is the exact opposite of the just-quoted

---

13. Letter from Chad Walsh to Eva Walsh, 24 June 1948, ibid.
14. Walsh, *Apostle*, 11.
15. Ibid., 12.

criticism. This gives him the rationale for an examination of Lewis: "When the authorities disagree, and disagree with such heat, one suspects that the subject of their disagreement is worth further study. That is why I have written this book."[16]

As one reads *Apostle to the Skeptics*, one is not treated to a volume of hero-worship. While it is obvious that Walsh admires Lewis and his writings, he brings a trained academic eye to his analysis. He praises Lewis's serious treatises and his imaginative works, but when it comes to his poetry, Walsh notes that Lewis failed to catch on in that sphere. His analysis of that failure is astute:

> It is clear that Lewis has never completely found himself as a poet. He has experimented with alliterative verse, free verse, parallelism, and elaborate stanzaic patterns, but somehow his poetry has not shaken down into an individual style. One can seldom read a prose book of his without feeling that no other person could have written it; his poetry seems to have been composed by half a dozen men, none having the talent of C. S. Lewis. Almost everything that he has said in verse he has said better in prose.[17]

The book's final chapter is a snapshot, from 1948, as to how the Christian faith fits into modern society, primarily in the English-speaking world. Walsh sees a reinvigoration of Christian faith post-WWII. There are many new voices coming forth to state the Christian case. But one voice stands out among the others. He ends the book with this comment:

> Of all the writers advocating Classical Christianity, none combines versatility, literary skill, and psychological insight so richly as C. S. Lewis. He is peculiarly capable of reaching and influencing the people who will influence the masses day after tomorrow. If Christianity revives in England and America it will not be the work of one man—and perhaps not really the work of man at all. But the odds are that it will bear strong traces of the Gospel according to C. S. Lewis.[18]

By all accounts, Lewis was satisfied and pleased with the finished product. He never minded legitimate critiques, and the overall positive evaluation of his writing could only increase his popularity, primarily among those in academia who would probably be the prime audience for the book. The

---

16. Ibid., ix.
17. Ibid., 61–62.
18. Ibid., 171–72.

friendship that began with an inquiry about whether he was going to write more science fiction, was solidified through personal contact and this first major book *by* an American who sought explain Lewis *to* Americans.

An Established Friendship

Personal correspondence between Walsh and Lewis was not as voluminous as with many other Americans, but it was ongoing and significant; further, they continued to meet whenever Walsh had a reason to visit England. A lot of their correspondence dealt with poetry. Even though Walsh had critiqued Lewis's personal poetry, he always sent him his poems for comment and sought Lewis's opinion on the trends in that field. In 1953, Lewis expressed regret over not being able to see Walsh when he thought he would, and, as with all the invitations he received to visit America, found himself in no position to take up the offer.[19] The next year, he remarked again on the hope they might meet. Lewis had switched his teaching duties from Oxford to Cambridge, but assured Walsh that since he continued to reside in Oxford, they could revisit all the old places together.[20]

Two months later, Lewis received an invitation from the Milton Society of America to be present for "A Milton Evening in Honor of Douglas Bush & C. S. Lewis" to be held in New York City. Walsh was part of that society and was going to be at the event. Lewis, though, had to beg off, regardless of the honor. He sent a grateful letter to the Society, albeit with his regrets. He also wrote Walsh at the same time, expressing his disappointment that his inability to attend would not allow them to meet again as soon as Walsh had hoped.[21]

In January 1956, Walsh's book *Behold the Glory* appeared. *Kirkus Review* gave it a solid recommendation, saying, "Professor Chad Walsh, of Beloit College, has earned a reputation as a penetrating Christian apologist, an advocate of the application of Christian principles to the problems of the day and, above all, as one who can use the English language with style and provocativeness." The volume was both "charming and stimulating," the review continued. "His general thesis running through all the essays is that the Divine Presence may be made manifest in many ways, many of them unexpected and surprising. . . . Good literature as well as good Christianity."[22]

---

19. Letter from Lewis to Chad Walsh, 21 February 1953, Hooper, *Collected Letters, Vol. III.*, 294–95.
20. Letter from Lewis to Chad Walsh, 5 August 1954, ibid., 501.
21. Letter from Lewis to Chad Walsh, 25 October 1954, ibid., 515–16.
22. *Kirkus Review*, 18 January 1956.

Lewis agreed, telling Walsh that this was his best book to date and that his writing style now evidenced greater precision. He opined that the new book was certainly better than *Apostle to the Skeptics*, but that was because Walsh had a much better subject this time, in his view.[23]

In 1958, Lewis recorded some talks for the Episcopal Radio-TV Foundation. They were broadcast in 1959, then made into his book *The Four Loves*, which came out in 1960. He decided from the outset to dedicate the book to Walsh, who when hearing of it, wrote, "I'm flattered and touched at your dedicating a book to me, and particularly pleased that you chose this one. I read the TV talks in typescript and had the feeling that this was going to be one of your most meaty and profound books. Very many thanks indeed! It means a great deal to me." That same letter also included a hope that Lewis, along with his wife, Joy, might make that American trip after all:

> There are recurrent rumors that you're about to make a trip to the States. Any truth in them? If at any time you are planning to be here, for heaven's sake let me know as soon as possible. We'd go quite a distance to see you and Joy—and might even hope to get you here as our guests. We're renting a great big Victorian monstrosity of a house, the kind that surely has a magic door into Narnia, and have plenty of room.
>
> Our love to you and Joy. Strange the way the lives of us four have crisscrossed and intertwined. And quite wonderful.[24]

Walsh came out with a novel in 1961 called *The Rough Years*. Its focus was on high-school life. Lewis read it and, as always, was honest in his appraisal. He began by acknowledging his ignorance of high schools in America, never wanting to say more than his knowledge permitted: "The school life depicted is so unlike anything in my experience that it was, for me, rather like a book about Martians." But he *did* delve into the characters Walsh had created, and offered some evaluation of how well he had made his points.[25]

Lewis and Walsh had the kind of friendship that was not threatened by honesty. They clearly expected candid assessments from one another. Their last face-to-face meeting took place in late 1961; Lewis's health was already in decline. His last letter to Walsh, on 21 April 1962, was only a

---

23. Letter from Lewis to Chad Walsh, 28 February 1956, Hooper, *Collected Letters*, Vol. III, 711, 713.

24. Letter from Chad Walsh to Lewis, 27 August 1958, Chad Walsh Papers, Folder 2—Correspondence, 12/18/45-4/26/64.

25. Letter from Lewis to Walsh, October [?] 1961, Hooper, *Collected Letters*, Vol. III, 1288–89.

short note about his semi-invalid condition. That appears to have been the final communication between the two, but the impact of Lewis continued on. A decade after Lewis's death, Walsh received a letter from a female correspondent that testified once again not only to the ongoing influence of Lewis on an American but also to the breadth of that influence across denominational lines: "As a Roman Catholic who is, at thirty-two, in process of rediscovering her baptismal faith, I have found C. S. Lewis of inestimable value for his lucid apologetics. My modernistic befuddlement is dispersing, I think, largely under the influence of his clear-sighted exposition of what he perceived to be bedrock truth."[26]

Chad Walsh is important to this study as the first American academic to write a book dissecting, in a friendly way, the C. S. Lewis phenomenon. For that alone, he deserves recognition. The fact that his initial contacts with Lewis and the resulting book were not the end of their relationship, but the beginning of a fifteen-year friendship, also makes him significant for this examination of how Lewis impacted the lives of individual Americans. Yet there is one more contribution Walsh made to the C. S. Lewis story: he was a principal participant in encouraging Joy Davidman Gresham to reach out to Lewis. Of all the Americans Lewis came to know, Joy was the one he learned to love the most—and Chad Walsh played his part in the development of that most intimate of all of Lewis's connections to Americans.

---

26. Letter from Theresa C. Strasser to Chad Walsh, 3 September 1973, Chad Walsh Papers, Folder 8—Miscellaneous Chad Walsh Correspondence.

3

A Story of Joy . . . and Grief

When I was fourteen I went walking in the park on a Sunday afternoon, in clean, cold, luminous air. The trees tinkled with sleet; the city noises were muffled by the snow. Winter sunset, with a line of young maples sheathed in ice between me and the sun—as I looked up they burned unimaginably golden—burned and were not consumed.

I heard the voice in the burning tree; the meaning of all things was revealed and the sacrament at the heart of all beauty lay bare; time and space fell away, and for a moment the world was only a door swinging ajar. Then the light faded, the cold stung my toes, and I went home, reflecting that I had had another aesthetic experience. I had them fairly often. That was what beautiful things did to you, I recognized, probably because of some visceral or glandular reaction that hadn't been fully explored by science just yet. For I was a well-brought-up, right-thinking child of materialism. Beauty, I knew, existed; but God, of course, did not.[1]

Helen Joy Davidman was born into a Jewish family in New York City in 1915. Her parents had been part of that immense migration that started in the late nineteenth century from all parts of Europe, but especially from areas that had not helped populate America previously. Joseph Isaac Davidman, her father, was born in Poland in 1887, but was a New York resident by the age of six. Her mother, Jeannette Spivack, left the Ukraine when she was five, also arriving in New York. They were Jewish, yes, but only ethnically. Neither

---

1. Davidman, "The Longest Way Round," Soper, *These Found the Way*, 13.

parent had much use for the Jewish faith, with her father being an outspoken atheist. Joy (as she was always called from childhood), eager to please a rather harsh, demanding father, decided at age eight that she also would be an atheist. This is why the "aesthetic experience" she had in the park that day could be so easily brushed aside.[2] As she put it in her later conversion testimony, "A young poet like myself could be seized and shaken by spiritual powers a dozen times a day, and still take it for granted *that* there was no such thing as spirit. What happened to me was easily explained away; it was 'only nerves' or 'only glands.' As soon as I discovered Freud, it became 'only sex.' And yet if ever a human life was haunted, Christ haunted me."[3]

What did she mean by that last sentence? Looking back, she could see that her "inner personality" always had been drawn to that figure in history, and she realized later that she had unconsciously quoted Jesus in everything she did. Yet as a Jew, even an ethnic one only, she "had been led to feel cold chills at the mention of his name." Men, in Christ's name, had persecuted her people through the centuries. "If nominal Christians so confuse their Master's teaching, surely a poor Jew may be pardoned a little confusion," she reasoned.[4]

Although her father had rejected religion, he maintained, by habit and/or convention, a strict morality. As Joy began to mature, she examined her father's stance more critically. "It never occurred to him," she concluded, "that, in the meaningless and purposeless universe of the atheist, moral ideas could only be something men had put together for their own convenience." She eventually decided that all morality was "a pipe dream," and if that were the case, one should live for pleasure—for what else was there to live for?[5] She believed in nothing: "Men, I said, are only apes. Virtue is only custom. Life is only an electrochemical reaction. Mind is only a set of conditioned reflexes, and anyway most people aren't rational like ME. Love, art, and altruism are only sex. The universe is only matter. Matter is only energy. I forget what I said energy was only."[6]

Despite this strong atheistic, materialistic belief system, Joy's poetic nature seemed to chafe under this strict outlook. Within her was a longing that she envisioned as a door "into Somewhere Else," an undiscovered country that C. S. Lewis would one day show her the true meaning of when she read his *Pilgrim's Regress*. She had a recurring dream, both as a child and

---

2. Dorsett, *And God Came In*.
3. Davidman, "The Longest Way Round," Soper, *These Found the Way*, 13–14.
4. Ibid., 16.
5. Ibid., 15.
6. Ibid., 16.

after she had grown: "I would walk down a familiar street which suddenly grew unfamiliar and opened into a strange, golden, immeasurable plain, where far away there rose the towers of Fairyland. If I remembered the way carefully, the dream told me, I should be able to find it when I woke up." Childish wishful thinking? If so, she wondered, "why should all human beings be born wanting something like that, unless it exists?"[7]

The young atheist wanted some kind of serious purpose for her life. The Great Depression affected her deeply; something must be done, and she should be a participant in finding solutions. So Joy joined the Communist Party as mostly an emotional decision. She didn't read Marx to find out what it was all about. She simply chose to believe socialism would, in some way, prove itself superior to capitalism. Joy Davidman became a communist for idealistic reasons, but her experience as a communist taught her instead to justify any means as long as it led to the proper end: heaven on earth. It was perfectly fine to lie to the rank and file and to develop a deep hatred of any who were deemed enemies of the Party. "Hatred, to us, was a virtue, and, much as we hated Fascism, we hated even more bitterly the anti-Fascist liberals who were our rivals for the support of labor." She recalled one editor at the *New Masses*, the magazine connected to the Communist Party, saying, "'We can see now that the *real* enemies are the Social Democrats!'" Even though, by nature, she was "the sort of woman who nurses sick kittens and hates to spank her bad little boys," she nevertheless found that "as a Marxist I would have been willing to shoot people without trial. In practice I willingly gave my spare time, my spare cash, my love of truth, and my artistic conscience. Fortunately for me, I was never asked to do anything more dangerous than that."[8]

Joy found her niche as a journalist and critic at the *New Masses*. She earned that position due to her award-winning volume of poetry, *Letter to a Comrade*, which was published in 1938. When the National Institute of Arts and Letters recognized her book with its Russell Loines Memorial Fund award and at the same time she won the Yale Younger Poet competition for the same volume, she was, in effect, on the A-list of American poets. She also published a novel, *Anya*, in 1940, a story about a late-nineteenth-century Jewish woman in the Ukraine, based on her mother's memories of real events. It was well received. While on the *New Masses*, she served as editor and publisher for *War Poems of the United Nations*, a collection of poems with an overtly pro-communist slant. Letters during this era reveal

---

7. Ibid., 17–18.
8. Ibid., 21.

her to be intellectually sharp, in tandem with an equally sharp tongue when she writes to aspiring authors.

In 1942, Joy met and married William Lindsay Gresham, a fellow communist who had fought in the Spanish Civil War. Bill Gresham was a freelance writer who would have a hard time making money (and keeping it when he did make it) his entire life. His Spanish experience hadn't soured him completely on communism, but it dampened his enthusiasm considerably. Joy herself was becoming restless with the Communist Party. She was supposed to be a doctrinaire communist, but she would make jokes at the Party's expense at times, and she followed her own path when it came to what she was expected to read: "I continued, in the teeth of the Party's contempt, to read fantasy; and I utterly failed to read the dreary books we called 'proletarian novels.' Though I reproached myself bitterly for it, moreover, I was bored at meetings." The birth of two sons, David in 1944 and Douglas in 1945, moved her even closer to a break: "My little son was a real thing and so was my obligation to him; by comparison, my duty to that imaginary entity the working class seemed the most doubtful of abstractions." Further, "I began to notice what neglected, neurotic waifs the children of so many Communists were, and to question the genuineness of a love of mankind that didn't begin at home."[9]

Her "renegade" reading had led her to Lewis's *The Screwtape Letters* and *The Great Divorce*. Both "stirred an unused part of my brain to momentary sluggish life. Of course, I thought, atheism was *true*; but I hadn't given quite enough attention to developing the proof of it. Someday, when the children were older, I'd work it out. Then I forgot the whole matter."[10] However, it was the beginning of a reexamination of just what she believed.

Conversion

The breaking point came on the day Bill called to inform her he was having a nervous breakdown and wouldn't be coming home. Joy was frantic. Waiting for some further word from him, fearing he had ended his life, she had to admit what her pride had not allowed before then: "I was not, after all, 'the master of my fate' and 'the captain of my soul.' All my defenses—the walls of arrogance and cocksureness and self-love behind which I had hid from God—went down momentarily. And God came in." She meant that last sentence literally. As she relates in her conversion story,

---

9. Ibid., 21–22.
10. Ibid., 22.

> There was a Person with me in the room, directly present to my consciousness—a Person so real that all my previous life was by comparison mere shadow play. And I myself was more alive than I had ever been; it was like waking from sleep. So intense a life cannot be endured for long by flesh and blood; we must ordinarily take our life watered down, diluted as it were, by time and space and matter. My perception of God lasted perhaps half a minute.
>
> In that time, however, many things happened. I forgave some of my enemies. I understood that God had always been there, and that, since childhood, I had been pouring half my energy into the task of keeping him out. I saw myself as I really was, with dismay and repentance; and, seeing, I changed. I have been turning into a different person since that half minute, everyone tells me.
>
> When it was over I found myself on my knees praying. I think I must have been the world's most astonished atheist. My surprise was so great that for a moment it distracted me from my fear; only for a moment, however. My awareness of God was no comforting illusion, conjured up to reassure me about my husband's safety. I was just as worried afterward as before. No; it was terror and ecstasy, repentance and rebirth.[11]

Joy's initial experience with God was not a complete one; it was a revelation of His existence, thereby wiping out her atheism, but it was not yet a commitment to Christ as the Savior.

Becoming a Christian was a hurdle for this Jewish ex-atheist. Joy had been used to hearing the word "apostate" attached to Jesus Christ. So her first impulse was to try to be a "good Jew" in the "Reformed" persuasion, but that did not work.[12] Shortly after her recognition of God's existence, she had returned to Lewis's writings, seeking more answers. He helped her see where she had gone wrong. "Without his works, I wonder if I and many others might not still be infants 'crying in the night,'" is how she phrased it in her testimony.[13] She had to set aside the delusion that all religions were the same. While she could see some wisdom in all, and good ethics in some, she concluded that only one "had complete understanding of the grace and repentance and charity that had come to me from God. And the Redeemer who had made himself known, whose personality I would have recognized

---

11. Ibid., 23–24.
12. Ibid., 25.
13. Ibid., 24.

among ten thousand—well, when I read the New Testament, I recognized him. He was Jesus."[14]

In order to complete her renewal of the mind, Joy then turned, for the first time, to all those Marxist works she had avoided reading earlier. She needed to dissect their reasoning to see if anything she had been taught could hold up under scrutiny. In a letter dating from 1948, one can see how she is linking what she has learned from Lewis to her critique of Marxism. "There are only two *really* atheistic philosophies: mechanical materialism and solipsism, and *both* are characteristic of the bourgeoisie," she reported to her correspondents. And she saw how Lewis incorporated both: "Lewis has personified them very neatly in *That Hideous Strength*, as the diabolists Wither and Frost. Wither holds that *only* his consciousness exists, therefore he has no social responsibility. Frost holds that only matter exists, and consciousness and free will are illusions . . . and therefore Frost too has no social responsibility."[15]

Later that year, she summarized for the poet William Rose Benét what she had discovered through her appraisal of Lenin's writings: "As for me, I had to have a direct and shattering experience of God, and then to plow my way through Lenin's *Materialism*, surely the world's most unreadable book . . . in order to find out that Marxism was philosophically nonsensical, logically unsound, historically arbitrary, and scientifically half false from the start."[16] In a later letter, Joy informed Benét that Lewis's writings, even his fantasies, were responsible for her being able to see clearly for the first time.[17]

The Lewis Link

How does an American Jewish atheist-turned-communist-turned-Christian end up as the wife of a famous Oxford don? The story is complex, but it begins with Chad Walsh serving as the link between Joy Gresham and C. S. Lewis. Walsh's *Apostle to the Skeptics* and an article he published in *The New York Times Book Review* caught Joy's attention. She wrote to him for the first time in June 1949, letting him know of her intense interest in Lewis's writings and the impact they had had on her thinking. He, in turn, encouraged her to write to Lewis directly. She responded,

---

14. Ibid., 25.
15. Letter from Joy to V. J. and Alice Jerome, 21 January 1948, King, *Out of My Bone*, 53–54.
16. Letter from Joy to William Rose Benét, 31 October 1948, ibid., 79.
17. Letter from Joy to William Rose Benét, 19 August 1949, ibid., 109.

> We more than share your feeling for Lewis; with us it was not the last step but the first that came from reading his books, for we were raised atheists and took the truth of atheism for granted, and like most Marxists were so busy acting that we never stopped to think. If I hadn't picked up *The Great Divorce* one day—brr, I suppose I'd still be running madly around with leaflets, showing as much intelligent purpose as a headless chicken. But I wouldn't have picked up *The Great Divorce* if I hadn't loved fantasy, and I wouldn't have loved fantasy if I hadn't, as a twelve-year-old moping in the school library, found *Phantastes*. . . .
>
> By the way, your remark that Lewis answered even asinine letters gave us courage to write to him—so we sent the unfortunate man five single-spaced pages of personal history and what not.[18]

Thus began a correspondence between Joy and Lewis that would lead to a reorientation of the rest of her life.

Writing to Walsh again the next year, and commenting on Lewis's logic with respect to how Jesus had to be either a liar, a lunatic, or the actual Son of God, Joy added her own commentary: "Anyone who thinks Jesus could have been a paranoid with delusions of grandeur has only to read up on *real* paranoids, in the asylum and out, and see what they sound like. History is full of self-appointed Messiahs, and they all sound the same, mad with pride. The humor and commonsense of Jesus never came from a disturbed mind." Toward the end of the letter, she informed Walsh that in her correspondence with Lewis, she had engaged him in debate on a couple of points where she had a disagreement with him. So even though she considered him her mentor in the faith, she continued to think for herself and challenged him on areas where she thought he might be wrong. This letter, though, reveals that Joy's newfound humility apparently was real, when she remarked to Walsh,

> Lord, he knocked my props out from under me unerringly; one shot to a pigeon. I haven't a scrap of my case left. And, what's more, I've seldom enjoyed anything more. Being disposed of so neatly by a master of debate, all fair and square—it seems to be one of the great pleasures of life, though I'd never have suspected it in my arrogant youth. I suppose it's *unfair* tricks of argument that leave wounds. But after the sort of thing that Lewis does, what I feel is a craftsman's joy at the sight of a superior performance.[19]

---

18. Letter from Joy to Chad Walsh, 21 June 1949, Chad Walsh Papers, Folder 4—Letters Between Chad Walsh and Joy Davidman.

19. Letter from Joy to Chad Walsh, 27 January 1950, ibid.

She didn't mind being proven wrong if the proof was arrived at through unassailable logical argumentation.

Bill Gresham purportedly had been converted along with Joy, but it didn't take too long to figure out that his "conversion" was just one more trendy philosophy he would follow for a while. His faith seems to have been only an external attempt to copy what Joy was experiencing. In a letter to his son David in 1962, Bill stated, "I am not a Christian and will probably never be one since I cannot understand the basic doctrines or accept them."[20] After his flirtation with Christianity, he plunged into Zen and Scientology. Their marriage was rapidly deteriorating. Bill would go into drunken rages. At times, he would lose control of himself completely—once shooting a hole in the ceiling, another time smashing his guitar to pieces, and still another time hitting one of the boys on the head with a bottle. Then there was the unfaithfulness sexually at a time when Joy was ill. The marriage became one in name only.

In early 1952, Joy's cousin Renée Pierce, along with her two young children, came to stay with the Greshams, running away from her own unhappy marriage to a violent, drunken man. Joy and Renée adjusted well to one another, and the latter helped a lot with the housework. The relationship with Bill, however, was not improving. Even though he was trying to stay away from alcohol, there were other issues. He was having trouble writing and earning money, and his infidelity led Joy to cut off all intimate relations. The stress was almost too much to bear, and she wanted some time away to think and to complete a manuscript she was working on, which later came out as *Smoke on the Mountain*. In fact, she wanted to see C. S. Lewis in person to ask his advice. As a Christian now, she didn't believe in divorce, and she was struggling with how to maintain her broken marriage.

Renée seemed to come to the rescue with a solution. She would be only too happy to continue to stay with Bill and the boys and take care of all domestic duties while Joy had her sabbatical from family problems. So a trip was arranged; Joy left New York for England in August 1952. It was a welcome respite from troubles, and she was anticipating some fruitful discussions with her spiritual mentor.

Joy's increasing reliance on Lewis can be seen in some of her letters. Writing to the poet Kenneth Porter, she had said, "I really belong with the Anglicans, and not Broad Church either—C. S. Lewis and Charles Williams are the teachers I follow. That is, I believe in the divinity of Christ and in the resurrection of the dead; the world around us seems to me, now, a process of growth rather than an end in itself. So of course material disasters don't

---

20. Dorsett, *And God Came In*, 71–72.

seem as terrifying as they once did."[21] Three months later, she confided to that same correspondent, "Since I am one of C. S. Lewis' converts I tend to follow him fairly closely, and nobody has yet been able to define *him*!"[22] Yet her mind was still her own (she also confided to Porter that she was arguing with Lewis over the issue of birth control) and she was continually undergoing a renewal of the mind that, while heavily influenced by Lewis, could never have occurred without her own commitment. This can be seen in one critique she offered Porter with respect to his poems:

> In many of them you are explaining and sympathizing with Jesus, rather than accepting him—you are, indeed, not following Jesus but trying to get him to follow you; using him as an agency of your own special revolutionary theory. I did this myself in the early days of my conversion; explained away what I didn't like in the Gospel, valued Jesus not as the gateway to my own salvation, but as a *means* which I could use to support my own ideas—until it dawned on me that unless Jesus was God he was nothing, just another man with a handful of random ideas, and that all I valued such a man for was the accidental support his ideas gave my own position. You see, I was still being my own God![23]

Such thoughts and conclusions mark a significant spiritual growth and maturity in her understanding. She now wanted Lewis to help her over her latest hurdles. A face-to-face meeting, in her view, was essential.

New Life in England

Michal Williams, widow of author Charles Williams, who had been one of Lewis's closest friends, wrote to Chad Walsh in November 1952 about meeting Joy Gresham: "I saw C. S. Lewis a few weeks ago & . . . nakedly & unashamedly listened to the great man cascading brilliance. He brought his brother & Joy Gresham along. I like Joy so much." Williams then analyzed her new friend: "She is most unusual. I think she may be going through some sort of crisis & I think her visit to England has done her good. She comes here quite a lot & we talk of mice & men & cabbages & Kings. She has great affection for you & Eva & says how lovely your children [are], & somehow I think she is a forlorn child & very brave & rather hurt by life."[24]

21. Letter from Joy to Kenneth W. Porter, 29 May 1951, King, *Out of My Bone*, 118.
22. Letter from Joy to Kenneth W. Porter, 16 August 1951, ibid., 122.
23. Letter from Joy to Kenneth W. Porter, 18 August 1951, ibid., 125.
24. Letter from Michal Williams to Chad Walsh, 11 [?] November 1952, Chad Walsh Papers, Folder 6—Correspondence of Chad Walsh with Michal Williams.

Joy got her heart's desire. She not only met Lewis and talked, but he invited her to spend Christmas with him and brother Warnie. Both he and Warnie hit it off with her from the start. It was while she was at the Kilns at Christmas that the letter came from Bill that didn't surprise her completely. It really was no good for them to continue, he counseled. Besides, he had now fallen in love with Renée and wanted to marry her. Would Joy please grant him a divorce? They could still be friends, he assured her. She shared the news with Lewis and asked his advice. He counseled divorce, given the fact of Bill's infidelity. Joy then returned to New York in January 1953, not sure what was going to transpire.

Chad Walsh received letters from both Lewis and Joy, giving an overview of the time they had spent together. Neither mentioned the impending divorce. Lewis's comments were shorter and more news-oriented. By not saying anything about Joy's domestic situation, Lewis was keeping a confidence.

Joy's letter, in contrast, was far more expansive on what it was like living in the Kilns for over two weeks. "First chance I've had to write to you—so much has been happening. I stayed with Jack and Warnie over a fortnight just before I sailed for home, and had a marvelous time; by the way, they both send their love. Quite an experience it was, Christmas with the Lewises!" She was impressed with Lewis's work ethic, even in what was supposed to be a break from the grind: "Being on vacation, Jack was taking life easy—he was merely writing his book on prayer (it's going to be a wonder, I've read part of it), correcting OHEL proofs, setting scholarship and fellowship exam papers, doing a college edition of Spenser for an American publisher, and finishing the *seventh* Narnia book. Also, of course, answering the endless letters." Not only that, but "this left him time to go over my own Decalogue book with me (about 50,000 words of it) and tell me how to fix it; he liked it quite well, thank heaven." She had an opportunity to see the galley proofs for his volume on the history of English literature: "I am the *first* person to see those galleys, and I feel very honored."[25]

Although studiously avoiding her marriage situation in that letter, she found, by the end of February, that she needed to confide in the Walshes. She told them of the potential divorce and added, "I can't pretend I'm sorry." She had hoped Bill's many problems would end if he became a Christian, but she had been disappointed. "Bill gave up being a Christian," she related, "as soon as he found out it meant living by a moral code and admitting and repenting one's sins." Not only that, but when Bill had met her upon her return, he "greeted me by knocking me about a bit.... Two days after he'd choked me, he asked in all seriousness, 'Have you ever known me to do a

---

25. Letter from Joy to Chad Walsh, 25 January 1953, King, *Out of My Bone*, 138–39.

brutal or unkind thing?'"[26] Lewis, she concluded, had been right. It was time to get the divorce. On the heels of that decision came another momentous decision: she would take the boys with her and make a permanent residence in England.

It was difficult for a divorced American woman trying to start a new life in a foreign country. But Joy had become a complete Anglophile and sought to fit in. Funds were always low, and her spirits were as well, at times. Bill promised to send money, and did when he could, but he wasn't being very successful in his writing career and refused to get a nine-to-five job. If not for C. S. Lewis, who was fast becoming her best and most trusted friend, she may not have survived. He covered the costs for the boys' education and helped her in any other way he could. Slowly, though perhaps more slowly on his side, they became more than friends. Still, it took a few more years before they came to the place where they would actually share their lives in marriage.

Lewis obviously enjoyed his interactions with Joy. They seemed to be on the same track intellectually. Joy wrote to Bill about how she and the boys spent time at the Kilns, which she deemed a great success. It was, she said, "a very relaxed and friendly visit, though physically strenuous enough; long walks through the hills, during which Jack reverted completely to schoolboy tactics and went charging ahead with the boys through all the thorniest, muddiest, steepest places; Warnie and I meanwhile toiling behind and feeling very old." Back at the Kilns, Joy was delighted that "Jack and Warnie taught Davy chess; he astonished them by learning it instantly and doing very well. Douglas, meanwhile, enjoyed himself sawing huge armfuls of firewood, which was *very* well received." There was a special surprise: "Jack gave them the typescript of the *next* Narnia book, *The Horse and His Boy*, which is dedicated to them; it's very good. I shouldn't dream of visiting Jack often—we're much too exhausting an experience for that quiet bachelor household; but a little of it's probably good for them, judging by their reactions."[27]

Increasingly, Joy would be by Lewis's side for a number of occasions, and she was becoming involved with critiquing his draft for his upcoming autobiography *Surprised by Joy*. "Sensation in the academic world" she wrote to Bill. "Jack is going to Cambridge. They've created a new chair specially for him—Professor of Mediaeval and Renaissance Literature. Serves Oxford right; they should have done it long ago."[28] Another letter to Bill: "Incidentally I've been reading Jack's autobiography in manuscript and I

---

26. Letter from Joy to Chad and Eva Walsh, 27 February 1953, Dorsett, *And God Came In*, 93–94.

27. Letter from Joy to William Lindsay Gresham, 22 December 1953, King, *Out of My Bone*, 166

28. Letter from Joy to William Lindsay Gresham, 17 June 1954, ibid., 201.

shan't send them to *his* old school, Malvern. Wow! He's as violent a satirist as Swift when he wants to be."[29] Still another: "I drank a pint of the Bird and Baby's special cider today to your happiness; as for Jack, he drank to the repentance and forgiveness of all sinners. After which we went out on top of Shotover Hill and helped the boys fly a kite, with fifty miles of England stretched out all round us."[30]

Joy even had access to Lewis's rooms in Oxford, where he let her work on a manuscript. She wrote of the bliss of viewing the deer park from one window and the flowers out of another. There was one hitch, though: the tourists. "They're really a menace," she informed Bill, "tiptoeing up and down stairs all day and poking into rooms, though they're not supposed to enter the Fellows' building. Yesterday two horrible German yentas tried furtively to enter Jack's room and froze when they saw me, their eyes roving from me to the lettered 'Mr. C. S. Lewis' over the door. I guess I didn't look the part. I challenged them; they squeaked, 'Ve chust vanted ve should see the house!' and fled."[31]

A real test for both Joy and Lewis arrived in October 1954 when her parents came for a visit. Still atheist, rigid, and demanding, they could prove to be a challenge. This wasn't exactly a "meet-the-parents" moment for the purpose of upcoming matrimony; it was couched in the language of meeting a good friend and mentor. Joy, when it was over, was delighted with how it went. They met twice, the first time in London as Lewis was taking part in a debate. "We took him to tea at the Piccadilly Hotel beforehand. (His suggestion; my organizing work; my parents' dough.) . . . Jack laid himself out to be charming to both my parents and succeeded admirably; when I complimented him on it privately he said pathetically, 'I'm doing my best!'" At the end of the tea, he invited them all to Oxford for lunch the next week. Joy's response? "Jack must be aiming for a halo."[32]

The second meeting went well also. She reported to Bill that the family had lunched with Lewis at Magdalen. Lewis asked Joy's mother what she liked best about Oxford, thinking it might be the impressive buildings, but was surprised when she instead lauded the shopping district. Overall, though, Joy was delighted with how the day went, especially when her parents told her afterward how much they liked Lewis. What was even more

---

29. Letter from Joy to William Lindsay Gresham, 6 July 1954, ibid., 207.
30. Letter from Joy to William Lindsay Gresham, 10 August 1954, ibid., 211.
31. Letter from Joy to William Lindsay Gresham, 27 August 1954, ibid., 214.
32. Letter from Joy to William Lindsay Gresham, 29 October 1954, ibid., 222–23.

unusual, she commented, was that he could joke with her father, something not many people could accomplish. He definitely had made his mark.[33]

Joy attended Lewis's inaugural address when he moved to Cambridge at the end of 1954, an event she compared to a coronation. There was a lot of hoopla surrounding the event. She considered it a great success, but, again, showing her independence of thought, she felt he was wrong in placing the historic break from the past at the point of the scientific revolution. "I don't know how the dons liked it," she wrote to Bill, "but the students ate it up. But I think, for once, he was sacrificing accuracy in the interests of a good show."[34] Commenting to Walsh on the same topic, she called his address "brilliant, intellectually exciting, unexpected, and funny as hell—as you can imagine." In the address, Lewis had referred to himself as a dinosaur, a leftover from a long-gone age, and had determined that Europe was now post-Christian. She thought he was being too gloomy: "How that man loves being in a minority, even a lost-cause minority! Athanasius contra mundum, or Don Quixote against the windmills. . . . I sometimes wonder what he would do if Christianity really did triumph everywhere; I suppose he would have to invent a new heresy."[35]

Joy's book, *Smoke on the Mountain: An Interpretation of the Ten Commandments*, was published in 1954. She thanked Walsh for noticing it and promised to send him the English edition with Lewis's preface. She was a little discouraged about it at first, since it wasn't attracting much notice. Lewis had agreed to do the preface in hopes that it would garner more attention as a result. He truly wanted Joy to succeed with it, and he thought it was an excellent treatment of the subject. "The quality of this book," he asserted, "which, I anticipate, will stand out more clearly the better it is known, is precisely the union of passionate heat with an intelligence which, in that passion, still modifies and distinguishes and tempers." He did have some differences with her, he writes, but one primarily:

> I do not of course agree with Miss Davidman at every point. In such a book every reader will have his own crow to pluck with the author. For my own part, what I would most gladly see altered are certain passages where she quotes myself for thoughts which she needed no sense save her own to reach and no pen save her own to express. But every old tutor (and I was not even that to Miss Davidman) knows that those pupils

---

33. Letter from Joy to William Lindsay Gresham, 4 November 1954, ibid., 224.
34. Letter from Joy to William Lindsay Gresham, 30 November 1954, ibid., 226.
35. Letter from Joy to Chad Walsh, 13 December 1954, ibid., 227–28.

who needed our assistance least are generally also those who acknowledge it most largely.[36]

So even that "criticism" was actually praise for her skills.

By April of 1955, she was happier with the book's acceptance, telling Bill, "It's doing fairly well here—has sold 3000 already, mostly on the basis of Jack's preface and some extraordinarily good reviews in church publications." She was coming to the view, though, that her talents were not primarily authorial: "I don't kid myself in these matters—whatever my talents as an independent writer, my *real* gift is as a sort of editor-collaborator . . . and I'm happiest when I'm doing something like that. Though I can't write one-tenth as well as Jack, I can tell him how to write more like himself! He is now about three-quarters of the way through his new book . . . and says he finds my advice indispensable."[37]

Joy helped in the move to Cambridge. To some friends she wrote of how Lewis was adapting to the move, revealing the emotional wrench it was for him at first, even though he handled his uneasiness with his usual sense of humor: "Poor lamb, he was suffering all the pangs and qualms of a new boy going to a formidable school—went around muttering, 'Oh, what a fool I am! I had a good home and I left!' and turning his mouth down at the corners most pathetical. He always makes his distresses into a joke, but of course there's a genuine grief in leaving a place like Magdalen after thirty years; rather like a divorce, I imagine." In the same letter, she shared her involvement with his endeavors, noting that he had "finished his autobiography—I've got the last chapters here now and must set my wits to work on criticism. I think it a first-rate job, though it will disappoint those who are curious for personal details; it is really chiefly the story of his conversion."[38] When Bill read the autobiography, he commented on how the death of Lewis's mother might have affected him. Joy agreed: "You're right about Jack's autobiography; I don't think he's ever got over his grief and horror at his mother's death—who would? There'd be no point in stirring up trouble by hunting for grief charges, though—even if he'd let me! Why disturb a satisfactory adjustment? Jack's sorrows, instead of breaking him down, seem to have strengthened him, made him something like a saint. And if he had any *more* energy he'd take off and fly."[39]

---

36. Lewis, Foreword to Davidman, *Smoke on the Mountain*, 10–11.

37. Letter from Joy to William Lindsay Gresham, 29 April 1955, King, *Out of My Bone*, 246.

38. Letter from Joy to Robert and Jackie Jackson, 19 January 1955, ibid., 235.

39. Letter from Joy to William Lindsay Gresham, 14 March 1956, ibid., 282.

It was Lewis's next work, though, that Joy had a direct hand in developing. The strange thing was that now that he had leisure to write whatever he chose, he had "dried up" and was deeply concerned about it. Then that changed. "Jack has started a new fantasy—for grownups," she wrote to Bill. "One night he was lamenting that he couldn't get a good idea for a book. We kicked a few ideas around till one came to life. Then we had another whiskey each and bounced it back and forth between us. The next day, without further planning, he wrote the first chapter! I read it and made some criticisms (feels quite like old times); he did it over and went on with the next. What I'd give to have his energy!"[40] That intellectual/inspirational exchange led to what Lewis considered to be his best novel, *Till We Have Faces*.

One senses that a bridge was crossed in their relationship in 1955. Their times together began to veer more toward the desire for togetherness in itself. Joy's letters from this period make it clear they were spending a lot of time together, along with her sons. Without being an official family, they were beginning to act like one. Joy rubbed some of Lewis's friends the wrong way because of her more abrasive personality. Others apparently didn't like her because she was American. Still others (there was some overlap here) were concerned about the burgeoning relationship due to her being a divorcee. Surely this was not a woman suitable for the foremost Christian writer of the era. Yet one of Lewis's friends, Peter Bayley, who also had been one of his students, saw the positive nature of the relationship. Lewis, he said, "seemed very different: much more muted, gentle, and relaxed. Even his voice and laugh seemed quieter. I felt that his sensitive nature had at last come through a tough masculine clubbability."[41]

Lewis was becoming more attached to Joy and very concerned about her state of affairs. In a letter to Walsh, he requested emotional support for her; she was rather depressed because she had to move out of her home. He requested that Walsh send a letter to her that might help cheer her up.[42] Harsher news, however, was looming, and it would lead C. S. Lewis into a firmer commitment and a love he had never expected.

Mrs. C. S. Lewis

A prelude to what was to come showed up in a letter to Bill in April 1956, as Joy expressed her sympathy for a problem with Renée's hip. She could

---

40. Letter from Joy to William Lindsay Gresham, 23 March 1955, ibid., 242.

41. Peter Bayley, "From Master to Colleague," 176.

42. Letter from Lewis to Chad Walsh, 28 February 1956, Hooper, *Collected Letters, Vol. III*, 711, 713.

empathize because when she took a walk with Lewis a few weeks previously, she developed a problem with her leg. It caused some lameness for a few days, and her biggest worry was that it might be rheumatism.[43] But before her health came to the forefront as the major issue, another hurdle appeared.

Joy wanted to become a permanent resident of England, but now her past membership in the Communist Party was being used by the government to send her back to the United States. The only strategy that would allow her to remain seemed to be marriage to a citizen. For Lewis, this was a decision point. If Joy had to return to America, not only would he lose the close relationship they had developed, but she would be facing an uncertain future with a potentially abusive former husband, and the boys would be uprooted from their school and all they had become accustomed to in England. He felt that would be devastating for them. For all these reasons, and in the teeth of what he knew would be fierce resistance from some of his friends, he offered to participate in a civil wedding ceremony, apart from the blessing of the Anglican Church, which he knew would be a problem anyway due to Joy's status as a divorced woman. He had no problem with remarriage in this circumstance, believing as he did that she had proper grounds Biblically for the divorce, but the Anglican Church did not recognize that exception. Lewis's "middle way" allowed Joy to remain; they were officially married on 23 April 1956, but knowledge of the marriage was limited to a select few. Neither did Lewis consider this a true marriage in God's eyes, merely one acknowledged by the state. Therefore, they would go on as before, living separately. How did Joy view this arrangement? Her biographer, Lyle Dorsett, says simply, "Joy respected Lewis's feelings on this, never mentioning it in her letters to America until the status of the relationship changed several months later."[44]

In the fall of 1956, Lewis was in the process of trying to secure a real marriage with the blessing of the Church. A man visiting a woman in her home late into the night so frequently could lead to suspicions about the relationship. He realized this could give rise to gossip and possibly be harmful to his Christian witness. It also was harmful to Joy's reputation, so he sought to make it right in everyone's eyes. The Church, though, remained obstinate and refused to give permission. Before anything could be fully resolved, though, the real blow fell. Joy fell one day in October when her hip seemed to give out; she was unable to walk and had to be rushed to the hospital in extreme pain. This was the beginning of a new phase in life.

---

43. Letter from Joy to William Lindsay Gresham, 13 April 1956, King, *Out of My Bone*, 285.

44. Dorsett, *And God Came In*, 136.

The diagnosis was a worst-case scenario: cancer had destroyed her left femur; she also had a malignant tumor in one breast. The prognosis was bleak. Joy broke the news to Bill, sharing how she hoped things would work out in case of her death, partly to forestall him from seeking to take back the boys: "I am only moderately afraid for myself. I've been very tired for a long time. But I am alarmed for the boys (I have told them nothing yet, of course). My will appoints Jack and his lawyer as their guardians, and I think it is essential for them to finish their education here—a break now would upset them irreparably. Jack has promised to see to their schooling."[45] Lewis alerted Chad Walsh to the turn of events, letting him know that what they thought had been merely rheumatism was actually cancer. Lewis praised her fighting spirit, but acknowledged that his personal world, now so linked to hers, was looking grim.[46]

In December, Joy wrote to the Walshes, informing them not only of her status with respect to the cancer, but also divulging the real relationship she had had with Lewis since April, which they now both decided to make public.

> One good thing has come of all this—I can now tell you that Jack and I are married; have been for a few months, and are going to publish an announcement soon. When I come out of here I shall go to the Kilns as Mrs. Lewis. I know you'll be glad for us and will not worry unduly about the ecclesiastical difficulty! We've been trying to get the Bishop to rule my former marriage invalid but he daren't. So Jack and I have been married only civilly; but I don't feel it matters a scrap, though I should like a friendly and independent clergyman to add something. Jack's love and strength are carrying me through this bad time miraculously. . . .
>
> There were three bad days of vomiting after the op. during which physical agony was combined with a strange spiritual ecstasy; I think I know now how martyrs felt. All this has strengthened my faith and brought me very close to God—as if at last I knew all the answers.[47]

Walsh responded shortly after, encouraging her that friends in America were praying for her—he, in fact, had prayed for her in his church the last Sunday—and expressed faith that she would soon be out of the hospital

---

45. Letter from Joy to William Lindsay Gresham, 19 October 1956, King, *Out of My Bone*, 297.

46. Letter from Lewis to Chad Walsh, 9 November 1956, Hooper, *Collected Letters, Vol. III*, 804.

47. Letter from Joy to Chad and Eva Walsh, 3 December 1956, King, *Out of My Bone*, 299–300.

and able to take on her new life as Mrs. Lewis. As for the problem with the Church's blessing, he urged her to look past that, saying, "I can understand why you would like the formal blessing of the Church, though you know also that a timid bishop can't keep this from being a thorough, Christian, and sacramental marriage. Thank God for the blessed fact that the ministers of this sacrament are the man and woman who marry."[48]

How was Joy handling her disease and the treatments for it? She had shown remarkable courage from the start, but some days could be overwhelmingly depressing. She fell into a crisis of faith in early February, as revealed in a letter to the Walshes where she admitted, "I am in rather a bad state of mind as yet—they had promised me definitely that the X-rays would work; I'd pinned all my hopes to having a year or so of happiness with Jack at least—and instead it seems I shall lie about in hospital with my broken femur waiting for death, and unable to do anything to make my last shreds of life useful or bearable." She began to wonder where God was in the midst of her agony. "I am trying very hard to hold on to my faith, but I find it difficult; there seems such a gratuitous and merciless cruelty in this. I hope that all we have believed is true. I dare not hope for anything in *this* world." In this state of mind, she bordered on self-pity:

> Miracles may happen, but we mustn't count on them. The worst of it is I feel perfectly well aside from mild intermittent pain in the leg. I fear all this will be horribly depressing for you; I shall go on praying for the grace to endure, and perhaps I'll be more cheerful next time I write. Jack is terribly broken-up. How horrible that I, who wanted to bring him only happiness, should have brought him this! Perhaps it would have been better for him if he'd never known me though he says not.[49]

A week later, however, she had rebounded spiritually. Writing again to the Walshes, she reported, "Everything looks much brighter than it did before. For one thing my prayers for grace have been answered." She even remarked that perhaps God knew she needed this kind of experience for her own spiritual health. And she included a light moment that showcased the strengthening of her bond with Lewis: "I was very merry last weekend and Jack and I had a gay time in my room with lots of sherry and kisses. *What a pity I didn't catch that man younger.*"[50] Lewis also wrote to Walsh the same day, rejoicing that she had rallied spiritually. The outward circumstances seemed to be improving, he thought, but knew, according to the doctors,

---

48. Letter from Chad Walsh to Joy, 16 December 1956, ibid., 301.
49. Letter from Joy to Chad and Eva Walsh, 5 February 1957, ibid., 305–6.
50. Letter from Joy to Chad and Eva Walsh, 13 February 1957, ibid., 306–7.

that he should not be too hopeful. Yet they were enjoying their relationship despite those circumstances. He could hardly believe how happy they were together, even though what they were experiencing was more like "a honeymoon on a sinking ship."[51]

These dire circumstances spurred Lewis on to find some way to marry Joy in the eyes of God as well as the state. One Anglican priest friend, Peter Bide, who had prayed for others for healing with some success, agreed to come to Joy's bedside and lay hands on her for healing. They also talked about the Church's refusal to conduct the marriage. Bide disagreed with the Church authorities. In a letter he later wrote to Joy's biographer, Lyle Dorsett, he explained why he decided to defy the Church and conduct the marriage ceremony anyway: "Joy desperately wanted to solemnize her marriage before God and to claim the grace of the sacrament before she died. It did not seem to me in the circumstances, possible to refuse her the outward and visible sign of grace which she so ardently desired and which might lead to a peaceful end to a fairly desperate situation."[52] So, on 21 March 1957, Bide married Lewis and Joy at the hospital and then proceeded to lay hands on her and pray for healing.

Shortly after, the doctors allowed her to go home to the Kilns, presumably to die. It was at this time that Bill Gresham became bolder about wanting to get the boys back, but Joy's new husband wasn't about to let that happen. He wrote two *very* direct letters to Bill on the same day, making it clear that was a bad idea. In the first letter, he pointed out the devastation such a move would have on the boys, urging him, if he really wanted reconciliation, to wait until they were grown.

The second letter, apparently written right after the first, and also apparently after talking things over with Joy, focused more on the effect a forcible removal of her sons would have on her. Lewis wanted to be sure Bill understood he was not writing with animosity but he had to be straight with him. Bill's letter couldn't have arrived at a worse time: Joy was in agony and the letter devastated her. Her fear over the boys being returned to Bill was like torture to her, Lewis reported. Surely, if he knew how cruel this proposal seemed to her, he would relent. Although he hated to sound threatening, he promised to place all legal obstacles possible in Bill's way, if necessary. Why, he wondered, would either of them want to pay all that money to lawyers? Near the end of the letter, he made a strong emotional appeal, telling Bill he now had the opportunity to soothe, rather than aggravate, Joy's miseries.

---

51. Letter from Lewis to Chad Walsh, 13 February 1957, Hooper, *Collected Letters, Vol. III*, 832.

52. Dorsett, *And God Came In*, 140.

Further, if he didn't try to take his sons back now, he might actually regain their respect later.[53] Those two letters seemed to accomplish the purpose; Bill never brought up the subject again.

The Miraculous Reprieve

Then came the miracle. At least, that's how Lewis and Joy saw it. The doctors also were surprised. The cancer went into remission against all predictions. Her bones strengthened. Bed-ridden for a while, she eventually not only got up and around, but walked again with the aid of a cane, needed only because one leg was now shorter than the other. She could wander in the woods outside the house; she even took to taking a shotgun with her to ward off trespassers. It was all so unexpected. Both knew it might only be a short time together, but they were going to make the most of it. As Lewis explained to more than one correspondent, there can be miraculous *reprieve* as well as miraculous *pardon*. Who knew how long God might allow them to develop their relationship even further and find out what marriage really could be? They threw themselves into it. "Jack and I manage to be surprisingly happy considering the circumstances," Joy wrote to the Walshes. "You'd think we were a honeymoon couple in our early twenties rather than our middle-aged selves!"[54]

In a letter to longtime American correspondent Mary Willis Shelburne, Lewis was quite open about the newfound freedom he was experiencing as a married man. He and Joy had gone to a hotel for a long-delayed honeymoon It was an odd sensation for him: "Here's another absurdity of the mind," he wrote to Shelburne. "I'm such a confirmed old bachelor that I couldn't help feeling I was being rather naughty ('Staying with a woman at a hotel!' Just like people in the newspapers!)."[55] One of the highlights of their brief marriage was their first airplane trip (for both) to Ireland in the summer of 1958, Lewis's place of birth. "Don't remember if I wrote you since we came back from Ireland," Joy related to Bill. "We had a heavenly time; beautiful sunny weather, miraculous golden light over everything, clear air in which the mountains glowed like jewels—there isn't a speck of dust in the whole country," she enthused with obvious exaggeration. "The country is

---

53. Letter from Lewis to William Lindsay Gresham, 6 April 1957, Hooper, *Collected Letters, Vol. III.*, 844–45.

54. Letter from Joy to Chad and Eva Walsh, 6 June 1957, King, *Out of My Bone*, 320.

55. Letter from Lewis to Mary Willis Shelburne, 15 April 1958, Hooper, *Collected Letters, Vol. III*, 935.

all rocks—granite hillsides like the roughest of New England, and dry stone walls everywhere—and completely lacks the lush garden quality of England; there's a good deal of austerity in its beauty, but it is the most beautiful place I've ever seen. Certainly the greenest!"[56] She also got to meet Lewis's relatives and friends, and felt more like a part of his extended family. It was a magnificent sensory experience for Joy, and an opportunity for Lewis to show off his homeland.

Lewis was actively writing during those few short years of marriage. Joy relates to Bill in a 1959 letter that "Jack has just sold *Sat[urday] [Evening] Post* an after-dinner speech by Screwtape, denouncing (among other things) 'democratic education.' I bet it'll make the fur fly." She also commented on the sales for the Narnia books, saying that they were doing better in England than in America, but that they would never get rich from them. "The good thing about them is that they don't dwindle with time—but I think it's only the most successful juveniles that go on for ever."[57] She was right in saying that the most successful children's books go on forever; that's precisely what has happened with Narnia. She was wrong, though, in her assessment that they would never sell enough for a large income and that American sales would lag behind, but no one can be held accountable for not knowing what the future will bring.

Lewis's biggest, and most successful, enterprise at this time was the publication of *The Four Loves*. This did not begin as a book idea; it was an outgrowth of some radio broadcasts he recorded for the Episcopal Radio-TV Foundation. One can say that this book, along with *Till We Have Faces*, might never have been published without Lewis's experience of being married to Joy. *The Four Loves* analyzes four types of love that Lewis felt should be contrasted: affection, friendship, eros, and charity. Without the intimate relationship with Joy, he could never have written so effectively, particularly on eros.

Joy continued to receive checkups from the doctors. In a letter to Lewis at Cambridge, she sent this encouraging news in March 1958: "I'm writing early a) because it's a short week, b) because the news is good. My blood count came out quite all right, the lump is a-shrinking & Ellis is very pleased with my response to the hormone he gave me—whose purpose is to counteract the effect of X-rays. I continue to feel as sassy as a jaybird (Americanism, needless to say) in spite of the weather."[58] By late 1959, though, there was no mistaking that the cancer was back.

56. Letter from Joy to William Lindsay Gresham, 8 August 1958, King, *Out of My Bone*, 339.

57. Letter from Joy to William Lindsay Gresham, 26 September 1959, ibid., 349–50.

58. Letter from Joy to Lewis, 8 March 1958, ibid., 331.

Through Grief and Beyond

"The blow has fallen," Lewis informed Walsh in October 1959. News that Joy's cancer had returned was a shock.[59] Prior to receiving this bad news, they had planned a May trip to Greece. Neither had ever been there, but for Joy, in particular, seeing Greece was an unfulfilled passion. Now they had to wonder if those plans should be canceled. She resisted; they went anyway, even knowing that it could drain the last drops of energy from her. Lewis wrote of it to Walsh shortly after they returned, wherein he remarked that though, at first, he doubted she would be able to make the trip, it turned out wonderfully. They had no regrets for making the trip. Lewis considered Joy "divinely supported" the entire time. She had been granted a lifelong desire and was grateful.[60]

Death—the last enemy the Christian faces before being ushered into the presence of God—came to Joy Lewis a few weeks later on 13 July 1960. Lewis wrote of it to many of his correspondents, but the letter to Walsh probably provides the greatest insight into her last moments. "It was a wonderful marriage," Lewis confirmed to Walsh. "Even after all hope was gone, even on the last night before her death, there were 'patins of bright gold.' Two of the last things she said were 'You have made me happy' and 'I am at peace with God.'"[61]

Shortly after Joy's death, Lewis began recording his feelings. Out of those daily jottings came an honest little book full of anguish, pain, and questioning of God's ways, yet ultimately coming to the conclusion that one must put one's life in His hands and allow Him to bring the healing, both now and in eternity. *A Grief Observed* was published in 1961 initially under a pseudonym, N. W. Clerk, which was a pun on an Old English term for "I know not what scholar." In those eighty-nine pages (more of a booklet than a book), we find Lewis struggling emotionally. Intellectually, he knew the answers to his questions, but he needed to work through the inner conflict that was making him doubt God's goodness.

Lewis's faith held. He lived only three more years, and was in bad health most of that time. By the end, he was fully resigned to death, even anticipating it. His understanding of his own faith, and his grasp of the door that opens into the next world, was enhanced by his relationship with an American, Jewish, former atheist, former communist woman who became the love of his life.

59. Letter from Lewis to Chad Walsh, 22 October 1959, Hooper, *Collected Letters*, Vol. III, 1095, 1097.
60. Letter from Lewis to Chad Walsh, 23 May 1960, ibid., 1152–54.
61. Letter from Lewis to Chad Walsh, 18 October 1960, ibid., 1198–99.

4

Walter Hooper: Keeper of the Flame

"I MUST MAKE IT absolutely clear from the outset that my acquaintance with Lewis was in comparison to that of many of his friends, a mere flea-bite." That was how Walter Hooper phrased it in speaking at a conference more than forty years after what he considered to be the absolute highlight of his life—a summer in Oxford with the man who had invigorated Hooper's Christian faith by his writings. A decade after first reading a C. S. Lewis book, the young lecturer in English literature at the University of Kentucky, in 1963, finally came face to face with Lewis—something he had dreamt of doing for a long time. Why was this meeting so important to him? He put it this way to his conference audience: "I wonder if, like me, you have found that in reading Lewis you enjoyed not just another author, but a meeting of minds that has gone on developing over the years. I expect I am one of the many who believes that his introduction to Lewis's writings was far from being accidental. That is because it changed the whole direction of my life, and hasn't ended yet."[1]

First Contacts

In 1953, Hooper was completing his degree from the University of North Carolina in Chapel Hill. He anticipated being drafted into the army shortly after graduation, but was told he had a couple of months before that would

---

1. Hooper, "Personal Testimony," originally presented at a conference in 2007, sent to the author via e-mail with original title of "Rockingham CC." All further references to this document will be titled "Personal Testimony."

happen. During that interregnum, he was introduced to Lewis for the first time, yet not to one of his books. Given a copy of J. B. Phillips's *Letters to Young Churches: A Translation of the New Testament Epistles*, he began with the introduction written by someone he had never heard of: C. S. Lewis. "I read the Introduction simply because it was there," Hooper recalled. It had an effect on him he never anticipated: "It made a total conquest of me." Why did this introduction—merely the preamble to what was supposed to be the substance, Paul's epistles in modern language—affect him as it did? He explained, "It was not so much what he said, but the *way* he said it. I wish I could describe it better, but what came through the introduction was not simply information about the Epistles but something about Lewis. I knew I'd stumbled upon someone whose faith was as certain as that of the Apostles. Lewis believed—or so it seemed to me—with the certainty of St. Peter and those who had been with Jesus."[2] In another essay, he provided even more detail about this first encounter:

> Will you think me a fool if I tell you that, all these years later, that piece of writing is *still* making a conquest of me? I remember where I was sitting when I read it, and I recollect its effect on me as if it happened yesterday. What did Lewis *say* that was so earthshaking? That's just the point. Nothing he said was particularly unusual. The difference, apart from his extraordinary lucidity and beautifully phrased paragraphs, was that he was *sure* of what he said.[3]

The army finally called Hooper and, when he went, he took along his first Lewis book, *Miracles*. Basic training does not provide a lot of free time, so it took Hooper a while to finish reading the book; his method for doing so was rather unorthodox. No matter whether he was engaged in bayonet practice or calisthenics, *Miracles* remained with him, tucked inside his shirt, "which made for a good deal of discomfort." He had to read it in small, digestible bites. "In those little ten-minute breaks between firing bazookas and throwing grenades, I managed to read a page or so. If a book can hold your interest during all that excitement, and while you're crawling under barbed wire in a muddy trench, it is a very, *very* good book."[4]

> And so amidst a thousand distractions, I read, page by page, my first book by C. S. Lewis. It remains in my memory as the greatest literary and theological experience of my life. I was savoring

---

2. Hooper, "Personal Testimony."
3. Hooper, "Original Encounter," 140.
4. Hooper, "Personal Testimony."

for the first time arguments about naturalism and supernaturalism, about miracles, about the doctrines of the incarnation and the resurrection. One of the most unforgettable moments of my life occurred under those pine trees at Fort Jackson when I came across Lewis's distinction between science and Christianity. I think I probably yelled out loud when I read in chapter 14 of *Miracles* "In science we have been reading only the notes to a poem; in Christianity we find the poem itself." . . .

I *knew* I'd never read anything like this. Indeed, had I not had this firsthand experience, I would not have believed it possible for anyone to express such deep truths in language of such brilliant clarity.[5]

With basic training finally behind him, he found himself stationed at Ft. Bragg, North Carolina, by November 1954, working for some of the chaplains. Dr. Bob Jones of Bob Jones University was scheduled to come to the fort, and since Jones had met Lewis in person on a trip to England, Hooper arranged to meet him. The strongly fundamentalist Jones normally would not have had much in common with an Anglican like Lewis, so there was no assurance that his opinions of Lewis would be favorable. Hooper wanted to talk with him regardless, seeking to get more insight into the writer who had so impacted his faith personally. When he had the opportunity to ask Jones what he thought of Lewis, he received this rather interesting reply: "That man," he said—there was a pause—"that man smokes a pipe, and that man drinks liquor—but I *do* believe he's a Christian!"[6]

Buoyed perhaps by that recommendation—albeit a somewhat strange one—of Lewis's genuineness, Hooper wrote to him for the first time that very month and was stunned to receive a quick response. Looking back on that first letter from Lewis, he realized that it showcased the essence of his character, "his lack of interest in himself and his huge interest in almost everything *outside* himself."[7]

Hooper's ongoing interest in all of Lewis's works led him to continue a sporadic correspondence over the next several years. By 1957, Hooper apparently was getting the itch to visit England and see his spiritual mentor. Lewis responded that he would be glad to meet him if he should come.[8] That visit did not occur as soon as Hooper would have liked. By the early 1960s, he had an idea for an academic book about Lewis and planned a

5. Hooper, "Original Encounter," 141–42.

6. Hooper, "Personal Testimony."

7. Ibid.

8. Letter from Lewis to Walter Hooper, 2 December 1957, Hooper, *Collected Letters, Vol. III*, 902.

trip to England, which led to an invitation to come visit when he arrived. Lewis, though, repeated the caution he had given Chad Walsh fourteen years earlier prior to his volume on Lewis: it would be far better to write about someone who had died, not someone still alive.[9] When Hooper then compiled a bibliography of all the writings of Lewis he could find, and sent it to him, the latter was impressed: Hooper, Lewis surmised, was a better scholar of his works than the author himself, who had apparently forgotten many of the works listed in the bibliography. He offered his help whenever Hooper might arrive.[10]

The Summer of '63

"I sold the only thing I had of value—my car—and went to Oxford in June 1963," Hooper later stated forty-plus years after the fact.[11] His long-anticipated meeting with C. S. Lewis almost a reality, he did not have too lofty of expectations for any truly deep friendship, hoping for no more than "a single conversation over a cup of tea." What transpired exceeded that modest hope. "I don't believe in luck, but I do believe in angels," he related, "and the coveted tea party turned out to be (if it needs a name) 'The Observations of a Late Arrival' or 'A Single Summer with C. S.L.'"[12]

Hooper arrived at the Kilns on a June afternoon in 1963. As he walked past a window on his way to the front door, he saw a man reading with his back to the window. Perhaps it was the fact that he was now so close to a goal in his life—meeting the man whose thoughts had so permeated his own—that he began to suffer from a sense of impertinence in himself. Who was he to sit down with a great thinker like Lewis? For whatever reason, as he approached the door, he started to have second thoughts. "I rang the bell and regretted bitterly that I was bothering Lewis. Never had I seen myself in so unfavourable a light—an ignorant, provincial Tar Heel calling on this great man!" What to do? "But it was too late to flee. Someone was unlocking the door, and there stood C. S. Lewis."[13]

The second thoughts vanished immediately upon meeting Lewis, who was gracious and inviting. In fact, it was tea time, so Hooper was asked to join him. Although Hooper liked tea, he was amazed at Lewis's consumption of it: "As soon as we'd finished one pot of tea, Lewis would go to the kitchen

---

9. Letter from Lewis to Walter Hooper, 2 July 1962, ibid., 1354–55.
10. Letter from Lewis to Walter Hooper, 15 December 1962, ibid., 1393–94.
11. Hooper, "Personal Testimony."
12. Hooper, "Introduction," *The Weight of Glory*, 3.
13. Hooper, "Personal Testimony."

and make another, and another. I was quite a shy young Southern American at that time, but after what seemed gallons of it, I asked if I might be shown the 'bathroom.' Remember, I'd only just arrived in England, and I did not then know that in most homes the bathroom and the toilet are separate rooms." What followed was a wonderful example of Lewis's sense of humor:

> With a touch of mock formality Lewis conducted me to what was really the bathroom. He flung down several towels, produced several tablets of soap, and before closing the door on me he asked if I had everything I needed for my "bath." "Oh, yes!" I said with some alarm. By this time I was very uncomfortable, and I finally got up enough nerve to go back in the sitting-room and say that it was not really a "bath" I wanted. Lewis was roaring with laughter, and he said, "Now that will break you of those silly American euphemisms. Let's start over again. *Where* do you want to go?"[14]

That embarrassing episode behind him, the two sat down to what Hooper remembered as a long and satisfying talk of the quality that he had never before experienced: "There I was, catapulted right into a far more interesting life than I'd imagined was to be had, and pretty soon we were talking about everything under the sun, Lewis constantly making verbal distinctions, and catching me out on logical points." As this conversation came to a close, Hooper was not sure how anything else for the rest of his life could measure up; he hated to see the time end. "In any event, the effect of all this clear talk was that by the time I had to leave I liked Lewis so much that I foresaw a life ahead of me that would be very dull compared to the few hours I'd just had. I remember to this day how *very* much I liked Lewis. He was beyond anything I hoped for, and certainly generous with his time." Lewis walked Hooper to the bus stop, where Hooper presumed he would be saying goodbye for the first and last time. Yet that was not the case: "I thanked Lewis for giving me so much of his time. He looked surprised, and said, 'you're not getting away! You're coming to the Inklings meeting on Monday.'"[15]

Hooper considered his first Inklings meeting to be a revelation similar to the one he had experienced with Lewis one-on-one. When he ventured to offer a viewpoint on the topic at hand, Lewis picked up on it and it became the focal point of the conversation. "Pretty soon I was saying things that certainly did not represent my usual, muddled way of talking," Hooper wrote. "We all know people who make us feel insecure and around whom we sound like fools. Lewis was the opposite. He brought you out. He encouraged you.

14. Ibid.
15. Ibid.

You were your best in his company."[16] Further, what had begun as a simple hope for a short talk over tea became a pattern for that first summer month, as Hooper and Lewis met three times a week: once at the Kilns, at church on Sundays, and with the Inklings.

Hooper records another incident that helped him learn more about Lewis's nature. Driven to one of Lewis's favorite pubs by his friend Dr. Havard, Hooper and Lewis got into a conversation about America. Lewis mentioned that Joy had told him that Southern men in America dominated their women. He wanted to know if Hooper agreed with that assessment. "I felt trapped," Hooper admitted. He did not want to contradict Lewis's deceased wife, but he really could not agree with what she had told him. "I tried to avoid a straight answer, but Lewis was persistent. 'Do you *agree* with her?' he asked. 'Well, no,' I said. 'Then, what do you disagree with?' he asked. 'Everything,' I finally said. 'She was totally wrong.'" He feared this honesty would destroy their relationship, knowing how much Lewis had loved his wife. He had a few minutes alone with Dr. Havard, told him what had occurred, and asked if his comments offended Lewis. "'Good heavens, No!' he said. 'He loved his wife, but he didn't always *agree* with her!'" Not only was that a relief to him, but the more he grew to know Lewis, the more he understood him: "I soon came to realise that for Lewis conversation was always *about* something, that the purpose of it was to argue towards truth. Furthermore, I sensed that this arguing towards truth has been one of the things Lewis enjoyed about Joy, perhaps was one of the main reasons they became friends in the first place."[17]

Hooper's memories of that summer with Lewis are peppered with anecdotes, such as the time they were discussing the nature of beauty—the distinction between "prettiness" and "beauty"—and Hooper mentioned actress Elizabeth Taylor as someone who fit the description of beautiful. He seemed to notice some hesitation on Lewis's part, as if he was trying to figure out who that person was, so Hooper told him he would know more about these things if he would only read the newspapers. Lewis's response? "'Ah-h-h-h!' said Lewis playfully, 'but that is how I keep myself "unspotted from the world."' He recommended that if I absolutely 'must' read newspapers I have a frequent 'mouthwash' with *The Lord of the Rings* or some other great book."[18]

What of the genuineness of Lewis's faith? What did Hooper learn about that in the summer of 1963?

16. Ibid.
17. Ibid.
18. Hooper, *Present Concerns*, 7.

Most Christians that I know seem to have two kinds of lives, their so-called "real" life and their so-called "religious" one. Not Lewis. The barrier so many of us find between the visible and the invisible world was just *not there* for Lewis. No one ever had less of a split personality. He was possessed of a blessed singleness of mind which sometimes made me gasp. It had become natural for him to live ordinary life in a supernatural way. If humour is based on perspective—seeing things in their right proportion and context—then God must have the greatest sense of humour of anyone. Lewis was close behind, for, being allowed for a while to see through his eyes, I found myself laughing more than I ever had.[19]

Then came the crisis.

Arriving at the Kilns on Sunday morning, 14 July, to go to church with Lewis, Hooper found him very ill and barely able to sit up. He even had trouble holding his tea cup. The next day, Lewis went into the Acland Nursing Home, where he was already scheduled for a blood transfusion. The unscheduled event for 15 July was his slipping into a coma. An Anglican priest came and went through Last Rites; the doctors thought he would not come out of it. Yet, quite unexpectedly, the next day he awoke and immediately asked for some tea. But he was not himself for many days. Writing to Chad Walsh near the end of the month, Hooper reported that Lewis was having "terrifying hallucinations." He would see books near him, but when he reached out for them, they would vanish. "He longs so earnestly for one complete night of sleep, to be woken by rolls of waves rushing upon him. I think he longs for the seas of Perelandra. To serve Jack is the highest privilege I have ever known, but every day is a near heart-break."[20]

It was at this point that Lewis, while still in the hospital, inquired whether Hooper could become his permanent secretary. Already he was dictating letters to him from his hospital bed that Hooper would then send on to Lewis's many correspondents. Although Hooper would have to return to America for the fall term of teaching, he promised he would come back at the beginning of the year to take up that post. Lewis's confusion of mind while recovering from the coma required that someone help him; Hooper was only too glad to be of service.

Shortly after Lewis emerged from his coma, Hooper realized he had no idea what had happened to him. Should he tell him how dire the situation had become? The doctors and nurses did not seem intent on letting Lewis

19. Hooper, "Personal Testimony."

20. Letter from Walter Hooper to Chad Walsh, 29 July 1963, Chad Walsh Papers, Folder 2—Correspondence, 12/18/45-4/26/64.

know, so he decided to take it upon himself to broach the subject. "Jack," he said one day, "do you remember that letter in which Screwtape tells Wormwood that Hell is not happy about wars because those who go into battle go knowing they might die. 'How much better,' said Screwtape, 'if *all* humans died in costly nursing homes amid doctors who lie, nurses who lie, friends who lie . . . promising life to the dying, encouraging the belief that sickness excuses every indulgence.'" Lewis looked steadily at him, reminding him, "I expect I know that letter better than you do." What was Hooper up to, he asked? "I then told him about the coma, the expectation of his death, and our worries about him. When I'd finished he said, 'I am glad you told me. What kind of friend would you be if you hid from me something which affects me more than anyone?' Thereafter, he was intrigued that he'd almost gone through the gate of immortality, but that God had decided to keep him here a little longer."[21]

The nurses at the Acland were concerned enough about Lewis's mental state that they refused to let him keep any matches on his person. The only little rebellion on his part was his desire to hide them from the nurses. Hooper tells of one incident that shows Lewis maintained a sense of humor despite his situation. Hooper, since Lewis was deprived of matches for his cigarettes by the nurses, sometimes would leave him a box of matches. But every time he did so, a nurse would come in immediately and snatch them away. Puzzled by how the nurses could know so quickly, Lewis queried Hooper, who admitted he was one who told them. "Informer!" roared Lewis. "I have what no friend ever had before. I have a private traitor, my very own personal Benedict Arnold. Repent before it is too late!"[22]

Hooper discovered another aspect of Lewis's character while he was recuperating. He came to the knowledge that Lewis kept hardly any of the money he earned through his many book sales. Beginning with the proceeds he received from *Screwtape* up to the present time, every penny was funneled to a substantial number of widows and orphans that Lewis supported. Lewis himself lived quite frugally—Hooper called it a "threadbare" existence—so he was stunned by such generosity. "'Why,' I asked plainly, 'did you give away *so* much?' The simplicity of his answer took my breath away. 'God was so good in having me,' he said, 'that the least I could do was give away most of what I made in His name.' When was the last time *we* said, 'God was so good in having me'"?[23]

---

21. Hooper, "Personal Testimony."
22. Hooper, "Introduction," *The Weight of Glory*, 6.
23. Hooper, "Personal Testimony."

Gradually, Lewis improved. Writing to Walsh in early August, Hooper gave this testimony to Lewis's renewed sharpness of mind: "It is so amusing to hear him talking with his nurses. They are completely bamboozled when he insists on defining terms, hammering away on the logic or illogic of their sentences. They usually slip away when the mental gymnastics become too tedious." As for his own increasing relationship with the famous author, he added, "I want to 'fill my mouth' with praises for good, dear Jack. Never have I liked anyone so much. And aren't we all glad to see a man so gifted with his Divine Alchemy that turns every literary work into a victory for Christ."[24]

When Lewis was released from the hospital, Hooper spent the rest of the summer living in the Kilns with him, writing the letters Lewis would dictate and waiting on him as needed. He called those final weeks with Lewis some of the most interesting of his life. He rejoiced to see his spiritual mentor reasoning cogently once again. He did get tired more easily, though. When he asked Lewis if he ever took naps, he received a characteristic Lewis response: "'Oh, *no*!' he exclaimed. 'On the other hand,' he went on, 'sometimes a nap takes *me*!'"[25]

The pattern for those last weeks together was for Lewis to dictate letters right after breakfast, since his correspondence was so constant and voluminous. When dictating, he would have Hooper then read the letters back to him before sending them, commenting, "It's as important to please the ear as the eye." This gave Hooper even greater insight into Lewis's mind: "We take it for granted that his writing is both beautiful to read and beautiful to hear, but this was hardly a matter of chance. He told me that when he was writing something—nearly always with a nib pen—he 'whispered' the words aloud to himself."[26] Hooper later analyzed the value of all these letters Lewis wrote for those many years:

> I found this when I was with him: that the letters, which he considered one other thing which one must endure about success of a sort, must be answered, if possible that very day. Yet those letters are some of the best. I think they were some of the best things for Lewis in the sense that they were a very pastoral thing to do. They also, I think, are one of the richest mines of his writing. How often he has learned to simply take what others would take ten pages in trying to write and condense to a brief paragraph, and yet in which everything is there. You cannot find an argument put more beautifully and precisely. For many people,

---

24. Letter from Walter Hooper to Chad Walsh, 5 August 1963, Chad Walsh Papers, Folder 2—Correspondence, 12/18/45-4/26/64.

25. Hooper, "Personal Testimony."

26. Ibid.

this will be the only way they will learn theology: to simply read it in that condensed form.[27]

As with the "bathroom" incident when Hooper first met Lewis, sometimes he was the target of Lewis's humor in those summer months. Hooper used Lewis as his authority for so many of his own views that he had developed the habit of constantly remarking, "As C. S. Lewis has said." Hooper explains, "Quoting one of his books one day, I suddenly realised how it must sound to him. 'As C. S. Lewis has said,' I said, 'Oh, but you *are* C. S. Lewis!' Thereafter he made it a joke between us, and whenever he wanted anything done, he might say, 'As C. S. Lewis has said "I would like a pot of tea." As C. S. Lewis has said, "You will go and make it." As C. S. Lewis has said, "I will drink it!"'"[28]

Lewis's poor health forced him to resign his professorship at Cambridge. That required the removal of all his books and personal effects from his rooms at the university. Unable to do this himself, Hooper and Lewis's stepson, Douglas Gresham, traveled to Cambridge to sort out his belongings. While there, Hooper met the Librarian of the Pepys Library. Upon his return to the Kilns, Lewis asked what he thought of the man, who had the reputation of being very boring. Hooper had to agree with that assessment, informing Lewis that "the man succeeded in interesting me by the sheer intensity of his boringness." That only provided Lewis with the opportunity to reveal even more of his heart when he responded that the man admittedly was "a great bore. 'But let us not forget,' he said, 'that Our Lord might well have said, "As ye have done it unto one of the least of these my bores you have done it unto me."'"[29]

That humility and willingness to serve others deeply impacted Hooper. He related another conversation with Lewis about the temptations he might feel from having been so successful. When he asked Lewis if he had ever thought about the danger of being worshiped by readers, he got this response: "One cannot be too careful *not* to think of it." Hooper called that the greatest example of humility he had ever witnessed.[30]

Perhaps nothing summarizes what Hooper came away with from that summer with Lewis better than these thoughts he shared with an audience in 2007:

---

27. Hooper, "What About Mrs. Boshell?" 47.
28. Hooper, "Personal Testimony."
29. Ibid.
30. Hooper, "Introduction," *The Weight of Glory*, 14.

Perhaps the greatest thing I received from Lewis was something he was unaware of giving. My impression of God grew a million times from simply being in Lewis's company and hearing him talk. I became acutely aware of his closeness to God, a love for God so deep and pure I felt almost baptised from being close to it. I told Lewis about that newspaper column that was very popular when I was growing up. It was called Ripley's "Believe it or Not," and I told Lewis about the grave of an unbeliever whose epitaph was, "Here lies an atheist, all dressed up but with nowhere to go." Lewis replied, "I bet he wishes that were so." It was one thing to read what Lewis wrote about God, but my experience was greatly deepened by Lewis's life. He prayed often during the day, and I sensed that it was as common to him as breathing. When I went to Church with him for Holy Communion I watched him from out of the corner of my eye. Lewis believed in the Real Presence—that Christ was truly present in the consecrated Host. When the priest at Holy Trinity Church lifted up the Host Lewis looked awe-struck. I became aware that my concept of God was miserably small and emaciated when I began reading Lewis's books. But being in his company I began to see that if this great man loved God so very, very much—then did I know God at all? Lewis was right. Modern man has succeeded in placing himself in the judge's seat and placing God in the prisoner's dock. But there was *none* of that cockiness in Lewis who seemed all but overwhelmed by God's holiness.[31]

As for Lewis's outlook on life and his prospects for his own future, he had reached the point where he could say, as the Apostle Paul had, that to live is Christ and to die is gain. Even though the doctors thought he could live for years yet, Lewis was ready to go. "I see myself," he said, "as a sentinel on duty. I'm willing to stay until I'm called—but, mind, I would sooner be called."[32]

Keeper of the Flame

When Hooper returned to the United States, he and Lewis kept in touch by mail. Lewis wrote on 3 September that his mind was recovering nicely and that he even authored a book review for the *Sunday Telegraph* newspaper. As for Hooper himself, Lewis reported, "You have won 'golden opinions from all sorts of people.'" Further, "I need not say you are missed."[33] A couple of

---

31. Hooper, "Personal Testimony."
32. Hooper, *They Stand Together*, 30.
33. Letter from Lewis to Walter Hooper, 3 September 1963, Hooper, *Collected*

weeks later, Lewis again praised Hooper and indicated how valuable he had been to him, as he missed his new friend's companionship: "No one has ever so endeared himself to the whole household," he told him.[34]

That same letter also went into details about how to manage the transition to permanent secretary when Hooper returned in the new year. Lewis desperately wanted his help, but despaired over being able to afford to pay him what he was worth. He recommended that the projected January return date be moved back to June, for Hooper's sake, since an English winter may not be to his liking. Lewis, as always, had little understanding of his financial situation, thinking he was on the verge of poverty when he was not. Hooper's response exhibited confidence that he would be just fine and not to worry too much about the pay. Writing back to him a few weeks later, Lewis gingerly approached the payment issue again, with great hesitation, embarrassed that he could offer so little. Regardless, he certainly did look forward to a reunion, one that he hoped could be permanent. Lewis affirmed that the day of Hooper's return would be one of joy for him. "Your absence," he remarked, "makes a cavity like a drawn tooth!"[35]

That was the last letter Lewis ever wrote to Hooper, who commented later,

> Lewis told me many times that I valued his writings too much, and he was always amused when he saw me scribbling something he said in my little notebook. "I know what the divine joke on you would be," he said near the end of the summer. "I might utter my last words and *you* won't be here to write them down!"
>
> As it turned out, I wasn't. I was in between classes at the University of Kentucky on 22 November 1963 when a colleague told me President Kennedy had been shot. Later that day we learned that the President was dead. Horrible as that was, I was still looking forward to joining Lewis in January. I was just drifting off to sleep in my bed that night when Lewis's step-son, Douglas, rang to tell me that Jack had died the same hour as President Kennedy.[36]

The news of Lewis's death not only meant that Walter Hooper's future was up in the air, but it meant the budding relationship that meant so much to him had come to an end. What connection now could he hope to have with Lewis's world? He wrote, "Lewis had been the centre of my life since

---

Letters, Vol. III, 1453–54.
    34. Letter from Lewis to Walter Hooper, 20 September 1963, ibid., 1456–57.
    35. Letter from Lewis to Walter Hooper, 11 October 1963, ibid., 1461–62.
    36. Hooper, "Personal Testimony."

I first came across his writings in 1953. And during the months we were together I had come to love him. Now everything seemed lost."[37] However, two of Lewis's friends whom Hooper had come to know, Dr. Austin and Katherine Farrer, asked him to come back to England and stay with them, believing there was something significant he could do in the aftermath of Lewis's death. They were right.

Hooper had never met Warnie in his brief sojourn the year before, but now they became good friends, so much so that Warnie asked if he would be willing to serve as editor of his brother's literary works. The trustees of Lewis's estate, Owen Barfield and Cecil Harwood, had no objections; in fact, they had already come to know and appreciate Hooper and enthusiastically embraced his new role, one that would last for decades. "If they felt any resentment about my being asked to edit their friend's writings I never detected it," Hooper wrote later. "They *said* they were pleased, and I believe they were because, while they were exactly Jack Lewis's age, they had been waiting for their retirement in order to pen the books *they* wanted to write. . . . In brief, responsibility for Jack's literary estate fell on them at an inconvenient time, and they welcomed the young man Jack had already asked to help him."[38]

His first task was to stop Warnie from setting fire to anything he considered extraneous. Hooper had to rescue many of Lewis's papers from the bonfire in the backyard of the Kilns one day. Some had been burned prior to his arrival. What, he wondered, had been lost to posterity?

> What papers went into the fire I never discovered. George Sayer believed that Lewis had written a sequel to *Surprised by Joy*. If so, it was never found. I wondered then, as I still wonder now, what happened to the correspondence between Lewis and Joy. Was it destroyed in this fire? In any event, let me say that none of this surprised me. Neither of the brothers felt the reverence for their manuscripts which we feel. When I was getting to know Jack Lewis I asked what he did with his manuscripts and he told me that after writing a book, such as *The Lion, the Witch and the Wardrobe*, he turned the manuscript over and wrote another book on the other side. He then threw the manuscript away. I did not *need* to express my horror for he saw it in my face, and from that point on he began giving me the manuscripts

---

37. Hooper, "Editing Lewis," a paper sent to the author via e-mail with Hooper. This is the source for quotes from it, although the essay also can be found in Michael Travers, ed., *C. S. Lewis: Views from Wake Forest* (Wayne, Pennsylvania: Zossima Press, 2008).

38. Ibid.

of whatever he had published or was about to publish, the first of which was *Letters to Malcolm*, now in the Bodleian Library. When Warnie saw the delight I took in the notebooks and various papers he gave me—those originally destined for the fire—he was delighted that I cared so much for them.[39]

Lewis had famously predicted that he would be forgotten a few years after his death. Walter Hooper set out to prove him wrong, ensuring that Lewis's books and essays would be reprinted time and again. But he knew he had a hard task ahead of him to make that happen. "What forced me to work harder with the editing was a chance comment I heard in a meeting with Lewis's publisher, Jock Gibb. He said, 'Every *new* book by an author helps sell the old ones.' It may not happen with every author but it certainly seems to be true of Lewis, and this has spurred me on as much as anything. 'Every *new* book helps to sell the *old* ones.'" One of Hooper's strategies was to collect as many of Lewis's essays as possible, which were not widely known, and publish them under new titles, thereby coming out with "new" C. S. Lewis books. That strategy worked. He wrote many of the prefaces and/or introductions to those books, but always kept one thing in mind as he did: "From the time I began editing Lewis I have tried to keep in mind that it is *his* work—*not mine*—and that I should not include in the preface or notes anything that contradict Lewis's own writings. This was hardly a difficulty for me because there are, I expect, few thoughts in my mind that did not come from Lewis."[40]

Hooper's attempt to keep a low profile while pushing Lewis's writings found confirmation in a rather humorous way one day when he received a visit from Charles Colson, the founder of Prison Fellowship (whose story will be found in the next chapter). "Before we went to the Bird and Baby for lunch Colson began praising *God in the Dock*. 'You must read it!' he said. '*Promise* me you will read it!' I didn't have the heart to mention that I'd edited the book for Charles Colson—rightly—was interested in what *Lewis* said."[41]

Lewis's works would no longer be available in English only. One of Hooper's initiatives was to put Lewis into the hands of non-English speakers also. He was welcomed in countries that were normally opposed to religious instruction, particularly behind the Iron Curtain.

> Owen Barfield put me in charge of translations, and I was deeply touched to find that Polish translators—under the heel

39. Ibid.
40. Ibid.
41. Ibid.

of Communism—were keen to translate Lewis's works. As they had almost no money I charged them the smallest amount possible—half a cent per book. I learned later that the moving force behind the Polish translations was the future Pope—John Paul II. But the Estate could easily afford to be generous to Poland for there was an enormous and growing interest in Lewis almost everywhere, especially in the States."[42]

Those final words, "especially in the States," are indicative of the aim of this study, which is to document Lewis's popularity in America. According to Hooper, the desire for his writings only increased in America in the years after he died. The new American publisher for Lewis, HarperCollins, was keen on selling what they called a "handbook" on Lewis, and they believed Hooper was the man who should write it. The publisher sought a 137-page volume; what they received in *C. S. Lewis: A Companion and Guide* (1996) was instead a 960-page tome that took four years to write, covering all aspects of Lewis's life. Why so long? What led Hooper to devote so much time and effort to it? "I don't know whether to bow my head in shame, or to laugh, at how wide of the mark my 'handbook' turned out to be. Why is it so long? . . . Lewis's life and writings were in some quarters taking on the quality of a soap opera, and after witnessing the liberty taken by the screenwriter of the film, *Shadowlands*, it seemed to me that the real C. S. Lewis was being replaced by a mythological one," he explained. "As a result, I thought I saw how a *factual* account of Lewis's life and his works might serve as a kind of *cordon sanitaire*—a quarantine barrier between the myth and the reality."[43]

Although quite tired after that effort, he nevertheless then threw himself into editing all of Lewis's personal letters. It took seven years to complete that task, with the resulting three volumes a testimony to the prodigious nature of Lewis's letter writing. Hooper said that when the editing ended, "I found myself arguing in my mind with Jack Lewis. 'How could you *do* this to me!?' I asked him. 'Jack, I bet I've spent more time editing your letters than you did writing them!' '*That*,' he seemed to reply, 'is why I chose you as my secretary. It's part of the deal.'"[44]

At the conference where he spoke in 2007, Hooper made an interesting claim: that he had won an argument with C. S. Lewis. In what way?

> Lewis was worried about what his brother would live on when he—C. S. Lewis—died, and this because he was sure that upon his own death his books would stop selling. "No!" I exclaimed.

---

42. Ibid.
43. Ibid.
44. Ibid.

"What'd you mean, 'no?'" he said. "This happens," he said, "to nearly all authors. After they die their books sell for a while, and then trail off to nothing." "But not *yours!*" I said. "Why not?" he asked. "Because they are too good—and people are not that stupid."

Well, you see who won that argument. And yet, if Lewis was wrong about anything, wasn't this precisely the one thing he *ought* to have been wrong about? But such was his humility, his attention always turned away from himself. And if Lewis got one thing not only right, but terrifically right, it was his prediction that I was stuck forever with the phrase even he could not cure me of—"As C. S. Lewis has said."[45]

In his introduction to a collection of Lewis essays under the name *The Weight of Glory*, Walter Hooper offered high praise for his spiritual mentor when he said, "I knew . . . that no matter how long I lived, no matter who else I met, I should never be in the company of such a supremely good human being again. Of all my memories this is the most indelible and is certain to remain so."[46] Hooper often emphasized to people that he only knew Lewis for three months, yet upon further reflection he wondered if he was doing a disservice to Lewis by using the word *only*. Sometimes one can develop an intimate friendship in a relatively short period, he mused, when other relationships that have gone on for years may never achieve that same level of intimacy. "I am ashamed to admit that I once thought that because the plans Lewis and I made together did not run on into the years, I was somehow cheated. If not wicked, it is ungracious."[47]

Like his mentor, Walter Hooper was anything but ungracious as he poured his life into assuring that Lewis and his thoughts would never be forgotten. Truly, he acted as the Keeper of the Lewis Flame.

---

45. Ibid.
46. Hooper, "Introduction," *The Weight of Glory*, 9.
47. Ibid., 15.

5

The Academy and the Ministry

Lewis's contacts with and/or influence on leaders in American higher education and in the American church world in general are numerous, far more so than any one chapter can catalogue. It is possible, though, to highlight some key figures, both during his lifetime and afterwards, who testify to Lewis's impact on their thinking, or even, in some cases, how his writings led to their conversion. There is significant crossover from American colleges and universities to the church world in the lives of many of the individuals who were affected by him. Chad Walsh, the English professor discussed in chapter two, is a perfect example: he was a professor all his adult life, but also an Episcopal priest. An attempt will be made, though, to create, however artificially, two distinct groups for the purpose of this study.

In the Academy

The Brady Beginning

As noted in chapter one, Charles A. Brady, an English professor at Canisius College in Buffalo, New York, was the first American academic to write articles about Lewis. He wrote in a Jesuit journal titled *America*. Brady's first article, "Introduction to Lewis," began with this attention-getting sentence: "Not many writers nowadays are on such terms of cordial insult with His Infernal Majesty as the ruddy Ulster-born professor of English literature at Oxford University, Mr. Clive Staples Lewis, has shown himself to be in what is by now the most phenomenally popular household book of applied religion of the twentieth century, *The Screwtape Letters*."[1] He then compared Lewis to G. K. Chesterton as a champion of Christian orthodoxy, and urged that his works needed to be read far and wide, not just within close-knit academic circles: "But it would be a shame if his critical work and scholarly essays were confined to the lamp-lit circle of those dull persons who subscribe to *English Studies* and *Modern Language Notes*. Mr. Lewis' veins run blood, not ink; there is no mildew in his bones; nor mere jargon on his lips."[2]

The second article, "C. S. Lewis II," aimed to illuminate the fantasy world of Lewis through his Space Trilogy, a fantasy world "on an intensely imaginative plane of great beauty," according to Brady. In this review, Brady sets Lewis against H. G. Wells, who wrote from more of a "white-man's-burden assumption" and who believed any inhabitants of other planets would naturally be sinister, and who would need either to be annihilated or exploited by the superior race—earth's humans. Lewis's approach was the opposite: "In fact, he puts the boot on the other foot, and virtuous beings of undoubted rationality reflect sadly on our earth as the Bent Planet, a star deflected from normality—where Maleldil, the Supreme Being, is a prince exiled from enemy-occupied territory, and rule is held by an evil usurper over us, members of the spiritual underground." Near the end of the review, Brady concludes, "His pages are a melodious sounding-board, a whispering-gallery haunted by the echoes of what is great in world literature."[3]

More than a decade later, in that same journal, Brady offered his critique of the Narnia stories. The passage of years did not dim his praise for Lewis's ability to transfer his imagination to the printed page. The Chronicles of Narnia, Brady believed, marked "the greatest addition to the imperishable deposit of children's literature since the *Jungle Books*. Narnia takes its place forever now beside the jasper-lucent landscapes of Carroll, Anderson, Macdonald and Kipling." Brady was particularly taken with Lewis's depiction of Aslan, realizing that most would recognize Christ in the majestic lion. But what about those who would not make the connection? No reason to worry, he asserted:

> It is probably not necessary for the secularized children who are lucky enough to get the Narnia books as presents to know this fact. For, among the many beauties of Dr. Lewis' achievement, are the other facts that the story is self-sufficient and that the echoes attract the mind's ear even when the mind's eye cannot tell for sure the source of the echoes. If the meaning is hidden, it

---

1. Brady, "Introduction to Lewis," 6.
2. Ibid., 7.
3. Brady, "C. S. Lewis II," 6.

> is only because the world, outside of orthodoxy, has temporarily lost the key. Like the adults, the children, too, must be coaxed inside again. Many are, I suspect, and more will be. One of the most trodden, if least acknowledged, roads leading to Damascus is the old imperial high road of the sovereign imagination.[4]

So impressed was he by the Narnian stories that he predicted that one day the decade of the 1950s, at least when it came to literature, would be remembered as the decade that saw the emergence of Narnia as the most significant achievement. Children will always respond to what Lewis has written, he confidently proclaimed, due to "the narrative sweep," "the heroic mood," and the way in which Lewis constantly brings out the "numinous." These stories would resonate far into the future, he felt, because Lewis "touches the nerve of religious awe on almost every page. He evangelizes through the imagination."[5]

Lewis responded to Brady, again thanking him for his positive review: He shared with Brady that he was getting a lot of letters from children. The depth of some of the letters surprised him because he did not expect that children would catch on to the theology that infused the books, but he believed that some of the children actually saw the truth more clearly than some of the adults who had read the books. He added that he thought Brady might be amused to know that the inspiration for the Narnia tales was the result of nightmares he had been having about lions.[6]

Vanauken's Severe Mercy

An American studying in Oxford, Sheldon Vanauken, became friends with Lewis not because he had him as a tutor (he never was one of Lewis's students), but because he reached out to Lewis for an explanation of the Christian faith and to try to convince him why he should become a Christian. He and his wife Jean—always called Davy—were on a quest for truth, even when, at the time, they did not realize it was a quest. They began reading some Christian authors, one of whom was Lewis. Vanauken began with the Space Trilogy because he was a literature major; Davy started with *The Screwtape Letters* because a friend had told her it was funny. Vanauken later remarked it was fortunate he read the trilogy first; it created a kind of alliance in his mind with Lewis. The last part of the trilogy, *That Hideous Strength*, showcased a totalitarian society that he hated as much as Lewis

---

4. Brady, "Finding God in Narnia," 3.

5. Ibid., 4.

6. Letter from Lewis to Charles A. Brady, 16 November 1956, Hooper, *Collected Letters, Vol. III*, 806–7.

did. "Much more important, perhaps, the trilogy showed me that the Christian God might, after all, be quite big enough for the whole galaxy."[7] Both Vanauken and Davy were so impressed with Lewis's intellect that they, for the first time, realized that a person could be intellectual and a Christian at the same time; those concepts were not inherently contradictory.

On an impulse, Vanauken penned his first letter to Lewis in late 1950. Explaining that he had "embarked" on a "voyage that would someday lead me to God," he was writing to find out if Lewis, who had already "linked certainty with Christianity," might be able to give him "a hint of how it's to be done." He continued, "Having felt the aesthetic and historical appeal of Christianity, having begun to study it, I have come to awareness of the strength and 'possibleness' of the Christian answer. I should *like* to believe it. I *want* to know God—if he is knowable. But I cannot pray with any conviction that Someone hears. I can't *believe*." His deepest question was how to believe, out of all the religions in the world, that just *one* could be true. Perhaps, he reasoned, because he lived in a "'real world' of red buses and nylon stockings and atomic bombs" and had never seen an angel or heard the voice of God, that it cannot be easy to connect with Him. Why write to Lewis? "Somehow you, in this very same world, with the same data as I, are more meaningful to me than the bishops of the faithful past. You accomplished the leap from agnosticism to faith: how?"[8]

One might not ordinarily expect an extremely busy Oxford don to reply to a total stranger, even if that stranger were currently residing in Oxford. After all, there was no academic connection between them; he was not Vanauken's tutor. Yet Lewis saw an opportunity to aid someone's honest quest for truth. He replied with a directness that was both bracing and refreshing for Vanauken. Lewis began by questioning the assumption that everyone really wanted Christianity to be true. Certainly Hitler and Stalin never wished to submit to an eternal standard established by God, and most people don't want a deity acting as judge over their actions, he asserted. They would instead, in their very heart of hearts, want to tell God to stay away from what they considered their private business. Lewis shared that this was his own reaction early in his life, a reaction against the idea that Someone transcendent would have the right to tell him what to do.

He then narrowed the choices for Vanauken and explained why he had chosen the Christian answer. The only real choices available, Lewis contended, were that of a materialist worldview, the early pagan religions (he didn't consider them to have a proper moral foundation), Hinduism,

---

7. Vanauken, *A Severe Mercy*, 84.
8. Ibid., 87–88.

or Christianity. Only the last of those, Lewis told Vanauken, "compels a high brow like me to partake in a ritual blood feast, and also compels a central African convert to attempt an enlightened universal code of ethics." He concluded his comments with a recommendation that Vanauken read Chesterton's *The Everlasting Man*, which he thought was the best apologetic on the market.[9]

Lewis's thoughtful letter encouraged Vanauken to write again that same month. He wished that God would not require so much to believe; why not instead be "as clear as a sunrise or a rock or a baby's cry?" He agreed with Lewis's assertion that most men, not only Hitler and Stalin, "would be horrified at discovering a Master from whom *nothing* could be withheld. . . . Indeed, there is nothing in Christianity which is so repugnant to me as humility—the bent knee." He would perhaps be willing to be humbled if he knew it meant that death was not a leap into "nothingness," and that it would mean "Materialism was Error as well as ugliness," and "above all, that the good and the beautiful would survive."[10] Lewis, in response, maintained that there could be no demonstrative proof of Christianity in the same sense as a mathematical proof. He then aimed at Vanauken's concepts of ugliness and beauty, noting that even the idea that something is ugly or that something else could be called beautiful must mean that there is some standard of judgment that Vanauken himself recognized. Where did this standard originate? His final comment probably was written with a twinkle in his eye, as he predicted, "I think you are already in the meshes of the net! The Holy Spirit is after you. I doubt if you'll get away!"[11]

While Vanauken was pondering these things, Davy was moving forward in her spiritual journey. All of her reading and her connections with new Christian friends were leading her toward conversion ahead of her husband. In her journal, she wrote, "Underneath I kept wanting to say 'I do, I do believe in Jesus—Jesus the Son of God and divine.'" What she added after that reveals her debt to a mentor: "I owe this to C. S. Lewis who has impressed me deeply with the necessity of Jesus to any thinking about God." Then, a mere two days later, she recorded this: "Today, crossing from one side of the room to the other, I lumped together all I am, all I fear, hate, love, hope; and, well, *did* it. I committed my ways to God in Christ."[12]

---

9 Letter from Lewis to Sheldon Vanauken, 14 December 1950, Hooper, *Collected Letters, Vol. III*, 70–71.

10. Vanauken, *A Severe Mercy*, 90–91.

11. Letter from Lewis to Sheldon Vanauken, 23 December 1950, Hooper, *Collected Letters, Vol. III*, 74–76.

12. Vanauken, *A Severe Mercy*, 95–96.

Two months later, Vanauken bent his stubborn knee and joined his wife in the faith. He reported his conversion to Lewis, who rejoiced, but who also issued a prescient warning about what to expect from the enemy of his soul, who would undoubtedly try to undermine Vanauken's newfound faith. Lewis told him not to be too alarmed should that happen: "The enemy will not see you vanish into God's company without an effort to reclaim you." The warning, though, was followed by an invitation to continue with their conversation on the faith and with an exhortation that they should pray for one another as both progressed on the Christian path.[13]

It was shortly after this that they met for the first time when Lewis invited Vanauken to dine at Magdalen. He recorded his first impression of Lewis upon meeting him in his Oxford rooms, saying that he appeared almost as "John Bull himself." He was "portly, jolly," had a "wonderful grin, a big voice, a quizzical gaze—and no nonsense." As he got to know him better, he considered Lewis "the most friendly, the most genial of companions." Although they had shared through letters, Vanauken felt that the real friendship began at that dinner, and it continued to grow. "It was a very deep friendship on my part," he wrote, and "no man ever did so much to shape my mind, quite aside from Christianity, which of course shaped my whole life. I have never loved a man more. And I must believe, from things he said and wrote to me, that he felt both friendship and affection for me. Later, he became very fond of Davy—or Jean, as he called her—too."[14]

For the remainder of the Vanaukens' residence in Oxford, their relationship with Lewis grew stronger. "We talked, Lewis and I, about everything under the sun, and beyond the sun, too. There were several good discussions of science-fiction, which we had both read a lot of. And of course we talked of Christianity and of Christian morality."[15] With their time in Oxford coming to an end, Vanauken arranged to meet Lewis one more time for lunch, on the very day they would leave to return to America. It was a bittersweet parting, yet Lewis managed to provide the proper perspective:

> We talked, I recall, about death or, rather, awakening after death. Whatever it would be like, we thought, our response to it would be "Why, of course! Of *course* it's like this. How else could it have possibly been." We both chuckled at that. I said it would be a sort of coming home, and he agreed. Lewis said that he hoped Davy and I would be coming back to England soon, for we mustn't

---

13. Letter from Lewis to Sheldon Vanauken, 17 April 1951, Hooper, *Collected Letters, Vol. III*, 106.
14. Vanauken, *A Severe Mercy*, 108–9.
15. Ibid., 110.

get out of touch. "At all events," he said with a cheerful grin, "we'll certainly meet again, here—or *there*." ... We shook hands, and he said: "I shan't say goodbye. We'll meet again." Then he plunged into the traffic. I stood there watching him. When he reached the pavement on the other side, he turned round as though he knew somehow that I would still be standing there. ... Then he raised his voice in a great roar that easily overcame the noise of the cars and buses. Heads turned and at least one car swerved. "Besides," he bellowed with a great grin, "Christians *never* say goodbye!"[16]

Vanauken accepted a professorship at Lynchburg College in Virginia. Correspondence with Lewis continued. One letter from Lewis is particularly insightful as to how he viewed himself as an agent to help bring Vanauken to faith. What stands out is the humility of someone who almost cannot believe God would use him for such a high purpose. He expressed a sort of wonder and awe that God would actually use him to help another person find the truth. He compared it to a boy's feelings the first time he would be allowed to use a rifle. How so? "The disproportion between his puny finger on the trigger and the thunder & lightning wh. follow is alarming. And the seriousness with which the other party takes my words always raises the doubt whether I have taken them seriously enough myself." He thought the proper way to look at his influence was to think of himself as "a fellow-patient in the same hospital" giving advice from the vantage point of having been in the hospital longer.[17]

Lewis's advice to Vanauken was soon to become almost as essential as it had been in helping lead him to his conversion. Only two years after returning to the States, Davy came down with a terminal illness; her liver had been severely damaged, possibly from a virus contracted during the time they had spent in the Caribbean early in their marriage. By mid-July 1954, the doctors were saying she had only one chance in ten of living another six months.[18] Unfortunately, that prognosis was accurate.

Davy died in January 1955. Over the next year and a half, Lewis wrote to Vanauken six times, each letter a combination of spiritual consolation and practical advice for carrying on in life without her. It was, unwittingly, a preparation for his own grief when Joy would die in 1960. Vanauken had written to Lewis of Davy's death and had asked if he could spread some of her ashes in Oxford. Somehow, that letter never reached him. When he

16. Ibid., 125.

17. Letter from Lewis to Sheldon Vanauken, 22 April 1953, Hooper, *Collected Letters, Vol. III*, 324–25.

18. Vanauken, *A Severe Mercy*, 155.

found out about the lost letter, Lewis was grieved that he had been unable accommodate that request. He was heartened, though, by how Vanauken described Davy's last days, as she died in full faith; their marriage bond was actually strengthened during her final illness.

Vanauken naturally wrote of his sadness, yet to Lewis this was not a bad thing. Sadness, he asserted, is not what harms people; rather, it is the accompanying "resentment, dismay, doubt and self-pity" usually associated with it. He rejoiced that Vanauken was experiencing none of those symptoms. He further reflected that perhaps an early death of a loved one might be the best way to lose one's youthful love. Why? "It must *always* be lost in some way," Lewis asserted. "Every merely natural love has to be crucified before it can achieve resurrection. . . . Your MS, as you well say, has now gone safe to the Printer."[19]

When Vanauken wrote again, he noted that he was "seeing the whole Davy," experiencing her anew at various times in their life together, and how in heaven he would have not only a remembrance of her, but the *real her* once again. He also commented on the change in what he called his "once-famous 'luck,'" in the wake of her death. Since becoming a Christian, he had suffered more life setbacks than before. Could Lewis provide any insight on that, he wondered?[20]

The response came quickly from Cambridge, where Lewis had recently taken up his new professorship. Do not worry about the hardships that come our way as Christians, Lewis counseled. God never promised we would avoid all suffering and hardships. As for the experiences he was having of Davy, so vivid and making her seem so present, Lewis had an encouraging word about that also: "What you say about the total Jean being apprehensible since the moment-by-moment Jean has been withdrawn . . . is most true and important." He advised Vanauken to see it as one of God's blessings, a little taste of what is to come when we see one another again in the heavenly realm.[21]

In another letter, Lewis addressed the temptation to act only after first thinking about what Davy would have liked. That is dangerous, he warned. "The real question is what she wills *now*; and you may be sure her will is now one with God's." Vanauken needed to be reminded that she was now living in an entirely different realm, seeing things with crystal clarity, unlike when she shared life with her husband. He needed to be aware of the danger of

---

19. Letter from Lewis to Sheldon Vanauken, 10 February 1955, Hooper, *Collected Letters, Vol. III*, 560–61.

20. Vanauken, *A Severe Mercy*, 185–86.

21. Letter from Lewis to Sheldon Vanauken, 20 February 1955, ibid. 564–66.

trying to preserve the way things were before; no one can preserve the past, Lewis counseled. "Death—corruption—resurrection is the true rhythm: not the pathetic, horrible practice of mummification." While sadness was natural, Vanauken had to avoid clinging to sadness out of some kind of duty; Lewis described that as a false duty. We do not live in perpetual sadness, Lewis reminded Vanauken; it will retreat eventually.[22]

A month later, Lewis responded to a letter in which Vanauken explained why he and Davy had decided never to have children. They had determined that children might come between them and destroy their close relationship. There is some indication Davy was rethinking that decision after she became a Christian. In that same letter, he even voiced some thoughts about the validity of suicide in his situation. This required Lewis to tackle two very significant issues in his response. Yes, he said, Christians do view marriage as the two becoming one, but this concept should not exclude others. Children are a God-given extension of the one flesh God established. He then took Vanauken to task for possibly denying Davy something she might have, in her innermost being, longed for. This letter is the source of the phrase that Vanauken later used when he wrote his book: a severe mercy. Here's how Lewis put it, in context:

> One way or another the thing had to die. Perpetual springtime is not allowed. You were not cutting the wood of life according to the grain. . . . You have been treated with a severe mercy. You have been brought to see . . . that you were jealous of God. And from *us* you have been led back to *us and God*: it remains to go on to *God and us*.

That is why suicide was out of the question. God expected Vanauken to go on. Besides, it was folly to think that he would be reunited with her in this way: "You might be digging an eternally unbridgeable chasm. Disobedience is not the way to get nearer to the obedient."[23] "After this severe and splendid letter," Vanauken commented, "I loved Lewis like a brother. A brother and father combined."[24]

By August of the following year, Vanauken seemed to have weathered the emotional and spiritual turmoil in the wake of Davy's death. As he wrote in *A Severe Mercy*, "I found I *could not* reject God. I could not. I cannot explain this. One discovers one cannot move a boulder by trying with all one's strength to do it. I discovered—without any sudden influx of love or

---

22. Letter from Lewis to Sheldon Vanauken, 6 April 1955, ibid., 591–93.
23. Letter from Lewis to Sheldon Vanauken, 8 May 1955, ibid., 604–6.
24. Vanauken, *A Severe Mercy*, 210.

faith—that I could not reject Christianity. Why I don't know. There it was. I could not. That was an end to it."²⁵

Vanauken returned to England, stayed for a few months, and had many opportunities to speak with Lewis once more about everything under the sun. He even visited Joy at the Kilns and remarked how cheerful she was despite her condition, and how she took an interest in everything. He returned to Virginia and life went on. They kept in touch for the rest of Lewis's years, and Vanauken made one more trip to England to see Lewis, in early November 1963. "We made tea there in the Kilns and talked about prayer and books.... He was his usual incisive self; though, because of his illness, he would doze momentarily during the talk. We set a date for a future meeting. When the day came, he was dead."²⁶ If there is any epitaph Vanauken wrote for Lewis, it would be this: "C. S. Lewis was a strong, genial, stimulating, loving presence in my life from Oxford days through Davy's death and the immensity of grief that followed. He was, above all, a friend."²⁷

Kilby the Collector

How does a young man who was born in nearly rural Tennessee and then received his bachelor's degree from the University of Arkansas become one of the most significant conduits of C. S. Lewis to Americans? The American South, many would surmise, in the early-to-mid-twentieth century, would not be considered a natural breeding ground for all things Lewis. Yet out of that atmosphere came Clyde S. Kilby, who did more than anyone else in America to establish a place where Lewis would find an American "home."

Kilby's graduate work took him outside his native South to the University of Minnesota and then to New York University, where he earned his doctorate in English literature. He arrived at Wheaton College in Illinois in 1935 and remained there for the rest of his teaching career. By the time he retired in 1981, he had created a virtual C. S. Lewis world at the small evangelical college, a collection not to be rivalled anywhere else in America, along with six other notable British authors, all, in one way or another, connected to Lewis.

Kilby's C. S. Lewis journey began in the early 1940s when he purchased *The Case for Christianity*, taken from the BBC talks that later were brought together as *Mere Christianity*. When Kilby later wrote his first book on Lewis, *The Christian World of C. S. Lewis*, he described his subject as having

25. Ibid., 190.
26. Ibid.
27. Ibid., 227.

"a mind sharp as a scalpel and as intent as a surgeon upon the separation of the diseased from the healthy."[28] In a later book about Lewis, *Images of Salvation in the Fiction of C. S. Lewis*, Kilby revealed just what it was that impressed him when reading Lewis: "I was overwhelmed by the powerful logic of works such as *Mere Christianity*, *Miracles*, and *The Problem of Pain*," he explained. "I felt that no Christian I had ever read, unless it were G. K. Chesterton, had spoken so clearly or so cogently for Christianity." As a theological conservative, Kilby said he had sought out "explicitly lucid and logical statements in defense of our faith." In Lewis, he found the author who met that need.[29]

It was in late 1952 that Kilby sent his first letter to Lewis. In it, he let Lewis know he was planning a trip to England the next year and asked if they could meet. The meeting took place on 1 July 1953, in Lewis's Oxford rooms. Later that year, Kilby penned an article detailing the time they spent together. Before he got to Lewis's rooms, he wrote, someone led him astray about the nature of the man he was going to meet. Kilby's wife was accompanying him, and he asked at the college gate "whether there was anything to the report that Mr. Lewis disliked women." Whoever he spoke with made it seem that there was some truth in the report, so his wife went shopping instead, and he met Lewis by himself.[30]

Upon knocking, Kilby was greeted warmly by the man who had meant so much to him in writing. First impressions? "He has a pleasant, almost jolly face, full though not fat, with a double chin. He has a high forehead and thinning hair. Actually, he is a much better looking man than the published picture of him." Kilby also liked Lewis's sense of humor, of a type understood best by a fellow academic: "He spoke of the making of a bibliography as just plain labor and laughed about the idea of the scholar's life as a sedentary one, saying that the physical labor of pulling big folios from the shelves of the Bodleian was all the exercise he needed."[31]

It was the sharing of minds, though, that stood out to Kilby as he looked back on this meeting. They spoke of the nature of the Renaissance, with Lewis's comments foreshadowing what he would say the next year in his inaugural lecture at Cambridge. They also talked about Palestine/the new nation of Israel and of Kilby's recent trip there. Lewis longed for the pleasure of visiting the Holy Land someday, and they speculated about the possible rebuilding of the Jewish temple and the reestablishment of sacrifices

28. Phemister, "A Mind Sharp as a Scalpel," 156.
29. Ibid., 157.
30. Kilby, "A Visit with C. S. Lewis," 11.
31. Ibid.

on that ancient spot in Jerusalem. Further, they discussed the relationship between Christian faith and art, as well as all things people consider secular. "He said the same relation existed between Christianity and art as between Christianity and carpentry." Of course, given Lewis's penchant for writing novels, they debated the exact nature of that specific species of literature. When Kilby quoted someone who had said a novel is no better than a well-told lie, Lewis objected: "As I expected, he disagreed completely with this claim, saying that one is far more likely to find the truth in a novel than in a newspaper. In fact, he said he had quit reading newspapers because they were so untruthful."[32]

When asked if he would be open to a visit to America, Lewis said that would have to wait until he retired. Kilby also sought to know if Lewis would be lecturing while he was in Oxford. "He said he had no lectures scheduled and bantered me as a college professor wanting to hear a lecture while on vacation. In fact, in all his talk there is an incipient good humor and genuineness that makes a conversation with him a real pleasure." The only awkward moment was when Kilby asked him to autograph one of Lewis's books he had brought with him. Although Lewis agreed to the request, he commented that he saw no sense in doing so. That led Kilby to conclude something about his character: "Both from reading his books and talking with him, I get the impression that he is far more fearful than most of us of the subtle sin of pride and tries in every way to escape it: thus his reticence to give an autograph."[33] Perhaps that is what should be expected from one who wrote a book detailing how Satan traps Christians. *The Screwtape Letters* may have been one of the hardest books Lewis ever wrote, but the message of it seemed to remain with him to the end.

Kilby very much liked *Till We Have Faces*, published three years after their face-to-face meeting. Lewis responded in February 1957 to a letter in which Kilby sought to know Lewis's personal take on this novel. What did he intend by it? Lewis's response was rather long and detailed, as he attempted to describe how he viewed the characters and the key points being made throughout. He then put it into context in a contemporary setting by comparing it to how when someone becomes a Christian and decides to become a missionary, others in the family may feel some outrage over the loss of a loved one. Lewis could understand and sympathize with that feeling. Just like his protagonist in the book, it would be easy for bitterness to arise, especially bitterness about a religion that has taken someone away.[34]

---

32. Ibid.
33. Ibid., 28, 30.
34. Letter from Lewis to Clyde S. Kilby, 10 February 1957, Hooper, *Collected Letters*,

Kilby used *Till We Have Faces* in courses with his students at Wheaton. In a paper he handed out in class, he remarked, "This is, I think, unquestionably the most difficult of all of C. S. Lewis's books. Yet it may be the best of his books." The paper analyzes the various aspects of the story and concludes with these paragraphs:

> My present reading of the story has suggested to me all over again something of its almost unlimited mythic quality. There seems to be hardly a page—sometimes hardly a sentence—which has not its overtone about which one must ask, Is there something else here? For instance, the unseen lover of Psyche suggests more or less the whole relationship between the Christian and Christ. Though unseen, He is our great love and worthy of the test to "forsake all others." Even the sexual relation, as Bible students well know, is one of the important metaphors of the New Testament. Also this whole palace picture often suggests the glories of heaven as seen in the book of Revelation and the final goal of the Christian as the bride of the Lamb, as Psyche herself suggests the perfection of the Church, "without spot or wrinkle."
>
> One characteristic of a great book, said Mortimer J. Adler, is that it will not let you down if you try to read it well. By this standard I think that *Till We Have Faces* is surely a great book.[35]

Kilby participated in a theological tussle Lewis was drawn into in 1958. It had to do with theologian Norman Pittenger, who decided to use the liberal magazine *The Christian Century* to attack Lewis's apologetic works. For the record, Pittenger later ended up denying most traditional Christian theology and declared himself to be openly homosexual. Both Lewis and Kilby saw the signs of apostasy in Pittenger from the start. Kilby contacted Lewis to let him know about Pittenger's critique, in case he was unaware of it. He did not know if Lewis would feel an answer was necessary, but he wrote down his own rebuttal, sent it to Lewis, and informed him he had sent it also to *The Christian Century* in the hope that the magazine would publish it. "If not published in that magazine, I shall see if *Christianity Today*, a magazine with which I am connected as a contributing editor, wishes to run the article."[36]

In response, Lewis assured him he had seen the critique and was preparing his own response. In the end, *The Christian Century* did publish

---

Vol. III, 830–31.

35. Clyde S. Kilby, "An Interpretation of *Till We Have Faces*," 1968-1969, submitted to the author by Carol Wald Saia, a former student of Kilby's.

36. Letter from Clyde S. Kilby to Lewis, 28 October 1958, C. S. Lewis Letter Collection.

Lewis's rejoinder and *Christianity Today* did the same for Kilby's, who informed Lewis, "Though my remarks were weak in comparison with your masterful answer published in the *Christian Century*, you were kind enough to commend what I wrote. My own statement was published in *Christianity Today* and has brought me notes of appreciation from many parts of the country, showing how widely you are known and admired here."[37]

In the same letter in which he informed Lewis of his response to Pittenger being published, Kilby then turned to his main reason for writing. He was asking permission from Lewis to "prepare a book of excerpts from your writings similar to the one you published on George MacDonald." He anticipated Lewis's reluctance to approve such a project, so he tried to offer a solid rationale that Lewis might entertain: "I realize that . . . your writings are available to the public, yet it seems to me that a collection of some of your most cogent remarks assembled topically and with good editorial judgment would promote the sale of your books."[38] Kilby received the typical Lewis response to this suggestion, which was to argue that it would never do to collect an anthology from a writer who was still alive. Neither would any publisher be interested, he claimed. Lewis apologized for being so blunt, but he just didn't think it would be the right thing to do.[39] Anthologies of Lewis's most poignant writings did appear later, after his death, which is apparently how he wished it to happen, if it were to happen at all.

As Kilby was wont to do, he later raised a point of criticism that another writer had with Lewis, seeking Lewis's reaction to it. In this case, it had to do with the concept of the *Tao*, the term Lewis used in *The Abolition of Man* to express the idea of a law of nature built into the universe by God. One writer seemed to suggest that Lewis was not clear about God "making" the *Tao*. In response, Lewis wrote, "If I had any hesitation in saying that God 'made' the *Tao* it wd. only be because that might suggest that it was an arbitrary creation. . . . I believe it to be the necessary expression . . . of what God by His own righteous nature necessarily is." In a P.S. to the letter, he added, "I think . . . *not* that certain things are right because God commanded them, but that God commanded them because they are right."[40]

Near the end of 1961, Kilby wanted to know if Lewis had any letters or other materials he could have for his proposed Lewis collection at Wheaton. This is the first indication of what Kilby eventually would accomplish

---

37. Letter from Clyde S. Kilby to Lewis, 15 January 1959, ibid.

38. Ibid.

39. Letter from Lewis to Clyde S. Kilby, 20 January 1959, Hooper, *Collected Letters*, Vol., III, 1013–14.

40. Letter from Lewis to Clyde S. Kilby, 11 January 1961, ibid., 1226–27.

with his vision of an American repository for Lewis's works. In typical Lewis fashion, he discouraged the attempt, saying he didn't have any material that would in any way contribute to the collection. He had not kept any private letters, so there was no reason for Kilby to trouble himself with a trip to Britain.[41] Stymied at this point, Kilby nevertheless kept the idea percolating in his mind.

After Lewis's death in November 1963, Clyde Kilby was one of the first academics to write of his legacy. He authored an article in *Christianity Today* in January 1964 that covered the landscape of what Lewis had given to the world through his writings. "The death of Clive Staples Lewis on November 22," he began, "removed from the world one of its most lucid, winsome, and powerful writers on Christianity. We have reason to thank God that such a man was raised up in our time to become, as Chad Walsh has put it, the apostle to the skeptics." After reminding his readers of the various contributions Lewis made to the realm of Christian reading and thinking, he concluded the article on this optimistic note: "He managed the difficult feat of successfully integrating his scholarship and his religion. If we add to these things the gifts of a lively imagination, a vigorous and witty mind, and a brilliance of language, we can discover why his books have sold widely and why his readers are steadily on the increase."[42]

Kilby quickly became the foremost publicist for Lewis on this side of the Atlantic. While American Walter Hooper was taking up the standard for Lewis overall as editor of his works and key promoter in Britain, Kilby was accomplishing the same thing in America. Before 1964 expired, he had published the first book on Lewis after his death, *The Christian World of C. S. Lewis*. That same year saw the beginning of the fulfillment of the vision for a collection of Lewis's papers and works to be housed at Wheaton. The collection, at first, consisted of the sixteen letters Lewis had written to Kilby, but with great vigor, he began to pursue the ambitious dream.

Kilby made many trips to Britain to collect letters and other materials related to Lewis. He became good friends with Warnie, who came to consider him as practically a member of the family. He provided Kilby with a list of his brother's many correspondents.[43] In his will, Warnie directed that the papers of both Lewises were to be given to Wheaton College.[44] That, in short, is how the most prestigious Lewis collection in America, surpassing in absolute numbers the collection at the Bodleian Library in Oxford,

---

41. Letter from Lewis to Clyde S. Kilby, 18 November 1961, ibid., 1296–97.
42. Kilby, "Everyman's Theologian."
43. Woodcock, "Kilby: Friend and Curator of the Oxford Christians," 23.
44. Phemister, "A Mind Sharp as a Scalpel," 158.

was born. The collection eventually expanded to include J. R. R. Tolkien (with whom Kilby worked personally in 1966), George MacDonald, G. K. Chesterton, Dorothy Sayers, Charles Williams, and Owen Barfield. When Clyde Kilby died in 1986, his legacy was more than what students might remember about him, valid as those memories are; what he left behind was a treasure that would keep on giving as long as any American remains interested in C. S. Lewis and those closest to him.

Other Notable Lewis Contacts

The three academics highlighted thus far in this chapter were given special treatment due to their overall significance in tracing the influence of Lewis on the American professorate: Charles Brady, because of his seminal role in introducing Lewis to those involved in higher education; Sheldon Vanauken, because of his personal relationship with Lewis as he prepared to teach at an American college and for his valuable memoir, *A Severe Mercy*; and Clyde Kilby, because he engineered the amassing of the largest Lewis collection in the States and housed it at his own Wheaton College. There were others, though, who had direct contact with Lewis, either by correspondence, personal meetings, or both. Their stories are worth telling also.

Probably the most notable American professor in this group who connected with Lewis during his lifetime was Nathan Comfort Starr. Two years Lewis's senior, the American Starr had actually been an undergraduate at Oxford at the same time as Lewis, just after World War I. They were unaware of one another, and only learned of the shared experience when they met for the first time after World War II. Thinking back on his undergraduate days, Starr later commented, "How I wished we had known each other then!"[45] Of course, Lewis would not have been the later Lewis, steeped as he was at the time in his atheism. Starr would go on to teach English literature at a number of American colleges and universities: Harvard, Radcliffe College, Colgate University, St. John's University, Rollins College, Williams College, and the University of Florida.

Starr's primary literary interest lay in Arthurian legends, and he later authored the book *King Arthur Today: The Arthurian Legend in English and American Literature, 1901–1953*, a study of modern Arthurian adaptations. He first wrote to Lewis in 1947 after being captivated by *The Screwtape Letters*, *The Abolition of Man*, and the Space Trilogy. Thanking him profusely for his writings, he offered praise for Lewis's "insistence on 'life made strong through divine grace' and his restoration of 'authentic vision' in beauty and

---

45. Starr, "Good Cheer and Sustenance," 222.

terror."[46] That letter brought an invitation to visit should he ever come to England. Since Starr was contemplating a trip to the British Museum and the Bodleian Library anyway for his studies on Arthurian legend, he arranged to go the very next year.

Once settled in Oxford for his research, he contacted Lewis to remind him of the invitation. At first, his hopes were dashed. The new term had just begun, which was demanding for an Oxford don, and Lewis had a bad cold besides. Unsure if he would get the opportunity to meet Lewis at all, Starr embarked on a strategy he hoped Lewis would appreciate, sending him a package of food he had brought with him from America that was scarce in England, accompanied by a short poem written in the style of Chaucerian English. Whether it was the poem, the food, or the eventual good health of the recipient—or a combination of them all—Starr got his appointment.

First impressions of Lewis as presented in this book all seem to have commonalities, whether recorded by Chad Walsh, Walter Hooper, Sheldon Vanauken, Clyde Kilby, or, in this instance, Nathan Comfort Starr, who wrote of this first meeting as follows:

> At the appointed hour, I went to his chambers and faced Lewis for the first time. He wore a tweed coat, much rumpled, and baggy gray trousers. I got the impression of a solidly built man, not at all fat, who moved lightly. It took me no time at all to realize that his mind moved as effortlessly as his body. There was no sense of the slight embarrassment that one sometimes feels on meeting a stranger. It seemed as if we had known each other a long time. I cannot now remember how we managed at once to get on such easy terms—what I said, what he answered, what caught us up so easily in friendship. I know only that the hour I spent in his rooms overlooking the Magdalen quadrangle was the most stimulating experience I had ever had—stimulating not through the sober discussion of weighty literary matters, though we had that, too, but chiefly because of the sheer joy of meeting a man of such enormous vitality, such electrical responses, such spontaneous wit, and such a generous outgoing to a stranger from across the Atlantic.[47]

When that first meeting ended, he got another invitation, this time to dine with Lewis in hall at Magdalen. Naturally, he accepted, and that led to another one—a meeting of the Inklings group at the Bird and Baby pub, where Starr was introduced to J. R. R. Tolkien and others. "More than

---

46. Ibid., 219.
47. Ibid., 221.

anything else," he remembered, "I received the impression of Lewis as the catalyst, the animating element in the group."[48] This series of events is reminiscent of how Lewis treated Chad Walsh that same year and Walter Hooper fifteen years later. He always welcomed his American colleagues heartily.

Upon his return to the States, Starr kept in touch with Lewis by mail. In one response, in 1950, Lewis looked back at Starr's visit and promised that the next meeting of the Inklings at the Bird and Baby would include a toast to Starr's health.[49] A year later, writing from his position as a professor at Rollins College in Florida, Starr implored Lewis to intervene publicly in a dispute with the progressive president of the college who was attempting to purge some of the professors who had "non-progressive" views. He was hoping Lewis's star quality might tip the balance back toward the traditionalists. Lewis, however, was not eager to join the fray, thinking his participation might do more harm than good. He didn't send a cable to any American newspaper to complain about the situation, he explained, because he was a foreigner and his intervention would probably be considered an intrusion; it also might stir up some anti-British and/or anti-God sentiments. Naturally, though, he sympathized with Starr's plight and ended the letter with the plaintive cry, "God help us all. It is terrible to live in a post-civilized age."[50]

Lewis's unwillingness to involve himself in the ideological struggles at Rollins did not damage the relationship. One year, in particular, yielded a number of letters between them, as Starr's book on King Arthur was published in 1954. Lewis awaited both the publication of the book as well as a chance to see Starr once more. When the book arrived, Lewis sent his positive appraisal almost immediately, encouraging Starr that his new book was not only "useful" and "friendly," but that it provided new information on Arthurian lore that he never had heard before.[51]

Starr determined to go to England again in 1960, as well as to Brittany for a meeting of the International Arthurian Society. He let Lewis know that he and his wife, Nina, would be coming and asked if they could meet with both Lewis and Joy. Lewis was eager to renew the face-to-face encounter they had had more than a decade earlier. Some things were different now, though, he told Starr: "There is still a weekly meeting at the Bird and Baby: but whether you can call it the Old Group when there is a new landlord and

---

48. Ibid., 222–23.

49. Letter from Lewis to Nathan Comfort Starr, 9 January 1950, Hooper, *Collected Letters, Vol. III*, 3.

50. Letter from Lewis to Nathan Comfort Starr, 29 May 1951, ibid., 120–21.

51. Letter from Lewis to Nathan Comfort Starr, 30 July 1954, ibid., 498.

Charles Williams is dead and Tolkien never comes is almost a metaphysical question, and one you will discuss much better on the spot."[52]

But by the time they arrived in August 1960, it was too late to meet Joy. "We had crossed the Atlantic on a slow ship, so we missed hearing the news that stunned us the day after we arrived. As soon as we reached Oxford I telephoned Lewis, saying we would very much like to call. I was horrified to hear him say that his wife had died the week before." Starr tried to beg off the meeting, not wanting to intrude upon Lewis's grief, but Lewis insisted that he very much wanted to see them. They did meet, and once again, Starr reported it was "a memorable talk."[53]

There would be one more meeting with the Starrs. Upon being informed they would be returning to England in 1963, Lewis wrote to indicate he would welcome them even though he was nearly an invalid.[54] As the time for that reunion approached, Lewis wrote again, letting Starr know he was still eager to receive them, but laying out the situation with his health: "Term will never again begin for me. Last July I was thought to be dying, oxygen-tent and Last Unction. . . . I am now retired and immobilised on one floor of this house. But glad to be visited (an hour or so) if such an extinct volcano as I now am is worth visiting."[55]

The visit took place in October 1963 at the Kilns. Although Starr was aware of Lewis's poor health, he was surprised that he saw no outward sign of physical or mental debility. "He seemed as robust as ever and captivated us by his electric vitality, his friendliness, and the marvelous range of his mind." He was amazed with Lewis's mind, noting, "He was prodigiously learned, but he never paraded his knowledge. He used his learning dynamically, in the cut and thrust of good masculine argument, yet I never heard him in a contemptuous or malicious mood." He and Nina left the Kilns that day, saying goodbye to Lewis, not knowing it would be the last goodbye. "Shortly thereafter we sailed for America and were appalled to read in the foreign edition of a New York newspaper that he had suddenly died. What a light was extinguished!" Starr's final thoughts about his friend were these: "I will always remember our first meeting in his rooms at Magdalen—the warm smile wrinkling up his eyes, his joie de vivre, his instantaneous outreach to an overseas visitor, his quick wit, his magnificent intellectual grasp.

---

52. Letter from Lewis to Nathan Comfort Starr, 22 April 1959, ibid., 1040.

53. Starr, "Good Cheer and Sustenance," 224.

54. Letter from Lewis to Nathan Comfort Starr, 30 July 1962, Hooper, *Collected Letters, Vol. III*, 1359.

55. Letter from Lewis to Nathan Comfort Starr, 4 September 1963, ibid., 1454.

He was the greatest man I have ever known. Perhaps what has endeared him to me most, he was the best of companions."[56]

William Brown Patterson, professor emeritus of history at the University of the South in Sewanee, Tennessee, has written highly acclaimed books such as *King James VI and I and the Reunion of Christendom* (1997), which won the Albert C. Outler Prize in Ecumenical History by the American Society of Church History.[57] Still actively writing in 2015, Dr. Patterson's most recent book is *William Perkins and the Making of a Protestant England*.[58] He has been a scholar of great repute from 1963 to the present. Where did he receive his most valuable training in logic and argumentation? From C. S. Lewis, of course.

Patterson's interest in the English Renaissance era led him to apply for the prestigious Rhodes Scholarship, an honor that was bestowed on him for study in Oxford from 1953–1955. He sought to go to Oxford specifically because Lewis would be his tutor. In making his application and arguing his case for the scholarship, he forthrightly said he wanted to study under the author of *The Allegory of Love: A Study in Medieval Tradition*, which was Lewis's first highly acclaimed academic book. He wanted to interact with a literary scholar like Lewis because he "dealt with writers and texts in their historical and cultural setting." Patterson added, "I also said that I wanted to study under a man whose views on the importance of religion and moral values were very consonant with—but much more highly developed than—my own."[59]

Patterson's recollection of his first impression of Lewis is similar to others' remembrances noted in this book, although it was not in Lewis's rooms at first, but rather spotting him out for a walk by the Cherwell River. He did not realize at first that it was Lewis: "He was wearing baggy trousers—corduroy, I think—and a shapeless tweed jacket over a loosely fitting sweater. On his head was an old tweed hat with its brim turned down. His shoes were heavy brogues. I identified him—to myself, of course—as one of the gardeners." But once he sat down with him as his student, his outward appearance gave way to what was inside the man: "Beneath Lewis's bluff, hearty, and inelegant appearance was, I soon found, a man of uncommon intelligence, vast enthusiasm for books and learning, and a deep, sometimes mystical devotion to the God he had come to know."[60]

56. Starr, "Good Cheer and Sustenance," 226.

57. Poe and Poe, *C. S. Lewis Remembered*, 268.

58. Patterson spoke and signed books at a "Symposium on Religion and Culture in Elizabethan England," at the University of the South, 27 February 2015; http://theology.sewanee.edu/news/event/symposium-on-religion-and-culture-in-elizabethan-england.

59. Patterson, "Personal Reflections," 89.

60. Ibid., 95.

For the better part of two years, Patterson had hour-long tutorials with Lewis each week. Tutorials centered on the student's reading of a text and a written essay in response to it. The student would read his essay aloud, and then the tutor would critique it. Reading an essay to Lewis put one in the crosshairs, as he would not allow any shabby thinking or inappropriate use of terminology. Patterson recalled, "He could quote back to me sentences I had just read, which he commented on for style as well as content. I once used the word 'fortuitously' to mean 'fortunately.' He reminded me that it meant 'by chance' and convinced me that 'we' should not let the word change its meaning to something for which there was already a perfectly good word available." Yet, harrowing as that might sound to a budding scholar, the goal was always to make the student the best he could be. "In all his criticisms he sought to lead me to strengthen an argument, to express an idea more clearly, or to anticipate a difficulty. All of this was aimed at improving my way of understanding the texts and expressing my point of view. Unless I asked him directly he would not elaborate on his own views, let alone try to impose them on me." The goal, for Patterson, was to write something Lewis could praise.

> An approving word from Lewis—as came, for example, in a session on sixteenth-century English tragedy—was something that made my efforts seem entirely worthwhile. I was very much aware that I was presenting my half-baked ideas to a world-class scholar, and as a result I tried to advance an argument that was as tenable and persuasive as possible. I ventured to suggest that a tragedy in Elizabethan England had a different quality from the tragedies of ancient Greece, partly because Christians thought of death, at least for the faithful, as an entrance into larger life. The ancients seemed to have no such hope, with the result that death seemed a stark and fearful alternative to earthly existence. We talked about several plays of Shakespeare and Sophocles, and he seemed surprisingly taken with my distinction.[61]

Patterson not only achieved his aim of being tutored by Lewis, but he also was able to converse with him on theological and moral issues, as he had hoped, although Lewis always insisted that those issues needed to be related to what Patterson was studying. The young scholar came away from these tutorials convinced that Lewis took his faith and the Scriptures very seriously. Patterson also picked up on the strong natural law tradition upon which Lewis based much of his thinking, the argumentation he used, for instance, in his *The Abolition of Man*. "He had little time," the young scholar concluded, "for

---

61. Ibid., 91.

theologians who were urgently trying to be responsive to changes in society and knowledge in what later came to be called a 'trendy' way."[62]

It was while Patterson was Lewis's student that the call came from Cambridge and Lewis left Oxford. But he did not neglect those who were his Oxford students, continuing to tutor them while in transition. He even wrote a letter of recommendation for Patterson for entrance into the Episcopal Theological School in Cambridge, Massachusetts. Patterson's ongoing education led him into the relationship between religion and politics, a subject not precisely in Lewis's field of interest, but he felt that what he received from Lewis was exactly the kind of preparation he needed. Lewis's tutorials helped him see "that no one can understand adequately the men and women of medieval and Renaissance Europe without a firm knowledge of the Christian ideas that pervaded the culture of those centuries."[63]

Reflecting on his time with C. S. Lewis, Patterson identifies what he calls three distinguishing characteristics of his famous tutor:

1. *Doggedness*: Lewis resolutely upheld those ideas and values he believed in. He stubbornly resisted Christianity before his conversion. Afterwards he was just as stubborn and persistent in its defense. What he defended, moreover, was no fashionable or trendy version; it was the solid heart of the matter. . . .

2. *Imaginativeness*: Lewis had a vivid, almost wild imagination, which he harnessed to interpret the sometimes strange, exotic, remote territory of the European Middle Ages and to create the lands of Narnia and the extraterrestrial life of his science fiction. His Christian faith became the organizing principle of much of his work, and he defended Christianity with great skill, but his faith was at bottom the faith of a poet, a storyteller, a magician in words. . . .

3. *Humanity*: In everything he wrote, Lewis was deeply aware of how ordinary people lived, what they thought, and what they were looking for in life. This is what makes his Christian writings so accessible and so influential. Lewis was not an aristocrat, nor was he an intellectual snob. He never liked the role of a celebrity. He could talk to you and me in our everyday language and understand us.[64]

That was Patterson's overall view of Lewis's strengths, but what did Lewis do for him, specifically? "The experience of studying at Oxford under

---

62. Ibid., 92.
63. Ibid., 96.
64. Ibid., 96–97.

C. S. Lewis was important to me in ways which I came to understand more fully as the years passed," he later concluded. "Thinking through literary, moral, and religious questions helped me to sort out my own ideas and values. Receiving his criticisms and advice on my essays certainly helped me to become a more effective writer. More than anything else, conversations with him gave me confidence in my own abilities."[65]

Thomas Howard was born into an evangelical household. His sister, Elisabeth Elliot, was a famous missionary and author, whose book, *Through Gates of Splendor*, chronicled the martyrdom of her husband, Jim Elliot, as he sought to take the Gospel to the Aucan Indians. The book then showcases her courage in going to that very tribe and leading to Christ the men who killed her husband. It was Elisabeth who gave her younger brother Thomas his first C. S. Lewis book, *The Screwtape Letters*. "I was about twelve at the time," he recalls. "But how odd it was—these letters from a seasoned old demon to a fledgling devil on how to leach away the faith of a Christian. I was galvanized, of course, but the author's name meant nothing to me (he wasn't one of the great Bible teachers who held the limelight in those palmy 1940s days of Philadelphia fundamentalism). Who he might be, no one could say, but what he wrote sounded as though he might be a Christian, so that was all right." Attending Wheaton College, Howard took a course in which he was required to read a number of Lewis's works—*Miracles*, *Mere Christianity*, and *The Abolition of Man*. His professor was Kenneth Kantzer, and, Howard notes, "I owe him a great debt for putting Lewis in front of us all."[66]

This exposure to Lewis led him on to Tolkien, which became the subject of a letter he sent to Lewis in 1958, after his Wheaton College experience. While in the army at Ft. Benning, Georgia, Howard wrote Lewis about *The Hobbit* and wanted his perspective on it. Lewis's response to a recent college graduate he had never met or corresponded with previously shows again his openness to American inquirers. He was particularly glad to illuminate for Howard the glories of Tolkien's writings, which he always praised, but he told him to set *The Hobbit* aside now and go to *The Lord of the Rings*. "*The Hobbit* is merely a fragment of his myth, detached, and adapted for children, and losing much by the adaptation. *The Lord of the R* is the real stuff."[67]

Five years later, just a few months before Lewis's death, Howard had the opportunity to speak with him at the Kilns. In a talk to the New York C.

---

65. Ibid., 93–94.

66. Howard, "We All Have the Same Difficulty," 143.

67. Letter from Lewis to Thomas Howard, 14 October 1958, Hooper, *Collected Letters*, Vol. III, 980–81.

S. Lewis Society seven years later, Howard said Lewis was "down to the last molecule what I would have expected." He described the sitting room "as sort of a hobbit hole." Although he was concerned he was wasting Lewis's time, Lewis seemed to be in no hurry at all to end the conversation. The Society's report on Howard's presentation summarized his talk with Lewis, noting, "They talked largely about Tolkien. Both agreed their favorite among CSL's own writings was *Till We Have Faces*. They discussed Purgatory and the nature of evil. On psychiatry, 'neither my bag nor his,' Lewis remarked that introspection is not the road to freedom." Howard's takeaway from this short time with one of his favorite authors, again provided in the Society's summary, was that there was "a great continuity between the man, his talking, and his writing. He sensed a certain toughness with himself and with other people in the right sense, as about the nature of God and evil: toughness in a kind of ruthless candor. CSL assumed the other person's candor, and that one actually means what one says." Howard's response: "'It's almost frightening!'" Further, Howard came away with a strong feeling that he had met a man possessed of "an authentic humility which has no interest in pressing its own credentials or calling attention to itself." Howard's final comment was "'You had the feeling of all rubbish being cleared away—of being left with tremendous clarity.'"[68]

Howard went on to obtain a doctorate in English literature and taught at Gordon College, an evangelical institution, for fifteen years. He left in the mid-1980s when he decided to become Catholic and finished his academic career at St. John's University. Along the way, he wrote many books, including *Narnia and Beyond: A Guide to the Fiction of C. S. Lewis* and *The Novels of Charles Williams*, an examination of the writings of Lewis's close friend and fellow Inkling. In an essay reflecting on Lewis's influence on his life, he thanked him for his writing style, which was "brisk, energetic, clean, and robust, as opposed to the earnest, swampy, and eager literature, written in terrible English prose, that fills religious bookstores in our own epoch." He also stated clearly, "There is no question about it—Lewis has been a spiritual mentor to me (although he would, I think, have jibbed mightily at the term) through his imaginative works. It is as though the entire universe has been unfurled and one has been vouchsafed a glimpse of glory and of the whole panoply of holiness."[69]

As he catalogued the treasures one finds in Lewis's imaginative works—from the heroic and beautiful characters in The Chronicles of Narnia to the multifaceted individuals that people his Space Trilogy novels—Howard

68. *The New York C. S. Lewis Society Bulletin #7* (May 1970), 2.
69. Howard, "We All Have the Same Difficulty," 144.

asked, "Who can read all of this and not himself be bidden to the gates of holiness? God (literally—certainly not I) only knows what I owe to Lewis here." And this parting thought: "I cannot write about all of this without the tears starting into my eyes. That, perhaps, as well as anything, speaks of my debt to Lewis as a spiritual mentor."[70]

The Generation That Knew Not Lewis

The Biblical Joseph was a Godsend—literally—to Egypt. His leadership allowed the Egyptians not only to survive, but to thrive during a drought. After Joseph's death, however, we are told that a generation came along "that knew not Joseph" and did not recall his greatness. That was a concern for many Lewis adherents after his death: would the upcoming generations lose the knowledge of what he had accomplished and how he had been the wellspring of spiritual life for so many? Would his works lie in the dust, never to be seen again? By God's grace, men like Walter Hooper and Clyde Kilby undertook massive efforts to ensure that would not occur. As a result, later generations continue to read and thrive under Lewis's tutelage.

The Americans highlighted in this chapter thus far either had met Lewis personally, had written to him, or both. Once he left this earthly scene, though, later academics would have to "know" him through his works only, and by the testimony of those who had interacted with him. A second generation arose that picked up the Lewis mantle in a way that few predicted. Building on the cornerstones laid by Hooper and Kilby, they continued to learn from Lewis, discuss/debate his ideas, and appreciate his writing skills.

Perhaps chief among these second-generation American scholars is James T. Como, whose first experience with Lewis was as a junior in college in the 1960s. He read an article in *National Review* highly appreciative of Lewis's work, and as he read it, he sensed within "a mounting, incredulous excitement mingled with a sort of personal rebirth of optimism." As an undergraduate, he had felt his faith come under fire; now there might be someone he could relate to who had weathered that fire. "Could it be?" he asked himself. "Could a man who so unashamedly expressed his Christian beliefs not be laughed at as a fool, scorned as a zealot, or patronized as an eccentric?" Further, "Could he not only be taken seriously but also, without apology, put the enemy to flight from the very center of its own strength, the university?"[71]

---

70. Ibid., 145.
71. Como, *Remembering C. S. Lewis*, 34.

Como went directly to Lewis's *An Experiment in Criticism*, which is not where most Lewis aficionados start. Yet it was the perfect starting place for Como, who said he was "undone" by "its clarity, cogency, explanatory power, and especially, its generosity of spirit."[72] As he later explained to the New York C. S. Lewis Society (of which he was a founding member[73]), he saw in Lewis's scholarly work "the same qualities present in his apologetic and creative works: simplicity; strength; firmness; courage; tolerance & open-mindedness; suspicion of cynicism; intellect (wit, judgment, use of analogy, & method of refutation); humility; concreteness; energy; gratefulness to God & enjoyment of God's plenty; sympathy; all summed up in love."[74]

After his introduction to Lewis, Como wrote his master's thesis on *Perelandra*; his doctoral dissertation also was on Lewis. Then he began traveling: to Wheaton, where he met Clyde Kilby and got acquainted with the budding collection there; to Oxford, where he became friends with Walter Hooper. "Reading Lewis, along with reading, thinking and talking *about* Lewis—these were like breathing pure oxygen, or rather like emerging from some depth into fresh air," he relates.[75] This is what led him to find others like himself, those who were fascinated with what Lewis had to offer. As he states in the preface to one of his books,

> C. S. Lewis is the sort of author—a "discovery" of the first order—that compels a reader to spread the word, so strikingly direct and familiar is his voice, so bracing his thought. You might have begun with what I call the "you, too?" reflex, "you, too?" being what you whispered with happy surprise three decades ago when you noticed someone else engrossed in a Lewis tome. You go on to gather fellow enthusiasts into a society dedicated to the study and enjoyment of his work. But because you do not want anyone to miss out on even the smallest morsel of him, and because you think you understand those morsels so well, after a while you presume to make the already-pellucidly-clear clearer still. Before you know it, you are writing, teaching, and lecturing about him. There are other authors, of course, who matter to you—some greater than he and many of very telling importance. But he abides, dwelling within and designing much of your own internal landscape.[76]

---

72. Como, "An *Apologia* on the Way," 85.
73. The founding of this society will be covered in a later chapter.
74. *The New York C. S. Lewis Society Bulletin #7* (May 1970), 1.
75. Como, "An *Apologia* on the Way," 86.
76. Como, *Branches of Heaven*, ix.

Como's first great literary contribution to the memory of Lewis was a book he edited originally titled *C. S. Lewis at the Breakfast Table*, which appeared in 1979 and incorporated essays by many of Lewis's closest friends, some of whom were members of that unofficial group called the Inklings. This study already has drawn on that book (now renamed *Remembering C. S. Lewis*) for personal testimonies by Americans Walter Hooper and Nathan Comfort Starr. It is now in its third edition, having been reissued in 2005. Como says, "Never in the late seventies did I suppose I would be writing a third preface to this book, let alone a quarter century hence; thirteen years after that first edition, when I wrote the second preface, I did not suppose there would be a third."[77] But interest in, and fascination with, C. S. Lewis continues unabated.

Como taught at York College of the City University of New York for more than forty years as a professor of rhetoric and public communication. One of his latest books is *Why I Believe in Narnia: 33 Reviews and Essays on the Life and Work of C. S. Lewis*. He has written a number of articles on Lewis in scholarly journals and has been a commentator on a number of television programs featuring Lewis; the York College Alumni Association chose him as the recipient of their 2014 Distinguished Faculty Award. He is another eminent scholar who was inspired by the combined intellectual rigor and spiritual insight from his mentor, C. S. Lewis.

Another American academic underwent a profound conversion, via Lewis, that changed the entire course of his career, making him one of the foremost Lewis authorities. Lyle Dorsett was teaching history at the University of Denver in the mid-1970s when he was challenged by a student who asked him if he had not said in class one day that intelligent people were not Christians. Dorsett's response was perhaps a little on the snarky side, as he corrected the student slightly: "No, I said that intelligent, *thoughtful* people are not Christians. They are agnostics."[78] Such was Dorsett's worldview at the time. The student then gave him a copy of Chesterton's *Orthodoxy* and talked Dorsett into reading some Lewis. He proceeded to tackle *Mere Christianity*, *The Screwtape Letters*, and *Surprised by Joy*. Shortly afterward, Clyde Kilby came to a campus nearby, so Dorsett decided to hear what he had to say about Lewis. "I do not remember what Kilby said, but I do know that his stories about his personal relationship with Lewis and his brother Warnie intrigued me." Cumulatively, all these events led him to acknowledge his new faith:

---

77. Como, *Remembering C. S. Lewis*, 21.
78. Dorsett, "Changed My Life," 95.

To make a long story short, Kilby's lecture and writings, several books by Lewis, and the witness and prayers of my wife and that University of Denver student, all conspired with some other factors to bring me to repentance and faith in the Lord Jesus Christ in the summer of 1976. In the wake of my conversion, I read more Lewis. Indeed, he became my teacher through his books, articles, and letters.[79]

Then a second spiritual revolution occurred. While researching for a biography on Lewis's wife Joy—eventually published as *And God Came In*—he discovered "that no one had embarked upon the larger effort of systematically and carefully recording the reminiscences of C. S. Lewis's surviving relatives, friends, and associates."[80] In conjunction with the Wade Center, he interviewed Douglas Gresham, Lewis's stepson, and then, upon Clyde Kilby's retirement, he was appointed director of the Wade Center, where he devoted himself to a seven-year marathon of oral history interviews with as many of Lewis's contemporaries as possible. In all, while directing the Center for those seven years, he conducted forty-two such interviews, which now form a significant collection in the Wade archives.

Dorsett stepped down from his position at the Wade in order to return fulltime to the classroom. He continued teaching at Wheaton for a while, then, in 2005, moved to Alabama to become the Billy Graham Professor of Evangelism at Beeson Divinity School at Samford University in Birmingham. He has authored eighteen books on various Christian ministry topics, but three are specifically devoted to Lewis: his biography of Joy, mentioned above; his co-editorship with Marjorie Lamp Mead of the Wade Center of *C. S. Lewis: Letters to Children*; and his more recent *Seeking the Secret Place: The Spiritual Formation of C. S. Lewis*. He has summarized Lewis's impact on his life in this way: "Serving as the curator of the Wade Collection and eventually as the director of the Wade Center opened opportunities for what I am tempted to call complete immersion in the writings and world of C. S. Lewis. Studying Lewis's life and writings (published and unpublished) opened my mind and enriched my soul. My career was shaped by my encounter with Lewis."[81]

Wheaton has continued to be a source of Lewis scholars over the decades. Another one, English professor emeritus Wayne Martindale, has told how *The Great Divorce* altered his entire view of heaven, along with what it meant to be in that eternal abode. His testimony starts rather amusingly

---

79. Ibid., 96.
80. Dorsett, *Seeking the Secret Place*, 9.
81. Dorset, "Changed My Life," 96.

when he writes, "I begin with a confession: I have not always wanted to go to Heaven." The problem was a toxic mixture of inaccurate myths, "fuzzy logic," and images of what heaven will be like that were not at all appealing, as he imagined "stuffy mansion houses and ghosts walking on golden (therefore barren and cold) streets." His biggest fear, though, was easy to identify: that heaven would be a most boring place. He equated it with the types of stultifying church services he was accustomed to attending, "with this exception: you never got to go home to the roast beef dinner. What a way to anticipate my eternal destiny."[82]

All that changed when Martindale picked up *The Great Divorce*:

> It awakened in me an appetite for something better than roast beef. It aroused a longing to inherit what I was created for: that which would fulfill my utmost longings and engender new longings and fulfill those, too. After reading *The Great Divorce*, for the first time in my life, I felt Heaven to be both utterly real and utterly desirable. It was a magnificent gift. Small wonder, then, that *The Great Divorce* has always been one of my favorite books because when I read it, it awakened me to my spiritual anorexia. I was starving for heavenly food and didn't even know I was hungry.[83]

Heaven has been a popular topic in Christian publishing, particularly in the past two decades. Martindale notices a commonality in those books:

> While anything approaching precision about a great book's influence is difficult at best, some observations rooted in fact may at least be suggestive. In surveying some of the popular books on faith and Heaven from my own shelves, I find that the following books (all published between 1995 and 2006) explicitly cite *The Great Divorce*: Randy Alcorn's *Heaven*, Anthony DeStefano's *A Travel Guide to Heaven*, John Eldredge's *The Sacred Romance*, Hank Hanegraaf's *Resurrection*, Max Lucado's *When Christ Comes*, Lee Strobel's *The Case for Faith*, and Joni Eareckson Tada's *Heaven*.[84]

Martindale, throughout his academic career, has written a multitude of articles on Lewis. In 1990, he and co-editor Jerry Root compiled what the book cover calls "an encyclopedic selection of quotes from the complete published works of C. S. Lewis," appropriately titled *The Quotable Lewis*. Then, in 2005, Crossway published his *Beyond the Shadowlands: C. S. Lewis*

---

82. Martindale, "The Great Divorce," 133.
83. Ibid., 134.
84. Ibid., 148.

on Heaven and Hell. The effects of Martindale's reading of *The Great Divorce* have lingered. He evaluates Lewis in these words: "Few writers bring to any subject Lewis's theological sophistication, historical grasp, imaginative range, and clarity of expression."[85]

David Downing had many questions as a young person. His parents were deeply involved in the Navigator ministry, and his father was a great help as he dealt with big issues such as the fate of those who have never heard the Gospel. Yet, as he went away to college at Westmont, an evangelical Christian institution in Santa Barbara, questions remained. One professor, though, aided his spiritual development tremendously by assigning Lewis's *Perelandra* as one of the required texts for a course. As was the case with Chad Walsh, Downing's world was turned upside down—or rather right side up—by this particular interplanetary novel. "What I wasn't expecting," he later wrote, "was a novel that would challenge me to reimagine my faith, that would tackle head-on some of the very questions that I had been grappling with since childhood."[86]

What grabbed him about *Perelandra* was how Lewis could put basic Christian doctrines and images into a new language and setting, thereby offering a fresh perspective on what Downing had heard all his life. For instance, in the novel, Lewis transforms angels into what he called "eldils," which could be perceived only as "majestic, awe-inspiring column[s] of light," more like "'thinking mineral[s]' than . . . creature[s] of flesh and blood." Downing explains further,

> Lewis has reimagined for us what it might feel like to actually encounter an angel. If Lewis had depicted a heavenly messenger clad in radiant garments, its identity would be so recognizable as to be dismissible. The word *angel* has been so overused that it may suggest nothing more than a Halloween costume or a cartoon character sitting on someone's shoulder. Lewis intended for his fiction to reenergize his readers' spiritual imaginations, to make *God* and *angel* and *soul* (and *heaven* and *hell*) terms of genuine wonder and terror, to make the Christian life a moment-by-moment cosmic adventure, not a once-a-week religious obligation.[87]

Downing's experience of reading Lewis's *Perelandra* reoriented his life, and he went on from there to dive into all of Lewis's writings. As with a number of the academics who connected with Lewis, he received a doctorate in

---

85. Ibid., 134.
86. Downing, "When the Science Is Fiction but the Faith Is Real," 99.
87. Ibid., 100.

English and became a university professor, beginning with his alma mater, Westmont, for fifteen years (where he was twice honored as Teacher of the Year), then on to Elizabethtown College in Pennsylvania, where he holds the R. W. Schlosser Professor of English chair. Lewis books have flowed from his fertile mind, with the first published in 1992, *Planets in Peril: A Critical Study of C. S. Lewis's Ransom Trilogy*, an apt start for someone whose Lewis path began with *Perelandra*. This first book was named as one of the Outstanding Books of the Year by the American Library Association and also was awarded the Mythopoeic Society's Book of the Year.

Downing's initial Lewis offering was followed by others. *The Most Reluctant Convert: C. S. Lewis's Journey to Faith* appeared a decade later. The American Library Association chose it as one of the Top Ten Books of the Year in the category of Religion, while The Evangelical Christian Publishers Association made it a finalist for a 2003 Gold Medallion Book Award in the category of Biography. His output increased with two more highly regarded books in 2005: *Into the Region of Awe* and *Into the Wardrobe*. In 2010, he came out with a novel called *Looking for the King: An Inklings Novel*, which incorporates Lewis, Tolkien, and Charles Williams as characters. His latest labor of love is an annotated edition of Lewis's first Christian book, *The Pilgrim's Regress*, which clarifies a lot of the more obscure individuals and movements mentioned in the book, making it more accessible and understandable to the modern reader.

Yet, after all of his Lewis experiences, Downing still looks back on that initial encounter with wistfulness:

> Though I have now read all of Lewis's books, most of them many times, I will never forget my first experience of the Ransom trilogy. Lewis said that when he encountered George MacDonald's *Phantastes* as a teenager, that classic work of Christian fantasy provided a spiritual cleansing that baptized his imagination. Lewis's books have performed the same service for me. And sometimes, like Lewis himself, I am apt to look up at twilight, see the evening star, and whisper in wonder, "Perelandra!"[88]

Another prolific author of Lewis works is Don W. King, professor of literature at Montreat College in North Carolina. His pathway to Lewis began with *The Lion, the Witch, and the Wardrobe*. He was a college student finishing his shift washing dishes at the campus cafeteria one day when someone walked up to him and gave him the book. "I doubt that I had heard of C. S. Lewis before then; I certainly did not know him well," he recalls. "Since I was a literature major, I was always hungry for something new to read, so I

---

88. Ibid., 101.

plunged into the book; to say that I was overwhelmed by Lewis's wonderful tale would be an understatement. All I know is that, in spite of the fact that we were in the middle of final exams, I read the other six Narnian tales over the next day or two—I was hooked."[89]

King's favorite Lewis book became *The Screwtape Letters* because "it so incisively describes the psychology of temptation form the hellish side." Screwtape, King notes, "is no Underwood-deviled-ham devil. Instead, he writes with a stiletto; by means of his lucid, diabolical epistles he offers a disturbing insight into the nature of temptation." What King most appreciates was how Lewis, in this book, avoided "prepackaged, spiritual truisms" and gave his readers more spiritual nourishment "than the devotional pabulum mass-produced by some Christian publishers. *The Screwtape Letters* is an antidevotional demanding we take serious stock of our spiritual lives," he concludes.[90]

His first Lewis book, published in 2008, was *C. S. Lewis, Poet: The Legacy of His Poetic Impulse*. He then began a laser-like focus on Joy Davidman Lewis, editing her letters in his 2009 work *Out of My Bone*. The year 2015 saw a burst of scholarship with three books appearing: Joy's poems collected into *A Naked Tree: Love Sonnets to C. S. Lewis and Other Poems*; *Yet One More Spring: A Critical Study of Joy Davidman*; and *The Collected Poems of C. S. Lewis: A Critical Edition*. In addition to his fulltime professorship and his publishing ventures, King also serves as editor of the *Christian Scholar's Review*.

He owes much to the influence of Lewis for all of his scholarly energy. At the conclusion of an essay detailing Lewis's impact on his thinking, King explains,

> All I know is that he has been a pivotal person in my literary, intellectual, and spiritual life. Each of us should find a writer we can read for the rest of our lives. It doesn't really matter whether the writer is well known to the rest of the world. What matters is that he or she *speaks* to us. For me that writer is C. S. Lewis; he combines literary excellence, hard-nosed thinking, and a winsome faith in Christ. It is no exaggeration to say he was the most articulate Christian writer of the twentieth century, especially in his appeal to readers across denominational lines. Although I never met him, through his books he became my greatest teacher and most influential mentor.[91]

---

89. King, "Writer We Can Read," 159.
90. Ibid., 160.
91. Ibid., 160–61.

In the Ministry

Cataloguing all the American scholars who were or are impacted by Lewis would be a greater task than this present study can attain to, so the previous section offered merely a sampling of some of the most prominent. The same can be said—even more so—for those outside the academy who are actively ministering the Gospel, whether as pastors, priests, writers, or in a parachurch ministry of some type. Rare is the evangelical pastor, for instance, who has not quoted Lewis from the pulpit at one time or another, or who has not at least read *Mere Christianity* or ensured that his children are introduced to The Chronicles of Narnia. The best that can be done is to provide representative individuals whose ministries have been deeply affected by what they have received from Lewis. Therefore, this section will focus on two men who are highly influential in the Christian ministry today, mostly as writers themselves, and then this chapter will end with the story of one of the most well-known conversions in twentieth-century America—a man who, as a political operative, was convicted and sent to prison, and then found new life in Christ through a reading of *Mere Christianity*. His conversion led to the establishment of a worldwide ministry.

Philip Yancey

He has sold fourteen million books, two of which, *The Jesus I Never Knew* and *What's So Amazing About Grace*, won the Evangelical Christian Publishers Association's Christian Book of the Year Award. Right out of college, in 1971, he joined the staff of *Campus Life* magazine as an editor, then moved on to *Christianity Today*, where he still serves as an editor-at-large. Yet Philip Yancey had to overcome what he calls a "toxic" church situation in his early years in the American South. It wasn't that he did not see some genuine Christianity in his church; it was that it was directed to whites only, leaving a scar on his soul. "Along the way I realized that God had been misrepresented to me. Cautiously, warily, I returned, circling around the faith to see if it might be true."[92] What could heal that scar? C. S. Lewis played a major role in the reaffirmation of Yancey's faith.

While attending a Bible college that was not at all top notch, and struggling to survive with temporary professors and missionaries teaching subjects that were beyond their depth, Yancey, as a cynical youth, delighted—he called it "a devilish delight"—in trying to overthrow the faith of his fellow students

---

92. "About Philip Yancey," official Philip Yancey website.

and "stumping professors with questions they could not answer."[93] Along the way, somehow, Lewis's Space Trilogy found its way into his hands, and from there, into his mind and heart. "It had an undermining effect on me," he reflected later. Lewis "made the supernatural so believable that I could not help wondering, *What if it's really true? What if there is a God and an afterlife and what if supernatural forces really are operating behind the scenes on this planet and in my life?*" As with many others who first picked up a Lewis book, his thinking was challenged. "The tremors strengthened into an earthquake as I went on to read *Mere Christianity* and *The Problem of Pain*, which dismantled my defenses and convicted me of the sin of pride."[94]

Yancey bought more Lewis books and continued to argue internally with the author's presuppositions and conclusions. Finally, though, he had to admit to himself that Lewis made sense. "I wrestled with them as with a debate opponent and reluctantly felt myself drawn, as Lewis himself had, kicking and screaming all the way into the kingdom of God. Since then he has been a constant companion, a kind of shadow mentor who sits beside me urging me to improve my writing style, my thinking, my vision." Lewis's influence never left even after Yancey became an established author himself. "Before writing any book, first I laboriously go through all of Lewis's to see what he said about the topic. . . . Lewis affirmed my calling as a writer. We live lonely lives, those of us who make a living by playing with words."[95]

On his website, Yancey offers this analysis of Lewis's relevance: "Other defenders of the faith—apologists they're called—have arisen since C. S. Lewis, but none has the continuing impact of the eccentric don who rarely traveled, never learned to drive, and yet somehow expressed his beliefs so clearly and winsomely that millions still turn to him for guidance. Some fifty of his books remain in print, with total sales exceeding a hundred million."[96] But he also has written of Lewis's relevance to him personally:

> I doubt C. S. Lewis ever anticipated that almost half a century after his death several million people each year would buy one of his dozens of books still in print or that Disney Studios would release movies based on Narnia with spin-off products available in every shopping mall. If informed of that fact during his life, he would likely have shrunk back in alarm. We writers are not Nouns, he used to say. We are mere adjectives, pointing to the great Noun of truth. Lewis did that, faithfully and masterfully,

---

93. Yancey, "Shadow Mentor," 211.
94. Ibid.
95. "C. S. Lewis: Mere Christian," official Philip Yancey website.
96. Ibid.

and because he did so, many thousands have come to know and love that Noun. Including me.[97]

Randy Alcorn

Another well-known Christian writer, Randy Alcorn, owes much to the influence of Lewis. He has authored more than forty books, and many of them bear the Lewis imprint, especially *Heaven* and a number of novels that capture the imagination in a way that Lewis undoubtedly would have approved. Some of those novels even have dual settings: what is transpiring on earth simultaneously with glimpses into heaven and the interaction between the earthly and heavenly realms. Alcorn began his ministry as a pastor for fourteen years, then founded Eternal Perspective Ministries, which his website describes as "dedicated to teaching principles of God's Word and assisting the church in ministering to the unreached, unfed, unborn, uneducated, unreconciled, and unsupported people around the world."[98] Yet where he is now is a long way from where he started.

Alcorn not only did not grow up in a Christian home, but his father, who owned a tavern, "despised Christians in general and pastors in particular." Both parents were on their second marriages, and the current marriage was so rocky and filled with fights that, as a boy, he half expected another divorce would occur. This combative and strained atmosphere left him empty inside, so he sought escape through comic books and science fiction. He owned a telescope and would spend long hours stargazing, seeking something grand in the universe. Viewing the Andromeda galaxy filled him with awe. "I longed to go there and explore its wonders and lose myself in something greater than myself," he recalls. "My wonder was trumped by an unbearable sense of loneliness and separation. I wanted to worship, but I didn't know whom. I wept because I felt so incredibly small. Unknown to me, God was using the wonders of the universe to draw me to himself."[99]

The Bible was practically an unknown book to him, but years later he picked one up and started reading at the very beginning in Genesis. It told him that God created the heavens and the earth; he felt excitement and began devouring the book. When he finally made it to the New Testament and discovered the Jesus therein, he was fascinated. "At first, I thought Jesus was fiction—a superhero like in the comics. But everything about Jesus had the

---

97. Yancey, "Shadow Mentor," 214.
98. "About Randy," EPM: Eternal Perspective Ministries.
99. Alcorn, "C. S. Lewis on Heaven and the New Earth," 105.

ring of truth. Then I realized something incredible. While reading the Bible, I had come to believe Jesus is real. By a miracle of grace, he transformed my life."[100]

This is where C. S. Lewis made his entrance. Alcorn was so hungry to learn more that he constantly visited a Christian bookstore looking for as much spiritual nourishment as possible. He found Lewis's *The Problem of Pain* first and was "stunned by his insight and clarity. He remembered what it was like not to know God, just like I did. He spoke of longing, like mine." Shortly after that first encounter, Alcorn discovered Lewis's science fiction—*Out of the Silent Planet*, *Perelandra*, and *That Hideous Strength*. For someone who had earlier immersed himself in science fiction books, this was a revelation—science fiction with a Christian ethos. He actually had stopped reading science fiction because his church "left me with the impression that using my imagination might be a sin, so I'd assumed science fiction was a thing of the past. Yet this same author with the great insights had also exercised his imagination by creating engaging science fiction."[101] His telescope, which also had been set aside, now came out of the cobwebs. "After reading Lewis's space trilogy, I went outside and once more gazed at the galaxy of Andromeda. Again I wept. But this time for a very different reason: gratitude. Now I knew personally the God who had spun into being the trillion stars and countless planets of the Andromeda galaxy and the Milky Way."[102]

His next Lewis adventure was a thorough reading of The Chronicles of Narnia. Although they were meant as children's books, Alcorn was taken aback by the theological implications Lewis sprinkled throughout these seven stories. In *The Lion, the Witch, and the Wardrobe*, he learned that God/Aslan is not tame, but is definitely good. *The Silver Chair* taught him that there was only one stream from which to drink to quench one's thirst. And in *Prince Caspian*, "I read a hundred pages of theology poured into two sentences: 'You come of the Lord Adam and the Lady Eve,' said Aslan. 'And that is both honour enough to erect the head of the poorest beggar, and shame enough to bow the shoulders of the greatest emperor on earth.'" He summarizes his Narnia lessons this way: "Lucy tells Aslan that he looks bigger than before, and Aslan says, 'Every year you grow, you will find me bigger.' I did then and I do now still find the never-changing God to be ever-bigger in my eyes."[103]

---

100. Ibid., 106.
101. Ibid.
102. Ibid., 107.
103. Ibid.

"It was Lewis who convinced me that the same person could write good nonfiction and fiction, and emboldened me to try," Alcorn testifies. "All my books are touched by Lewis, because ultimately the books we write are the overflow of the books we've read." He has a wish, another longing he wants fulfilled one day:

> In *The Four Loves* I learned about friendship. By then I knew what Lewis knew, that an author can become a friend, someone you can rejoin at will, picking up right where you left off. I look forward to meeting Jack Lewis and exploring the new earth, where there will be time for us all to walk and talk, with new friends who are also old friends, in the joyful presence of King Jesus.[104]

Charles Colson

Pride. That was the driving force in Charles Colson's life for more than four decades. He grew up in the Boston area, but his family was not one of the Brahmin elite. His father worked hard to get a law degree, succeeded, but never was invited to the fraternity of the top lawyers; instead, he struggled to stay afloat financially. Sometimes, Colson's parents would sell furniture and other items to make enough money to pay the bills. Religious instruction was minimal at best at a local Episcopal church. Colson felt the distance between his family and the upper crust and sought to break through the artificial ceiling that threatened his future. A work ethic is admirable, and the desire to make something of oneself, generally speaking, is fine. But not if it becomes an all-consuming desire.

Raised practically in the shadow of Harvard, Colson's hard work made him the valedictorian of his senior high school class. He did so well that he was offered a full ride to Harvard. Then he did the unthinkable; he rejected it in favor of Brown University. It was a pride factor. He liked being able to walk away from the offer with his head held high. It was a statement about the standoffishness of the elite; even their full ride seemed like condescension to him, as if someone from the wrong side of the tracks should be overwhelmed by their willingness to allow him into their presence.

At Brown, he joined the Naval ROTC, but told his supervisor he wanted to be a Marine. Informed that he would have to prove himself, he set out to do just that, and earned that honor. After that, he became a successful lawyer in his own partnership, then a cagey political operative who was willing to bend the rules of propriety, if by doing so his candidate would

---

104. Alcorn, "Learning to Love God," 41–42.

gain an advantage. Throughout the 1960s his star rose, and he was noticed by Richard Nixon, who eventually brought him into his administration as a treasured member of his inner circle. When Nixon ran for reelection in 1972, Colson was the chief strategist for his campaign, a highly successful one, with Nixon winning forty-nine of the fifty states. Colson should have been at the peak of his career; he should have been deliriously happy. Yet that was not the case.

It was election night, 1972, and Colson, with his wife and son, were at the Victory Party at Washington's Shoreham Hotel. Exuberance should have been the rule, but as he surveyed the room, he could not pick up on an air of triumph. "The faces before us were unsmiling, looking, in fact, disappointed and even imposed upon."[105] After a few rude conversations from people who wanted some kind of payback for their support, Colson was somewhat sickened by the prevailing attitude. "I wasn't imagining the sour mood," he recalled. "But something was also wrong in me." Relating the tale of that evening in his autobiography, *Born Again*, he continued,

> My insides were as deadened as the air in the room and the slow beat of the music. My lack of exhilaration made no sense. Being part of electing a President was the fondest ambition of my life. For three long years I had committed everything I had, every ounce of energy to Richard Nixon's cause. Nothing else had mattered. We had had no time together as a family, no social life, no vacations. So why could my tongue not taste the flavor of this hour of conquest?[106]

He was a spent volcano, he reasoned. It was time to move on, which he did in a few months, back to his private law practice. But his connection to the Nixon administration would follow after him in an affair called Watergate.

There is no need to resurrect all the details of the controversy that led to a president's resignation and a number of his close associates being convicted and sent to prison. It is enough to know that the long shadow of this scandal led to public accusations against Colson. He was innocent of anything in the Watergate scandal itself, but his tactics as a political operative were scrutinized carefully. By the end of the saga, he also was imprisoned, the charge being that he had spread false stories to undermine the reputation of a critic of Nixon's Vietnam policy, Daniel Ellsberg, who was on trial for leaking secret documents known as the Pentagon Papers to the *New York Times*.

105. Colson, *Born Again*, 13.
106. Ibid., 14.

As the accusations mounted, and the media went into a frenzy, Colson felt besieged and became deeply upset. One of the companies he represented as a lawyer was the Raytheon Corporation, headquartered in Boston. The president of Raytheon, Tom Phillips, had told Colson a few months before that he had given his life to Christ. In the midst of the Watergate turmoil, Colson decided he needed to see Phillips. He wasn't even sure why. This meeting would be the catalyst for turning Colson's life around, and the key to that meeting was C. S. Lewis.

As Colson and Phillips conversed on the latter's conversion experience, Phillips decided to bring Lewis into that conversation, bringing out his copy of *Mere Christianity* to share some salient points with Colson. He began to read Lewis's description of pride, which he said was at the foundation of all other sins; he called it an anti-God state of mind. That hit Colson where it hurt most. He had been proud all his life of his achievements; now Lewis was telling him it was his chief problem: "As he read, I could feel a flush coming into my face and a curious burning sensation that made the night seem even warmer. Lewis's words seemed to pound straight at me." Phillips kept reading aloud, coming to the place where Lewis noted that pride always looks down on people, and that if you are always looking down, you are blind to what may exist above you. "Suddenly I felt naked and unclean, my bravado defenses gone," Colson lamented. "I was exposed, unprotected, for Lewis's words were describing me. As he continued, one passage in particular seemed to sum up what had happened to all of us at the White House: 'For Pride is spiritual cancer: it eats up the very possibility of love, or contentment, or even common sense.'"[107]

Colson, as he listened, replayed his entire life in his mind, and saw that what Lewis had written was true: pride was killing him; his arrogance had led to his downfall.

> Now, sitting there on the dimly lit porch, my self-centered past was washing over me in waves. It was painful. Agony. Desperately I tried to defend myself. What about my sacrifices for government service, the giving up of a big income, putting my stocks into a blind trust? The truth, I saw in an instant, was that I'd wanted the position in the White House more than I'd wanted money. There was no sacrifice. And the more I had talked about my sacrifices, the more I was really trying to build myself up in the eyes of others. I would eagerly have given up everything I'd ever earned to prove myself at the mountaintop

---

107. Ibid., 113.

of government. It was pride—Lewis's "great sin"—that had propelled me through life.[108]

Phillips gave Colson that copy of *Mere Christianity* and urged him to read all of it. Before leaving, Phillips prayed over him, another new experience for Colson, who was struck by how that prayer was so personal, as if Phillips really knew the One to whom he was speaking. These weren't the formal prayers he had heard in the Episcopal church; Phillips was informally talking to a Friend. Colson got into his car and tried to drive away, but as he did, he was blinded by his own tears. He had to pull off the road. His words need to tell the rest of the story:

> With my face cupped in my hands, head leaning forward against the wheel, I forgot about machismo, about pretenses, about fears of being weak. And as I did, I began to experience a wonderful feeling of being released. Then came the strange sensation that water was not only running down my cheeks, but surging through my whole body as well, cleansing and cooling as it went. They weren't tears of sadness and remorse, nor of joy—but somehow, tears of relief.
>
> And then I prayed my first real prayer. "God, I don't know how to find You, but I'm going to try! I'm not much the way I am now, but somehow I want to give myself to You." I didn't know how to say more, so I repeated over and over the words: *Take me*.
>
> I had not "accepted" Christ—I still didn't know who He was. My mind told me it was important to find that out first, to be sure that I knew what I was doing, that I meant it and would stay with it. Only, that night, something inside me was urging me to surrender—to what or to whom I did not know.
>
> I stayed there in the car, wet-eyed, praying, thinking, for perhaps half an hour, perhaps longer, alone in the quiet of the dark night. Yet for the first time in my life I was not alone at all.[109]

He followed Phillips's advice to read *Mere Christianity*, only it was not a mere reading, but a careful, logical, analytical study of what Lewis was saying, as Colson sought to decide if he could accept the truths about Christ presented there. Was Lewis perhaps just someone who approached God on the intuitive, emotional level primarily? He found instead that he was "face-to-face with an intellect so disciplined, so lucid, so relentlessly logical that I could only be grateful I had never faced him in a court of law."[110] Colson's

---

108. Ibid., 114.
109. Ibid., 116–17.
110. Ibid., 121.

analysis started with the question, "Is there a God?" and went on from there to why evil can exist in a God-created world, then to the person of Jesus Christ. "As a lawyer I was impressed by Lewis's arguments about moral law, the existence of which he demonstrates is real, and which has been perceived with astonishing consistency in all times and places. It has not been man, I saw for the first time, that has perpetuated moral law; it has survived *despite* man's best attempt to defeat it."[111]

What about the existence of evil? Lewis pointed to the free will God had given man. "To understand this I came back to where Tom Phillips started: pride and ego. As Lewis put it, 'The moment you have a self at all, there is a possibility of putting yourself first—wanting to be the centre—wanting to be God.' How devastatingly I now saw that in my own life."[112] As to the nature of Jesus, Lewis's famous argument about Him being either a liar, a lunatic, or actually God hit home with a thunderclap. Again, it is best to let Colson tell this part of his story:

> There was my choice as simple, stark, and frightening as that, no fine shadings, no gradations, no compromises. No one had ever thrust this truth at me in such a direct and unsettling way. I'd been content to think of Christ as an inspired prophet and teacher who walked the sands of the Holy Land 2,000 years ago—several cuts above other men of His time or, for that matter, any time. But if one thinks of Christ as no more than that, I reasoned, then Christianity is a simple palliative, like taking a sugar-coated placebo once a week on Sunday morning.[113] . . .
>
> Once faced with the staggering proposition that He is God, I was cornered, all avenues of retreat blocked, no falling back to that comfortable middle ground about Jesus Christ being a great moral teacher. If He is not God, He is nothing, least of all a great moral teacher. For what He taught includes the assertion that He is indeed God. And if He is not, that one statement alone would have to qualify as the most monstrous lie of all time—stripping Him at once of any possible moral platform. . . .
>
> I realized suddenly that there is less heresy in rejecting Him altogether, dismissing Him as a raving lunatic, to use Lewis's word, than to remake Him into something He wasn't (and isn't). Jesus said take it, all or nothing. If I was to believe in God at all,

---

111. Ibid., 122.
112. Ibid., 123.
113. Ibid., 125.

I had to take Him as He reveals Himself, not as I might wish Him to be.[114]

That settled it. Charles Colson set aside his pride and bowed the knee to Jesus Christ as His Lord and Savior.

Jesus, of course, never promised that acceptance of His lordship would erase all the troubles of this life. Colson still had to face the accusations, the prison time, and the disbelief and even open ridicule once his conversion became public. Sentenced to one-to-three years, he served seven months, released early due to his eighteen-year-old son being convicted of a drug charge. The judge who had sentenced Colson was now showing some mercy. Maybe it was also due, in part, to what Colson had accomplished while in prison. His Christian faith was both tested and strengthened during those months in confinement. He set up prayer meetings and Bible studies with fellow inmates, creating what he termed a prison fellowship. One of Nixon's former lawyers, Herb Kalmbach, was in the same prison. Colson shared his faith with Kalmbach, read him the chapter in *Mere Christianity* on pride, just as Tom Phillips had done with him, and Kalmbach gave his life to Christ.[115]

Upon his release, a strong urging within Colson, based on what he felt were inadequate ministry attempts in the prisons, led him to establish an organization called Prison Fellowship, which is now an international ministry devoted to bringing the light of Christ to the prisoners. As time went on, he also created a daily radio program called *BreakPoint*, which brings the Biblical worldview to bear on many social and governmental issues. The Wilberforce Forum was another Colson idea, named after the famous British statesman William Wilberforce, who ended the slave trade, and eventually slavery, in the British Empire. The Forum became the backbone of the *BreakPoint* program, and continues to offer seminars and other means for disseminating Biblical principles.

As one peruses his many books, one finds C. S. Lewis mentioned prominently in nearly all of them. In his 1992 book *The Body*, Colson shows how Lewis continued to figure prominently in his conversations with non-christians. While having dinner with a journalist friend, the topic went to how to live with one's conscience. Colson then introduced Lewis's natural law arguments. Lewis, he said, provided "a common ground and language with which to discuss the spiritual realm."[116] Later, in the same book, he offers this praise of Lewis: "Today, many writers reveal in their work the incoherence, shattered logic, and relativistic chaos that mark a culture which

---

114. Ibid., 127.
115. Aitken, *A Life Redeemed*, 263.
116. Colson with Vaughn, *The Body*, 337–38.

has lost its understanding of concepts like sin, redemption, forgiveness, and grace. So when a writer who is a Christian beautifully crafts words and stories that spring from a world-view informed by truth—he or she is salting modern culture. C. S. Lewis did this brilliantly, his cogent, tough-minded logic riding on wings of lucid prose."[117]

Colson's *How Now Shall We Live?* is replete with Lewis quotes, not only from *Mere Christianity*, but also from *The Screwtape Letters*, *The Abolition of Man*, *Miracles*, *God in the Dock*, *The Discarded Image*, and his insightful essay, "The Humanitarian Theory of Punishment." He even uses Lewis to help solidify the main point of the book, as near the end he writes,

> In popular culture, as in every field, the best way to reach a nonbelieving audience is not so much by works that preach Christianity explicitly as by works that express a Christian worldview indirectly. "We can make people attend to the Christian point of view for half an hour or so," said C. S. Lewis, "but the moment they have gone away from our lecture or laid down the article, they are plunged back into a world where the opposite position is taken for granted." Therefore, "what we want is not more little books about Christianity, but more little books by Christians on other subjects—with their Christianity latent."[118]

Much the same can be found in his 2007 book, *God and Government*, where Lewis is ever-present, with pertinent Lewis quotes at the beginning of a number of the chapters. As with the previous book, near the end, Colson brings Lewis into the picture to drive home a primary thesis: "I'm not advocating that religious groups or leaders boycott the White House or the palaces and parliaments of the world. That's where the political action is, and Christians need to influence policies for justice and righteousness. . . . But Christians (and others as well) need to do so with eyes open, aware of the snares. C. S. Lewis wrote that 'the demon inherent in every [political] party is at all times ready enough to disguise himself as the Holy Ghost.'"[119]

There are also similarities between the way Lewis and Colson lived out their Christian witness. Beginning in 1992, Colson sensed that Christians across the Catholic-Protestant divide needed to create a bridge and work together in the spirit of "mere Christianity." In the same way as Lewis sought to minimize the differences among Christians and wrote of the "common" beliefs of all Christians, Colson worked to bring Catholics and Protestants together to speak to those commonalities. Prison Fellowship, at

---

117. Ibid., 374.
118. Colson and Pearcey, *How Now Shall We Live?* 474–75.
119. Colson, *God and Government*, 349–50.

first, experienced a reduction of one million dollars in annual donations, as some Protestants "protested" this outreach, but Colson remained firm on the need for this venture.

Another way in which the connection between Lewis and Colson is seen is through how they handled the profits from their works. Lewis famously put all the profits from his books into a trust that would then be distributed to those in need. Colson's approach was much the same. In fact, when he was awarded the prestigious Templeton Prize in 1993—the religious equivalent of the Nobel Prize, and which had been awarded previously to individuals such as Billy Graham, Mother Teresa, and Alexander Solzhenitsyn—he requested that the one-million-dollar check be made out to Prison Fellowship. This was in keeping with his practice. His biographer notes, "It was out of the question for Colson to ask for the check to be made out to himself. By the same logic he . . . refused to accept speaking fees and royalties from his books, having them paid directly into Prison Fellowship's bank account. This is Colson's code of financial honor."[120]

Colson also was present in England in 1997 for various events anticipating the centennial celebration of Lewis's birth. Standing in the pulpit of Great Saint Mary's Church in Cambridge, he delivered the keynote address for an event honoring Lewis. There was no question in anyone's mind whom Colson considered to be one of his greatest spiritual mentors.

Charles Colson died of complications from a brain hemorrhage in April 2012, but he left behind a vibrant ministry that continues to this day. Jesus Christ took a proud, arrogant man and transformed him into one of the most prominent Christian leaders in America, but He had invaluable aid in this transformation from His faithful servant, C. S. Lewis.

---

120. Aitken, *A Life Redeemed*, 373.

6

Writing to Americans

THIS EXAMINATION OF C. S. Lewis's contacts with Americans and the influence he had on their lives has centered on individuals with whom he developed relationships, either in person or via letter, or both. Joy Davidman became his beloved wife. Chad Walsh, the first American to write a book about him, was a friend to whom he dedicated *The Four Loves*. Sheldon Vanauken, a young man he led to the Lord, looked to Lewis as his mentor, and it was Lewis who helped him weather the spiritual storm of his wife's untimely death. Vanauken's *A Severe Mercy* has become a Christian classic, loved by many, and inspired by Lewis. Walter Hooper, although he knew Lewis personally only for a few months, became a trusted friend and companion whom Lewis sought to make his permanent secretary, a goal interrupted by Lewis's death. Yet Hooper went on to perform the valuable service of editing Lewis's works, publishing his letters, and generally ensuring he would always be read by later generations. Clyde Kilby carried out much the same task in America by collecting everything Lewis wrote and that was written about him, and by establishing a center at Wheaton College devoted not only to all things Lewis, but also to those who influenced his thinking, some of whom were members of the informal Inklings group.

From that close circle of Lewis's friends and personal acquaintances, this study then turned to a second generation of American scholars whose thinking and whose lives have been touched by Lewis's writings. These academics have flooded the market with books and articles that delve into the Lewis phenomenon from a variety of viewpoints. Similarly, those involved in Christian ministry, whether as pastors or writers themselves, also have been deeply affected by Lewis. One famous convert, Charles Colson, went from the heights of political power to the humility of a prison sentence. As noted in the previous chapter, that experience led to his conversion largely through his reading of Lewis's *Mere Christianity*.

Lewis, though, had many other American correspondents, most of whom were not scholars, pastors, or political figures. Many were women who wanted his advice on a variety of issues; he also had a constant supply of letters from children who wanted to interact with the author of the Narnia series. As busy as he was, he answered all these letters, believing it was an obligation from God. At times, he bemoaned the sheer volume and the time it took to write all those responses. An arthritic hand made the task even harder. Although Warnie would type a lot of his correspondence, he would disappear on occasion for one of his drinking bouts, which only added to Lewis's burdens. Taking all that into account, it really is quite remarkable that he would take so seriously each letter that was written to him, and respond with just what was needed for that particular person.

Walter Hooper collected as many of these letters as he could find, and the result is three large volumes covering Lewis's entire life. Hooper noted in his preface to the third volume that even though he had made every effort to find all of Lewis's letters, he knew that there would be others appearing afterward. So even though those three volumes cannot claim to be comprehensive, what we do have is immense and valuable. Reading through Lewis's letters to all those Americans who wanted to connect with one of their favorite authors is fascinating, as they reveal a man who, although he would have preferred a less hectic existence, sought to help guide those who wanted to converse with him. He developed affection for certain regular correspondents who seemed to love the interplay of debate and the sharing of views, and Lewis did it all with the same sparkling wit and clarity that mark his published works.

As with the treatment of American academics and those involved in ministry in the last chapter, this chapter will focus on representative correspondents, those with whom Lewis had an ongoing relationship throughout the last decade and a half of his life, including some of his letters to children. Taken as a whole, Lewis's letters to average Americans add significant brushstrokes to the portrait of a man who remains an enduring influence in a country he never visited.

Warfield M. Firor

There is more information on Warfield Firor than many of Lewis's American correspondents because Firor was a celebrated surgeon at Johns Hopkins and an elder in his Presbyterian church. He was two years older than Lewis and lived for another twenty-five years after Lewis's death in 1963. There is some overlap in his life with the academics in the previous chapter because he was also on the faculty at Johns Hopkins, but his primary career was as a neurosurgeon. He received a gold medal from the American Medical Association in 1939, and after his death, Johns Hopkins established the Warfield M. Firor Chair of Surgery. A description of his activities on the website for his personal papers collection at Johns Hopkins states,

> Firor played a major role in the national effort to raise the level of training in surgery and lectured on medicine throughout the United States. He conducted research on the effects of tetanus toxin on the spinal cord and investigated the treatment of diseased adrenal glands with hormone implants. Among Firor's surgical contributions was the introduction of intestinal antisepsis in preparation for colon surgery.[1]

Some of Firor's correspondence with Lewis appeared in the first chapter, where we learned that Firor was continually inviting Lewis to visit him in America. He tempted him with a standing invitation to his cabin in the Rocky Mountains. Lewis's responses indicated a desire to take up that invitation, but there were always too many responsibilities, at least to his way of thinking, that stood in the way. Also noted in the first chapter were the many gifts of food that Firor sent Lewis's way after the war when Britain, with a Labour government, suffered under a strict rationing policy. Although many of Lewis's American correspondents sent such gifts, for which he was constantly sending out letters of gratitude, Firor became notable for his steady flow of one of Lewis's favorite foods—ham.

Those hams started appearing in late 1947. After the arrival of the first one, Lewis replied that the ham had lifted morale and that the cheese that accompanied it reminded him of the days when he used to have cheese—he had forgotten how it tasted.[2] A scant three months later, after the arrival of another ham, Lewis sent another thank-you letter, and when another one arrived just two months after that, Lewis informed Firor that his generosity left him with no words left to say to express his gratitude.[3]

Lewis decided to share this largesse with the Inklings, rather than hoard it all for himself. He informed Firor that the group got together to

---

1. Alan Mason Chesney Medical Archives of the Johns Hopkins Medical Institutions.

2. Letter from Lewis to Warfield M. Firor, 1 October 1947, Hooper, *Collected Letters, Vol. II*, 806.

3. Letter from Lewis to Warfield M. Firor, 2 March 1948, ibid., 836.

dine on his ham, and that, along with some scrounged-up burgundy and port, soup, and fish, they created a banquet the likes of which they hadn't experienced, Lewis remarked, for at least the past five years.[4] Attached to the letter was a "Ham Testimonial" signed by all the Inklings who were present that evening to enjoy the feast.

Only a month after the Inklings' "Ham Testimonial," the arrival of more packages from Firor led to another grand feast at an Inklings meeting. Lewis described it with his typical wit, as he related how the group contemplated making the best use of Firor's gift. "It will give you an illuminating sidelight on English life today when I tell you that the first resolution passed for the impending banquet was 'Every man to bring his own piece of *bread*'"![5]

Even as Firor kept inviting Lewis to come to America, Lewis offered the same invitation to Firor, in reverse. Unlike Firor's unrequited invitations, though, Lewis received the news in 1949 that Firor was indeed coming to visit. He was to be in England for another reason and could work Oxford into his schedule. Lewis was delighted that he would be able to meet his benefactor and thank him in person. He warned him, however, of the dire conditions in post-war Britain but assured him of a rousing welcome from the group he had blessed so materially.[6] Even if they could not offer him gifts equal to what he had sent them, he could rest assured that he would be welcomed by a very grateful assembly of Inklings.[7]

Firor did make it to Oxford that July. He spent the night at Magdalen College as Lewis's personal guest. The next evening was the scheduled Inklings meeting; Firor was able to attend, meet the others who had benefited from his giving, and received the hand of gratitude and fellowship from the band of brothers. That was the only time Lewis and Firor would meet in person, but it solidified their friendship as more than just a giver and a recipient of gifts. Firor even made it clear he did not want Lewis to tax himself anymore with thank-you letters. The correspondence between the two deepened after this meeting, as they shared on more weighty topics than ham.

During Firor's visit with Lewis, they had begun to converse on more spiritual matters. After his return to America, their first correspondence reflected more on one particular topic they had started to discuss in person: the exact nature of praise as worship. How did speaking of God's glory make Him more glorious than He already was? A rich man knows quite well that he is rich, so why tell him? God knows He is a glorious God, so how does

---

4. Letter from Lewis to Warfield M. Firor, 12 March 1948, ibid., 838–39.
5. Letter from Lewis to Warfield M. Firor, 16 April 1948, ibid., 849–50.
6. Letter from Lewis to Warfield M. Firor, 22 January 1949, ibid., 908–9.
7. Letter from Lewis to Warfield M. Firor, 22 March 1949, ibid., 926–27.

it add anything to declare it? Praise, Lewis concluded, is a natural reaction from a created being who sees the glory of God. It is appropriate.

The letters then shifted to the issue of human mortality and how to deal with old age from a Christian point of view. If old age and death were an option for people, Lewis pondered, how many of us would choose them, even if we still retained the truth that this life is not our final destination and true happiness would only be found after death? Not many, he supposed. He was beginning to come to grips with his mortality, he wrote, and that was a good thing. He needed "to loosen a few of the tentacles which the octopus-world has fastened on one," he confided. Lewis remarked that a realization of one's mortality is actually a "partial waking" from "the old stupor" that blinds people spiritually. "But it is a *very* partial waking," he reasoned. The Christian, Lewis believed, needed to be ready at all times to detach from this life, knowing that what awaits in the next will be far better.[8]

The themes of physical death and death to self-will intertwined in his next letter, with the emphasis on the latter. The New Testament makes it clear, Lewis asserted, that we must die to the world. He expressed concern that he had not begun that process because it is those good things in the world that can be a stumbling block. He ended the letter with thanks to God that we are not left on our own with the world's false promises: all the terrible circumstances of life would be brought to bear to teach us this undeniable truth: "this tent is not home."[9]

Another letter to Firor, rather lengthy, was devoted to a critique of education, at least the way it was being carried out at that time. What is most interesting about this particular letter is that it contains sentiments about education that one might not expect from such an esteemed scholar. While Lewis certainly believed in high standards (witness the testimony of those he tutored), he also saw a bad trend in the early years when children needed more time to be children. He was deeply concerned that education had turned into more of a competition, even of a ruthless nature. While competition itself was not evil, he told Firor that children needed time to be children. Why, he complained, did one's entire childhood and the college years always have to be a constant exam preparation? Was this really good for the children? What kind of nation would this produce psychologically, morally, and spiritually?[10]

---

8. Letter from Lewis to Warfield M. Firor, 15 October 1949, ibid., 985–87.

9. Letter from Lewis to Warfield M. Firor, 5 December 1949, ibid., 1005–8.

10. Letter from Lewis to Warfield M. Firor, 12 March 1950, Hooper, *Collected Letters*, Vol. III, 15–18.

A number of letters touch on Lewis's concerns for how England was being governed. Although he never liked politics, he had a definite concept of good governance, and he was not seeing it under the Labour party. In one letter, he confessed to Firor that he sometimes felt ashamed that he took so little notice of the news. Yet he did worry about the possibility of another war, and entering a war with the type of government England currently had would be a nightmare, in his view.[11] In late 1951, he rejoiced at the ouster of Labour and was relieved that the change to Conservative government wasn't accompanied by a revolution.[12]

Lewis also wrote to Firor about the progress of his sabbatical year, in which he had to complete his volume on English literature of the sixteenth century. It was going well and he was confident he could finish it in 1952. But he did have one fear that can plague a scholar: what about possible hidden errors? He then compared his work with Firor's, noting that Firor perhaps had it better because his writing on medical issues was more empirical. But if Lewis were to make a grave error in his volume, and it went into print with that error intact, he harbored the concern that it would undoubtedly be sent to a reviewer who might be "the only man in England" who would spot that error. Lewis then made, maybe for the first time, his inaccurate prediction about the future status of his writings: "I am going to be . . . one of those men who *was* a famous writer in his forties and dies unknown."[13]

Lewis's connections with Firor were on many levels: as a professional man who was at the top of the medical profession, he and Lewis were on the same plane intellectually; as a humble man who gave out of his largesse to help Lewis and the Inklings through a hard time in England, he mirrored Lewis's own selflessness in giving; as a spiritual man who thought deeply about issues such as the proper worship of God and dying to self, they were following a common Lord and Savior.

Vera Mathews Gebbert

Vera Mathews was an unmarried woman about thirty years old when she first wrote to Lewis in 1947. In the 1940s, she had some success writing plays, having them produced in Dallas and New York City. She married Karl H. Gebbert in 1952, but they divorced two years later. One son, Charles, was born from that marriage; Vera Gebbert never again married.[14] Her cor-

---

11. Letter from Lewis to Warfield M. Firor, 6 December 1950, ibid., 66–67.
12. Letter from Lewis to Warfield M. Firor, 20 December 1951, ibid., 149–50.
13. Letter from Lewis to Warfield M. Firor, 20 December 1951, ibid., 149–50.
14. Basic biographical information taken from Vera Gebbert's obituary.

respondence with Lewis lasted from that first letter in 1947 until late 1962. Lewis's responses started out as more formal thank-you letters for the various packages she sent him during England's rationing era, but they gradually became more personal. He offered consolation for her divorce, brought his sharp mind to her aid as she attempted to do more writing, followed her various moves to a number of states, commented on politics, education, and theological issues, and expressed a sincere wish that they could meet in person. Gebbert did visit England twice during Lewis's lifetime, but circumstances denied them that face-to-face encounter.

Gebbert's gifts of food seemed to arrive nearly as often as those of Warfield Firor's. Lewis was showered sometimes with so many American parcels of goodwill that he had more than enough for the household. On those occasions, he would find someone else who might be more needy. On one occasion he confessed to Gebbert that he had re-addressed one of her packages and sent it to a woman who was in great distress financially. He did not want Gebbert to think, though, that her thoughtfulness went unappreciated; he merely wanted to share her generosity with others.[15] Another time he infused his thanks with some humor, pointing out that if she were to continue to send packages at her current rate, "the Customs people will begin to suspect that what you are really doing is to run a black market shop in Oxford, with me as your distributing agent!"[16]

As with all of Lewis's American correspondents, his books were the inspiration for writing to him. There is no clear indication, though, which of Lewis's books spurred Gebbert to write her first letter. When she requested a photo of Lewis, he had to admit he was not sure if he had any or where they might be, but he promised to look.[17] This was typical of Lewis's lack of self-promotion; when he finished writing a book, he would then quickly move on to the next one, with nary a thought of injecting himself into some kind of campaign to increase sales.

From other letters, we get some idea of how important Lewis's works were to Gebbert. She definitely liked *That Hideous Strength* because she hoped to see it made into a motion picture. In a pre-computer-generated-imagery world, Lewis's response is understandable: "The difficulty about filming *That Hideous Strength* is the rarity of tame angels and bears in this

---

15. Letter from Lewis to Vera Mathews, 1 October 1949, Hooper, *Collected Letters, Vol. II.*, 984–85.

16. Letter from Lewis to Vera Mathews, 21 December 1950, Hooper, *Collected Letters, Vol. III*, 73–74.

17. Letter from Lewis to Vera Mathews, 18 October 1948, Hooper, *Collected Letters, Vol. II*, 884–85.

country!"[18] She also had read the volume dedicated to the memory of Charles Williams, to which a number of English authors had contributed.[19] Lewis then sent her an autographed copy of *The Lion, the Witch, and the Wardrobe* as soon as it appeared in print.[20]

Gebbert, in 1952, wrote to ask when his next book might be forthcoming. Lewis had to lower her expectations, due to the publishing deadline on his history of English literature volume, which he had been working on steadily for fifteen years. "When it is actually done I expect my whole moral character will collapse. I shall go up like a balloon that has chucked out the last sandbag," he responded wearily.[21] When he gave his inaugural lecture at Cambridge, knowing her desire to read anything he had written, he pledged to make sure she received a copy from him personally.[22]

As noted at the beginning of this section, Gebbert had had some success as a playwright, and she sought to continue her writing career as an author of fiction books. Who better to give advice than the author of *Screwtape*, *The Great Divorce*, and the Space Trilogy? In a December 1951 letter, she ventured a question: Would he provide a critique of a story she had written? He agreed, but wanted her to know his limitations: short stories were not his specialty.[23]

Two months later, he gave her his honest appraisal, wondering if his honesty might in some way damage the relationship they had developed over the years. Yet he knew he had to be honest; it was the only way to help her improve, and integrity demanded it. His critique was blunt, but he hoped she would consider that a compliment because "the naked truth is not for fools." The story was not going to work, in his opinion. He did encourage her, though, by noting, "There is nothing amateurish about the actual *writing*." He asked at the end if, after reading his critique, they would still be friends.[24] When he received a positive response to his question, he was thankful, and he encouraged her to continue to write and send him her drafts.[25]

Gebbert attempted to move from short stories to novels. Naturally, she wanted to inform Lewis of her new project. Again, he was encouraging,

---

18. Letter from Lewis to Vera Mathews, 9 April 1949, ibid., 933.

19. Letter from Lewis to Vera Mathews, 28 August 1950, Hooper, *Collected Letters*, Vol. III, 48–50.

20. Letter from Lewis to Vera Mathews, 20 September 1950, ibid., 53–54.

21. Letter from Lewis to Vera Gebbert, 23 May 1952, ibid., 193–94.

22. Letter from Lewis to Vera Gebbert, 25 June 1955, ibid., 623–24.

23. Letter from Lewis to Vera Mathews, 12 December 1951, ibid., 148–49.

24. Letter from Lewis to Vera Mathews, 17 February 1952, ibid., 164–67.

25. Letter from Lewis to Vera Mathews, 22 March 1952, ibid., 172.

declaring that her theme had promise, but based on Lewis's next letter to her, she apparently indicated that she was not really as interested in the subject of her novel as she ought to be. That brought a caution from her writing mentor, as he directed her toward thinking about subjects that interested her more. If you are bored with what you are writing, he counseled, why would you think it would interest others?[26] Besides, he told her, even if she never published a book, as long as her son grew up to be the kind of man they both hoped he would be, she would have accomplished a great deal in life. Being a published author was not necessarily more important.[27]

Lewis followed all the twists and turns of Gebbert's life, always with genuine interest and concern for her future. He was informed of her marriage and her move from Beverly Hills to Idaho.[28] And when the happily-ever-after marriage scenario fell apart, he was supportive, and given his view that divorce was strictly limited by Scripture, apparently the causes for this divorce must have been valid. In two separate letters, he commented on this development and sought to lift her spirits. In the second, he, in essence, provided absolution for the action when he asserted, "I suppose I must congratulate you, as you must thank God, about the divorce.... I am most deeply sorry for all you have been through."[29]

Sharing certain aspects of personal life went both ways. Lewis felt comfortable enough with Gebbert over time to let her in on certain home-life experiences, such as when Joy and her sons stayed at the Kilns for a visit over Christmas in 1953. Commenting on the physical and financial trials of life in one letter, Lewis declared his preference "for a planet without aches or pains or financial worries," but he would not be happy with a race of "pure intelligence." God gave us our senses and affections, and he thought it would be perfectly acceptable to allow a little nonsense in his perfect planet: "I must have a little fooling. I want to tickle a cat's ears and sometimes have a slanging match with an impertinent squirrel."[30]

At the end of December 1957, he had no trouble letting Gebbert in on the improvements in Joy's health and what that meant for his life, as well as his own physical ailments, which he was taking in stride. He was in less pain, but he doubted he would ever be able to go out for a "real walk" again. "You'd think this would be dreadful, but it isn't. With the power, nature kindly removes most of the desire. If I were merely forbidden (say by police

26. Letter from Lewis to Vera Gebbert, 13 February 1957, ibid., 832–33.
27. Letter from Lewis to Vera Gebbert, 11 March 1959, ibid., 1028–29.
28. Letter from Lewis to Vera Gebbert, 23 May 1952, ibid., 194.
29. Letter from Lewis to Vera Gebbert, 17 December 1954, ibid., 542–43.
30. Letter from Lewis to Vera Gebbert, 25 June 1955, ibid., 623–24.

order) to go more than a mile from this house on foot, no doubt I'd find it intolerable. But as I can't, I find I don't mind."³¹

Two years later, when Joy's cancer returned and the future looked bleak, he did not hide this from Gebbert, but felt at ease explaining how his life was being affected.³² Then came an intensely personal letter, written only two days after Joy died: "Alas, you will never send anything 'for the three of us' again, for my dear Joy is dead. . . . You will understand that I have no heart to write more, but I hope when next I send a letter it will be a less depressing one."³³

In late 1952, Gebbert announced that she and her husband (from whom she would be divorced two years later) were going to be in England, and she dearly wanted to meet Lewis in person. Both he and Warnie were delighted with the proposed visit, and even offered the Kilns as one of their accommodations.³⁴ She arrived in England, but at the time they had arranged to meet, she contracted the flu, and had to cancel. After she returned to the States, Lewis wrote of his regret at missing her when she had been so close at hand. The flu had not been her only problem on the journey; the ocean voyage had left her seasick as well.³⁵ He both comforted and exhorted her in another letter, hoping that her last journey would become a memory that fades away and that if she were to come again, she might take a flight instead, "crossing *over*" the ocean "rather than *on* it."³⁶

Gebbert finally was able to return to England in 1961, and was living temporarily in London. She hoped this time a meeting would work out, but Lewis was in particularly bad health, thereby shutting off that possibility once again. He was deeply disappointed; after writing to her for so many years, he would have liked the opportunity to spend some time with her in person, but he had to inform her that his many medical appointments were making it untenable.³⁷ He still held out hope that he could extend an invitation, and intended to do so, but his medical condition again interfered with those plans.³⁸

Occasionally, Lewis would write about politics, government, and/or economics—all, of course, closely intertwined. In one of his first letters to

---

31. Letter from Lewis to Gebbert, 16 December 1957, ibid., 907.
32. Letter from Lewis to Vera Gebbert, 17 January 1960, ibid., 1122–23.
33. Letter from Lewis to Vera Gebbert, 15 July 1960, ibid., 1170–71.
34. Letter from Lewis to Vera Gebbert, 30 September 1952, ibid., 231.
35. Letter from Lewis to Vera Gebbert, 9 December 1952, ibid., 257–59.
36. Letter from Lewis to Vera Gebbert, 18 December 1952, ibid., 266.
37. Letter from Lewis to Vera Gebbert, 25 October 1961, ibid., 1289–90.
38. Letter from Lewis to Vera Gebbert, 29 January 1962, ibid., 1314.

Gebbert, in 1947, he referred to the Labour government as "Mr. Atlee's Iron Curtain."[39] He also contrasted the blessings she had in America with the current state of England, saying, "Try living in 'free' England for a bit, and you would realize what government interference can mean! And not only interference, but interference in a 'school marm' form which is maddening." Then he added this quip: "There are times when one feels that a minister or two dangling from a lamp post in Whitehall would be an attraction that would draw a hard worked man up to London!"[40]

Lewis also had a few choice comments about modern education, a concern of his, quite naturally, due to his profession, and one he had attacked frontally in his *The Abolition of Man*. In 1954, someone informed him of an incident in an American school that involved him directly—or at least one of his books. He let Gebbert know about it, telling her that one American girl apparently had been expelled for reading *The Screwtape Letters*.[41] Five years after that incident, he remarked on the deplorable state of education in both England and America, opining that both countries offered very little in the way of a solid education. He was fortunate that his father had sent him to a private tutor after his own miserable experiences at schools.[42] In his very next letter, in response to her information about the kind of school her son was attending, he again took aim at the way English schools were being run, devoid of a real understanding of education. The educational authorities seemed to think that spending money on better facilities would guarantee a great education, but Lewis pointedly remarked that genuine education in the hands of a very good teacher could take place in a ramshackle building, while the best facilities in the world could never make up for the tutelage of bad teachers.[43]

Surprisingly, little in the way of doctrinal issues or advice on how to live the Christian life is contained in letters to Vera Gebbert. Only near the end of the correspondence does anything pop up that is related to such issues. In a 1959 letter, Gebbert stated her opinion that the symbol of the Cross ought to be abolished because of the sad connotation of it. Lewis's short reply to that statement reminded her of the other side of the symbol: it was also a testimony to Christ's victory.[44] After Joy's death, Lewis wrote of

39. Letter from Lewis to Vera Mathews, 24 November 1947, Hooper, *Collected Letters, Vol. II*, 812.

40. Letter from Lewis to Vera Mathews, 6 April 1949, ibid., 932–33.

41. Letter from Lewis to Vera Gebbert, 17 December 1954, Hooper, *Collected Letters, Vol. III*, 543.

42. Letter from Lewis to Vera Gebbert, 8 May 1959, ibid., 1046–47.

43. Letter from Lewis to Vera Gebbert, 16 June 1959, ibid., 1057–58.

44. Letter from Lewis to Vera Gebbert, 8 May 1959, ibid., 1046.

the resurrection of the dead, commenting that "the state of the dead *till* the resurrection is unimaginable. Are they in the same *time* that we live in at all. And if not, is there any sense in asking what they are 'now'?"[45] His wording led to some confusion on her part, so he had to clarify what he meant in his next letter, explaining that he shouldn't be misunderstood as questioning whether eternal life was real; he was saying merely that there is no way we can possibly imagine what it must be like. "But don't let us trouble one another about it. We shall know when we are dead ourselves."[46]

In 1964, Vera Gebbert moved to Washington, D.C., where she found success in the field of real estate administration. She died in December 2014, at the age of ninety-eight, having lived long enough to be aware of the fiftieth anniversary of Lewis's death.[47]

Edward A. Allen and Belle Allen

Edward A. Allen, a resident of Westfield, Massachusetts, along with his mother, Belle Allen, not only regularly corresponded with Lewis, but they were, along with Warfield Firor and Vera Gebbert, the Americans who contributed the most in material goods to Lewis in the post-war rationing period. Edward Allen's prodigious giving was chronicled to some degree in the first chapter, but it is important to address that subject again here, as it provides more insight into how Lewis interacted with those whom he considered generous beyond the usual bounds.

A most interesting tidbit about Allen appears in one of Lewis's first letters to him in 1948 in which Lewis exclaims how pleasant it was to know that Allen wasn't really all that knowledgeable about Lewis's literary fame. To Lewis, this was a demonstration of American generosity beyond just seeking to help someone whose writings had been well received. Lewis was amazed that he had been singled out by Allen to be the recipient of his virtually uninterrupted flow of goods.[48] Why did Allen decide to bestow all these gifts on Lewis? One can speculate that perhaps it began with the influence of his mother, Belle. As one examines the letters Lewis wrote to both of them,

---

45. Letter from Lewis to Vera Gebbert, 5 August 1960, ibid., 1177.

46. Letter from Lewis to Vera Gebbert, 16 October 1960, ibid., 1197–98.

47. While researching Lewis's letters to Vera Gebbert in late 2014, I was unaware that she was still living. While there is no guarantee she would have been in any condition to be interviewed, it would have been a grand opportunity if such an interview could have been arranged.

48. Letter from Lewis to Edward A. Allen, 20 April 1948, Hooper, *Collected Letters, Vol. II*, 850–51.

one notices that comments on spiritual questions are directed more to her than to Edward.

Most of the correspondence, though, was with Edward. His constant flow of gifts taxed Lewis's ability to express gratitude in new and innovative ways. Lewis would sometimes, as noted above with Vera Gebbert, feel that he was being helped too much, and he would seek to find another recipient for a gift he received. As with Gebbert, he wrote a letter to Allen explaining what he decided to do with one of his gifts, and offered his rationale for why he thought it proper. The beneficiary, in this case, was his good friend Tolkien. As a matter of conscience, Lewis explained, he wanted to bless Tolkien. And besides, since it was the Lenten season, it would be good for his—Lewis's—soul to make this sacrifice. And a sacrifice it was: "A last lingering look at the label shows me only too well the treat which I have forfeited!"[49]

More so than with any of his other American correspondents, Lewis and Allen exchanged views on the political developments in both countries. He unburdened himself on Allen with regard to what he considered the foolishness of England's Labour government. He had a hard time grasping why they couldn't see the folly of their policies. All one had to do was compare with one's personal finances. How did the principles of national finance somehow become different than those for individuals? "Supposing you strike a bad patch, what is your domestic policy of spending? Surely, Rent, insurance, food, clothes, general necessities, and luxuries, in that order. Here it is hard to get envelopes but perfectly easy to get champagne and gin."[50] It was folly personified. It also confounded him that England's government would not acknowledge all the help it was getting from America.[51]

To Belle, who was deeply concerned over the world's entrance into the atomic age, Lewis helped her consider the morality of the development and use of the atomic bomb, which he considered a complex issue. He had been in church the Sunday after the first bomb had dropped on Japan and had heard the minister ask all the parishioners to pray that America would ask for forgiveness for using it. In fact, the minister called it a "great crime." But was it quite that clear-cut? Was that impulse toward viewing it as a crime merely an emotional reaction at the expense of rational analysis? "But, *if* what we have since heard is true," he continued, "that the first item on the

---

49. Letter from Lewis to Edward A. Allen, 12 March 1949, ibid., 925–26.
50. Letter from Lewis to Edward A. Allen, 24 January 1949, ibid., 909.
51. Letter from Lewis to Edward A. Allen, 24 March 1949, ibid., 927.

Japanese anti-invasion programme was the killing of every European in Japan, the answer did not, to me, seem so simple as all that."[52]

Ten years later, writing to both Allens, the topic of nuclear weaponry resurfaced. Yes, it was madness to depend on such things, Lewis agreed, but what choice did one have? The Labour Party's solution of unilateral disarmament seemed to Lewis to be an offer to the Soviets to proceed with their plans for conquering the world. Warnie had his own solution, Lewis related: at the end of any war, the winners should execute the leaders of the losers, thereby providing an ample incentive never to start a war in the first place.[53]

Since tensions with Stalin's Soviet Union had become the center-stage of the Cold War, Lewis provided Allen with a tentative analysis of the difference between the German and Russian threats, based on his understanding of how those two peoples had acted historically. Germany, he said, had "always been a big fighter" so nothing less than "a full-dress war" would ever do. It was not so with Russia, no matter whether Tsarist or Communist. The Russian, he ventured, "grabs things here and grabs things there when he finds them unguarded." Rearmament and a willingness to resist perceived Communist advances might be all that is needed, he suggested. He felt certain that one lesson had to be learned, reminding Allen, "Both your country and mine have twice in our lifetime tried the recipe of appeasing an aggressor and it didn't work on either occasion: so that it seems sense to try the other way this time."[54]

As post-war rationing finally disappeared under the new Conservative government, Lewis was happy to report to Allen that tea was no longer going to be rationed. He added that the government was also now allowing pork to be put back in sausages. That last comment may sound comical; Lewis agreed, as he followed up by jesting, "This I should think will probably turn the younger generation into lifelong dispeptics, for it has grown up to think of a sausage as an ounce of soya bean flour fried in a skin!"[55]

Allen was the only American with whom Lewis got into any kind of extended discussion of military matters. Lewis wrote of one British general in the 1920s and 1930s who had done his best to warn his superiors that they needed to be thinking about more modern approaches to war, such as using tanks and airplanes. He had been correct and had resisted the temptation to gloat when proved right. His analysis had been based on the inevitability of

52. Letter from Lewis to Belle Allen, 28 December 1950, Hooper, *Collected Letters, Vol. III.*, 76–77.
53. Letter from Lewis to Edward A. Allen and Belle Allen, 10 December 1960, ibid., 1215–16.
54. Letter from Lewis to Edward A. Allen, 3 April 1952, ibid., 178–79.
55. Letter from Lewis to Edward A. Allen, 21 February 1953, ibid., 294.

another war. Lewis agreed that another war had been inevitable; sin was the root cause of all wars, and sin cannot be entirely eliminated from the world.[56]

Belle Allen was the recipient of the more direct spiritual ponderings, probably because she was more attuned to them. She confessed to Lewis that she had a hard time reading his *The Pilgrim's Regress*. He was sympathetic to her plight, understanding how she might have become lost in its allegorical symbolisms. It was his first attempt at writing a religious book, he acknowledged, and he had written it more for an academic readership. "In those days I never dreamed I would become a 'popular' author and hoped for no readers outside a small 'highbrow' circle." Then he made a suggestion few authors would ever make willingly, assuring her she should not "waste your time over it any more."[57]

Edward and Belle Allen are two "unknowns" in most historical accounts, but they figure prominently in the history of C. S. Lewis and his associations with Americans.

Mary Van Deusen

Lewis's correspondence with Mary Van Deusen, a happily married woman—unlike Vera Gebbert—began in 1949 and ended just one week before his death. It has been difficult to find any solid information on her background and the circumstances of her life other than her husband's name was Van and they had a daughter, Genia Goelz, with whom Lewis also exchanged a few letters. The Van Deusens lived in New York and in Hendersonville, North Carolina, but it is unclear whether they did so simultaneously, with one being a second home, or if they moved back and forth between the two at different times. The only other piece of personal information, gleaned from Lewis's letters to her, was that she became an oblate—a layperson living in general society but affiliated with a religious order, promising to abide by that order's rules in one's own home—within the American Episcopal church.

Her correspondence with Lewis, while including some attention to personal matters, nevertheless was overwhelmingly theological. As Lyle Dorsett, one of the Lewis scholars highlighted in the previous chapter, noted, Lewis "felt completely comfortable" writing to Van Deusen. He could share his concerns for Joy and be assured of Van Deusen's prayers for her. On the intellectual level, he could enjoy "jousting with her because she was neither easily offended nor unable to return his intellectual serve." And

---

56. Letter from Lewis to Edward A. Allen, 20 December 1954, ibid., 544–45.
57. Letter from Lewis to Belle Allen, 19 January 1953, ibid., 282.

while he did offer her counsel, it was not a one-way street; she "did much more than take." She actually "stimulated his thinking and had a book or two to recommend to him."[58]

Van Deusen's letters, from the start, seemed to be a relief to Lewis, inundated as he was with some other rather needy individuals. He provided Van Deusen with quite personal details of the struggles he had endured trying to placate Mrs. Janie Moore. He even noted that Chad Walsh, despite their friendship, knew little of his private life, yet he was willing to share with Van Deusen what it had been like in the Lewis household. It was a place rarely "at peace for 24 hours," due to "senseless wranglings, lyings, backbitings, follies, and *scares*. I never went home without a feeling of terror as to what appalling situation might have developed in my absence."[59]

Van Deusen was one of the Americans who frequently invited Lewis to visit, promising accommodations and beautiful scenery. He always begged off, of course, explaining why his circumstances would never allow it, but one senses he would have liked to have accepted the offer. His Oxford schedule, he regretted, precluded him from accepting her hospitality.[60]

Upon reading *Surprised by Joy*, Van Deusen ventured to say she would have liked to have lived a life like his. That brought this response: "I doubt if you wd. really have enjoyed my life much more than your own. And the whole modern world ludicrously over-values books and learning and what (I loathe the word) they call 'culture.' . . . Never forget this: souls are immortal, and your children & grandchildren will still be alive when my books have . . . passed away."[61] Be happy with the life you have, he seemed to be saying.

During the period when Lewis thought Joy was going to die, he wrote Van Deusen, asking for her prayers. As he was also going through some physical difficulties at the same time, he had to apologize for his short letters, but he was comforted that he could turn to her for prayer support.[62] He considered her a friend. Two months later, he gave her an update, writing, "Sometimes, at Joy's bedside, we have more happiness and even gaiety than I wd. have thought possible. Other times, great misery. I value your prayers."[63]

In late 1962, she wrote to him of her distress at having to pack up and move to a new home, apparently due to a noise factor where they were

---

58. Dorsett, *Seeking the Secret Place*, 152.

59. Letter from Lewis to Mary Van Deusen, 18 April 1951, Hooper, *Collected Letters, Vol. III.*, 107.

60. Letter from Lewis to Mary Van Deusen, 29 February 1952, ibid., 169.

61. Letter from Lewis to Mary Van Deusen, 2 April 1956, ibid., 732–33.

62. Letter from Lewis to Mary Van Deusen, 5 January 1957, ibid., 824–25.

63. Letter from Lewis to Mary Van Deusen, 7 March 1957, ibid., 838–39.

currently living. He sympathized with the upending of one's life in that way, but attempted to help her get God's perspective on the situation. Keep in mind the people in the world who are in pain, starving, and being tortured, he reminded her. Yet he did understand her discomfort; he could empathize because he shuddered at the possibility of having to move as well. "By nature I demand from the arrangements of this world just that permanence which God has expressly refused to give them." What he disliked most was feeling as if a chapter of life has come to an end. "I would like everything to be immemorial—to have the same old horizons, the same garden, the same smells and sounds, always there, changeless. . . . That is, I desire the 'abiding city' where I well know it is not and ought not to be found. . . . The useless word is 'Encore!'"[64] It was a reminder that this earthly home is only temporary.

Lewis did what he could with Van Deusen's family situation. Her daughter, Genia, had a lot of questions about the faith, on which Lewis guided her directly. He also gave advice on Genia's marriage, at Van Deusen's request. Apparently, at one point, Genia felt she had married someone who was not up to par intellectually. Lewis, writing to Van Deusen, cautioned against such an attitude and sought to help the daughter recognize the blessing she had. Based on what he had been told, it seemed to him that her husband was a very good man. What Genia needed to understand was that every marriage has its ups and downs. The circumstances that come along provide an opportunity to grow in the faith.[65]

He followed up that letter with one much more direct, as he detected Van Deusen was about to make a big mistake in her advice to Genia. She was counseling Genia to work on her husband to make him better. Lewis sought to throw some cold water on that suggestion, considering it dangerous to approach her husband with that condescending attitude. He realized he was putting his relationship with Van Deusen on the line by critiquing her advice to her daughter, but continued nevertheless, challenging Van Deusen to think about how priggish her advice might be perceived. She needed to see things from the husband's point of view, particularly since Genia had suffered a series of physical ailments that could have tested any new marriage. He cautioned her that all those jokes about interfering mothers-in-law might be based on experience and closed the letter by stating his hope that he hadn't made Van Deusen into an enemy with his comments, but he felt he had no option but to offer them.[66]

---

64. Letter from Lewis to Mary Van Deusen, 21 November 1962, ibid., 1382–83.
65. Letter from Lewis to Mary Van Deusen, 23 July 1953, ibid., 350–51.
66. Letter from Lewis to Mary Van Deusen, 14 September 1953, ibid., 360–61.

Then he waited, to find out if his directness had caused a rift. It did not, and in the process, he learned something valuable about Van Deusen's character: she was willing to take correction given out of sincere concern.[67] It was that maturity on her part that made her such a welcome correspondent. He now knew he could say anything to her, in an honest and forthright way, and she would receive it in the proper spirit.

The bulk of Lewis's Mary Van Deusen correspondence dealt with some rather weighty church issues and theological questions. When she was considering joining a religious order within the Episcopal church—the Congregation of the Sisters of the Holy Redeemer—she sought his advice. Her decision, he counseled, ought to be based on at least three factors: whether she could vouch for the activity lending itself to holiness; whether it was more valuable than what he called "a harmless, if rather fussy, hobby"; and whether she could be assured the group was not merely "a pestilent coven of snoopers & busybodies." She would have to figure that out for herself, he said, but he would be praying she would come to a proper decision.[68]

They also wrote to one another about the importance of church, how to worship, discussion of particular doctrines, and insights on other aspects of living the Christian life. Lewis commented how Christians must be part of a church despite their individual preferences, telling Van Deusen (who seemed to have Lewis's perspective on the proper type of worship) that those who leaned more toward personal solitude in worship had to recognize the importance of corporate worship in church as well. On the other hand, those who naturally were drawn to church services had to be exhorted not to neglect personal devotions. The church, he reminded her, is made up of many different types of people, and God likes it that way. We need to learn from one another.[69]

Prayer was often a topic in their letters. Van Deusen raised the issue in her very first letter in 1949, wondering if he would be interested in writing a book on prayer. At the time, he demurred, but one of his final books, published after his death, was *Letters to Malcolm: Chiefly on Prayer*. She brought the subject up again in the context of praying for healing. Lewis responded with his understanding of the nature of prayer, saying it is a request, and as with all requests, the answer can sometimes be "no." But even if the request seems to have been answered, "you cannot prove scientifically that the thing wd. not have happened anyway." So it had to be removed from the scientific realm: "It remains a matter of faith and of God's personal action:

---

67. Letter from Lewis to Mary Van Deusen, 3 October 1953, ibid., 368–69.
68. Letter from Lewis to Mary Van Deusen, 5 November 1953, ibid., 374.
69. Letter from Lewis to Mary Van Deusen, 7 December 1950, ibid., 67–69.

it would become a matter of demonstration only if it were impersonal or mechanical."[70] Prayer, though, is never impersonal or mechanical because we deal with a personal God.

Lewis distinguished between two types of prayer in one's life: the Garden of Gethsemane type in which one simply seeks to know God's will and the type found in the Scripture where if you believe something will happen, it will. How to know which kind of prayer to pray? He theorized that both types have their place and that Christians should trust God to provide the second type, which believes something definitely will happen, when He calls for it.[71]

The two also corresponded on matters dealing with living the Christian life. When Van Deusen asked Lewis if following certain religious practices—whether prayer, Bible reading, church attendance, or whatever—could help the search for truth, he issued a caution about where such reasoning might lead to the false idea that once a person has found the truth, they need not carry out those practices anymore. Instead, he urged her to think of all those practices as "not a stair but a bannister . . . not the thing you ascend by but it is a protective against falling off and a help-up." He explained further, "The stair is God's grace. One's climb from step to step is obedience. . . . It is possible to get up without any bannisters, if need be: but no one wd. willingly build a staircase without them because it would be less safe, more laborious, and a little lacking in beauty."[72]

A Christian's obedience to God was another topic covered in these letters. Lewis was concerned that people misunderstood the term, seeing it as somehow a sign of weakness. Obedience seemed to imply to many a type of submissiveness that was unhealthy. Not at all, Lewis replied: "That's all . . . nonsense, isn't it, about obedience being 'weak.' One doesn't think nurses, sailors, & soldiers weak: and when we believe spiritual things to be as important as operations, storms at sea, and 'last stands' we shall see obedience as a strong thing there too."[73]

Lewis made an unusual confession to Van Deusen in one letter. The great apologist for the faith gave an insider's view of what it is like having to be faith's defender. He said he envied her for not having to think about apologetics all the time. He would have liked a reprieve himself, but his many correspondents kept bringing up issues that he would then have to dissect and for which he would have to provide solid answers. "It is very wearing, and not v. good for one's own faith," he stated bluntly. What did

---

70. Letter from Lewis to Mary Van Deusen, 5 January 1951, ibid., 81–82.
71. Letter from Lewis to Mary Van Deusen, 28 November 1953, ibid., 378–79.
72. Letter from Lewis to Mary Van Deusen, 29 June 1953, ibid., 342.
73. Letter from Lewis to Mary Van Deusen, 26 January 1954, ibid., 418–19.

he mean? "A Christian doctrine never seems less real to me than when I have just (even if successfully) been defending it. It is particularly tormenting when those who were converted by my books begin to relapse and raise new difficulties."[74]

Suffering, and the Christian's response to it, often arose in this correspondence. Lewis accepted the Biblical perspective that God suffers when we do. He realized that not everything works out in the manner we might expect, but we are ignorant people,lacking God's omniscience. He then expressed a slight regret: "I wish I had known more when I wrote the *Problem of Pain*."[75] He spent more time fleshing out the theology of suffering in a later letter, starting with the concern that his life had improved over the past year. A more blessed life ordinarily would not be a concern to someone, but Lewis admitted to being a little frightened by the good turn of events; he instructed Van Deusen that they both had to remember to be cautious "lest we become soft and self indulgent and cease to recognise one's dependence on God." Suffering, though, he was convinced, was not always sent by God as some form of punishment, but if it ever does come from the hand of God, there is a good reason.[76]

As with his other regular correspondents, Lewis was willing to discuss political and governmental issues whenever anyone wanted to know his views. Van Deusen, who was contemplating setting up a ministry that would involve a certain amount of planning, asked him what he thought of making extensive plans, and then what application might be made to government planning. Lewis replied that, in general, good planning is nothing less than the Christian virtue of prudence. However, if applied to government, there could be a problem. "Where benevolent planning, armed with political or economic power, can become wicked is when it tramples on people's rights for the sake of their good," he opined.[77]

More specifically, Van Deusen wanted to know what Lewis thought of the communist threat of the early 1950s. It had come to light in America that a number of communists had been placed in the federal government, dedicated to undermining the government and passing on secrets to the Soviet Union (which is how that nation got an atomic bomb so quickly). Lewis incorporated his response into the middle of an analysis of the possible weakness of democracy. If we go along with the concept of government by majority vote, he asked, what is the recourse if the majority establishes

---

74. Letter from Lewis to Mary Van Deusen, 18 June 1956, ibid., 762.
75. Letter from Lewis to Mary Van Deusen, 12 September 1951, ibid., 134–35.
76. Letter from Lewis to Mary Van Deusen, 31 January 1952, ibid., 162–63.
77. Letter from Lewis to Mary Van Deusen, 7 February 1951, ibid., 90–91.

something wrong? For instance, "If the Communists in this country can persuade the majority to sell in to Russia, or even to set up devil-worship and human sacrifice, what is the *democratic* reply? When we said 'Govt. by the people' do we only mean 'as long as we don't disagree with the people too much'"? But of one thing he was certain: if the government were to require Christians to obey laws that were directly opposed to the faith, they would "have to disobey and be martyred. Perhaps *pure* democracy is really a false ideal."[78]

Just a few months before this response, Van Deusen had encouraged Lewis to get the book *Witness* by Whittaker Chambers, who had been an underground communist agent in the 1930s, but who had then turned his back on communism and found God. Later, as a senior editor for *Time* magazine, Chambers had even referenced Lewis in an essay he wrote called "The Devil." As one reads that essay today, one can see the connection with *The Screwtape Letters*. Chambers's book that Van Deusen wanted Lewis to read was a bestseller in 1952, as it exposed not only the communist underground, but positively pointed to the need for Western civilization to return to its Christian foundations. Many have described *Witness* as one of the most elegantly written autobiographies of the century. When Van Deusen suggested he get the book, Lewis merely answered, "I'm afraid I can't find a W. Chambers book. It's better not to send the book. They all get lost in the pile on my table."[79] This could be one of the great lost opportunities of the twentieth century. One would have loved to know Lewis's response to that book, which, although written as an autobiography, is a wordsmith's delight. But it was not to be.

Mary Van Deusen's final letter to Lewis arrived in November 1963. He wrote back to her one last time just six days before he died, updating her on his health, the concerns he had for his two stepsons, his disappointment that it looked like England was about to saddle itself with another Labour government, and providing a personal perspective on the evils of progress: the local authorities, he complained, were about to destroy a favorite tree near his home so that the road would be straighter. "There are times when I wonder if the invention of the internal combustion engine was not an even greater disaster than that of the hydrogen bomb," Lewis commented sadly.[80] Their lively correspondence ended with those words, but at least we now have Lewis's half of that correspondence from which we can gain a greater depth of understanding of his character.

78. Letter from Lewis to Mary Van Deusen, 21 February 1953, ibid., 295–96.
79. Letter from Lewis to Mary Van Deusen, 25 November 1952, ibid., 252–53.
80. Letter from Lewis to Mary Van Deusen, 16 November 1963, ibid., 1479–80.

Mary Willis Shelburne

The first collection of C. S. Lewis correspondence to be published appeared in 1967 under the title *Letters to an American Lady*. Clyde Kilby edited this slim volume and explained in his preface that the identity of this American lady was being withheld at her own request. She was still living at the time and wanted to remain anonymous. She required that all references to her family issues were to be excised from the letters as well. Kilby did offer some information on her—that she was from the American South, had once been financially independent, but "she had fallen upon privation and, what was worse, serious family problems." Lewis felt such compassion for her situation that, once the law allowed it, he "arranged through his American publishers a small stipend for her," which continued even after his death.[81]

We now know this lady was Mary Willis Shelburne (1895-1975), Atlanta-born (surname Walker) but raised in Richmond, Virginia, where her family became rather prominent. She first married in 1920 to William Boyer, who died sometime before 1933 because that was when she remarried to Jacob Shelburne. He, in turn, died in 1942, leaving her a widow twice over. Shelburne, in the 1930s, began writing poetry and found some measure of success, finding herself, by 1940, on the board of the Poetry Society of Virginia. In 1951, shortly after contacting Lewis for the first time, a book of her poetry was published under the title *Broken Pattern*. She received aid in getting it published from Kenton Kilmer, the son of poet Joyce Kilmer and father to the Kilmer children, to whom Lewis dedicated *The Magician's Nephew*. She donated her collection of Lewis letters to Wheaton College upon her death in 1975.

Shelburne wrote more letters to Lewis than any other American correspondent; consequently, he wrote more to her than any other, since he felt duty-bound to respond to each letter he received. It is quite clear by the tone of the correspondence that she was an increasingly needy person, both financially and spiritually. Her anxieties seemed to be legion, and Lewis did his best to address them with tact and empathy. Did he ever tire of her constant flow of letters seeking help? There are indications that she could sometimes wear him down with her incessant demands for answers. Despite the temptation to be frustrated with her, he nevertheless maintained the ministry to which God had called him.

The correspondence began slowly in late 1950 when she wrote to tell him of her appreciation for his books. Occasionally, they corresponded about his books, such as when she shared that the Kilmer children were

---

81. Kilby, *Letters to an American Lady*, 9.

reading his Space Trilogy, a piece of information that alarmed Lewis because they were still children. He was particularly concerned that the final one, *That Hideous Strength*, might be unsuitable for their ages, since it contained a greater description of evil and pointed to some serious sexual problems.[82] He even informed her about his upcoming *Till We Have Faces*, letting her know that he thought he had handled the female lead character appropriately, having passed it through some female reviewers who approved of his approach.[83]

When *Time* magazine reviewed *Surprised by Joy* and included a photo of Lewis, he let Shelburne know his feelings: "The review is of course a tissue of muddles and direct falsehoods—I don't say 'lies' because the people who write such things are not really capable of lying. I mean, to lie = to say what you know to be untrue. But to know this, and to have the very ideas of truth & falsehood in your head, presupposes a clarity of mind wh. they haven't got. To call them liars wd. be as undeserved a compliment as to say that a dog was bad at arithmetic."[84]

As mentioned above, Shelburne experienced family problems, primarily with her daughter and son-in-law. The letters Lewis sent to her indicate that the son-in-law might have been the source of most of the problems, at least from Shelburne's perspective. At one point, it appears as if he tried to keep her away from her granddaughter, a development Lewis thought abhorrent. He advised her to be patient and took the opportunity to prod her toward a closer walk with the Lord, hoping that in this time of stress, she would experience His presence even more than before.[85]

By 1961, Shelburne was in serious financial straits, and her daughter and son-in-law invited her to live with them. She wasn't sure what to do, so naturally she turned once again to Lewis for advice. The first thing, he counseled, was to have a right attitude. They were acting as if they wanted to make up for the perceived injustices earlier in the relationship. She should accept that, he said, adding, "Remember that He has promised to forgive you *as*, and only *as*, you forgive them." He told her to look to herself rather than focus on them: "Try not to think . . . of *their* sins. One's own are a much more profitable theme."[86] When Shelburne made the decision to accept their offer, Lewis encouraged her to be patient, to learn humility, and to be

---

82. Letter from Lewis to Mary Willis Shelburne, 22 February 1954, Hooper, *Collected Letters, Vol. III*, 432–33.
83. Letter from Lewis to Mary Willis Shelburne, 4 March 1956, ibid., 715–16.
84. Letter from Lewis to Mary Willis Shelburne, 8 February 1956, ibid., 701–2.
85. Letter from Lewis to Mary Willis Shelburne, 26 October 1955, ibid., 667.
86. Letter from Lewis to Mary Willis Shelburne, 9 January 1961, ibid., 1224–25.

sacrificial in spirit: "As the comic beatitude says 'Blessed are they that expect little for they shall not be disappointed.'"[87]

Shelburne had been an Episcopalian all her life, but decided, in the early 1950s, to convert to Catholicism. Lewis, of course, believed in the concept of mere Christianity, in which he focused on all the essential points in which the various denominations could come together in agreement. When she announced to him that she was now a Catholic, he congratulated her on her decision even though he could not join in that commitment. The last thing he wanted was controversy over denominations. "In the present divided state of Christendom, those who are at the heart of each division are all closer to one another than those who are at the fringes."[88] In accord with those sentiments, he continued to counsel her for another eleven years.

Lewis often wrote to her of the true nature of the faith, the assorted trials Christians must endure, and how they needed to develop greater trust in God's provision for daily needs. Those were the issues at the forefront of her many letters, so we get an even better glimpse into Lewis's mind when we read the responses he sent back. Shelburne's greatest needs, which Lewis addressed almost endlessly, seemed to be her anxiety over her relationship with God and stress over financial worries. By mid-1953, she was job-hunting and distressed over her prospects. She felt she was losing her independence and sought to avoid becoming dependent on her daughter and son-in-law. He empathized with her concern, but reminded her that everyone is dependent, to some degree, on others and that "the state of being indebted to no one, is eternally impossible." As noted in a previous chapter, Lewis quite often felt, falsely, that he was living on the edge of poverty, since he paid little heed to the details of his finances. He confessed to Shelburne that he often was fearful about money problems himself. "Poverty frightens me more than anything else except large spiders and the tops of cliffs." He could understand her fear, but he also knew that God promised to take care of His children.[89]

Shelburne struggled with the sense that she was not forgiven. Lewis tried to deal with that one pretty directly, reminding her that one's feelings should not counter what one knows to be real. Feelings are not our guide, he exhorted her; instead we are to rely on our genuine repentance over sin. The devil was trying to upset her faith. "You can't help *hearing* his voice (the odious inner radio) but you must treat it merely like a buzzing in your ears

---

87. Letter from Lewis to Mary Willis Shelburne, 24 February 1961, ibid., 1242–43.
88. Letter from Lewis to Mary Willis Shelburne, 10 November 1952, ibid., 248–49.
89. Letter from Lewis to Mary Willis Shelburne, 10 August 1953, ibid., 358–59.

or any other irrational nuisance."[90] The next year, he addressed the feeling of not being *worthy* of receiving God's forgiveness. "Of course we aren't. Forgiveness by its nature is for the unworthy," he stated plainly.[91]

On the topic of suffering, Lewis had a lot to say as well, particularly since Shelburne always felt as if she were in that condition. Again, Lewis drew from his personal experience, letting her know that in the various stages of his life—in school, in the army, and as a junior fellow at Oxford—he had endured the same. She needed to remember what it was like for Jesus, and that Christians should imitate Him. While offering this advice, he characteristically sought to show he had not yet achieved everything he was advising, admitting, "But don't think I don't know how much easier it is to preach than practice."[92]

Shelburne also feared death, a topic he dealt with more often as both grew older and Lewis began to feel his own mortality, suffering from greater physical problems himself. He did his best to help Shelburne face her own demise with the proper Christian spirit and perspective. His letters become peppered with reminders that all humans have to face this ultimate test, but that Christians have a glorious eternity awaiting them. He joked about imminent death in a 1957 letter thusly: "What on earth is the trouble about there being a rumour of my death? There's nothing discreditable in dying: I've known the most respectable people do it!"[93] Commenting in another letter on horrible visits to the dentist, he told her to keep in mind they both had to recognize that "as we grow older, we become like old cars—more and more repairs and replacements are necessary. We must just look forward to the fine new machines (latest Resurrection model) which are waiting for us, we hope, in the Divine garage!"[94] And why not have the same attitude as the apostle Paul? "If we really believe what we say we believe—if we really think that home is elsewhere and that this life is a 'wandering to find home,' why should we not look forward to the arrival."[95]

After Joy's death and the realization that he would no longer be healthy in his final years, he wrote to Shelburne about the hope of the resurrection of the body. He kept his sense of humor even as he suffered greater physical distress, telling her, with respect to their bodies, "Like old automobiles, aren't they? Where all sorts of apparently different things

---

90. Letter from Lewis to Mary Willis Shelburne, 21 July 1958, ibid., 962.
91. Letter from Lewis to Mary Willis Shelburne, 7 July 1959, ibid., 1064.
92. Letter from Lewis to Mary Willis Shelburne, 31 March 1954, ibid., 447–49.
93. Letter from Lewis to Mary Willis Shelburne, 3 July 1957, ibid., 865.
94. Letter from Lewis to Mary Willis Shelburne, 30 September 1958, ibid., 975.
95. Letter from Lewis to Mary Willis Shelburne, 7 June 1959, ibid., 1055–56.

keep going wrong, but what they add up to is the plain fact that the machine is wearing out. Well, it was not meant to last forever. Still, I have a kindly feeling for the old rattle-trap."[96]

In his final year, Lewis's comments on death appeared more frequently, as he sensed his time was near. In March 1963, he conveyed to Shelburne his lack of concern about moving from this world to the next.[97] A letter in June remarked on her obvious fear of dying; Lewis's response was the most direct one yet: "Can you not see death as the friend and deliverer? It means stripping off that body which is tormenting you: like taking off a hair-shirt or getting out of a dungeon. What is there to be afraid of? . . . Has this world been so kind to you that you should leave it with regret? There are better things ahead than any we leave behind. . . . Of course, this may not be the end. Then make it a good rehearsal. Yours (and like you a tired traveler near the journey's end)."[98]

A week later, he sent another missive to Shelburne, but this time there was some rejoicing in it, as she seemed to be responding better to his pleas for her. He trusted her mind had been renewed somewhat, since "only a few months ago when I said that we old people hadn't much more to do than to make a good exit, you were almost angry with me for what you called such a 'bitter' remark. Thank God, you now see it wasn't bitter: only plain common sense." He did have a word for her should she precede him in the race for the heavenly realm: "If this *is* Good-bye, I am sure you will not forget me when you are in a better place. You'll put in a good word for me now and then, won't you?" Then he added, "It will be fun when we at last meet."[99]

Lewis's final word to Shelburne on the subject of death came three days later, about two weeks before he fell into a brief coma, followed by his resignation from Cambridge and his death four months after that. This final word showcases once again his facility with phrases that are memorable, as he encouraged her one more time: "I think the best way to cope with the mental debility and total inertia is to submit to it entirely. . . . Pretend you are a dormouse or even a turnip. . . . Think of yourself just as a seed patiently waiting in the earth: waiting to come up a flower in the Gardener's good time, up into the *real* world, the real waking. . . . We are here in the land of dreams. But cock-crow is coming. It is nearer now than when I began this letter."[100]

---

96. Letter from Lewis to Mary Willis Shelburne, 26 November 1962, ibid., 1383–84.
97. Letter from Lewis to Mary Willis Shelburne, 19 March 1963, ibid., 1415–16.
98. Letter from Lewis to Mary Willis Shelburne, 17 June 1963, ibid., 1430–31.
99. Letter from Lewis to Mary Willis Shelburne, 25 June 1963, ibid., 1431–32.
100. Letter from Lewis to Mary Willis Shelburne, 28 June 1963, ibid., 1434.

Mary Willis Shelburne did not precede Lewis in death; she lingered on for another twelve years. Her financial worries continued. Walter Hooper, in 1968, visited Shelburne. He recounts, "When I went to see her, it was about whether or not the Lewis estate should try to continue the payments which C. S. Lewis had been making to her, because she had told him how very poor she was. If you've read C. S. Lewis's letters you will gather that the lady was of very gloomy cast of mind. . . . So I was not very surprised when I walked into her flat in Washington, D.C. Her first words were, 'Don't expect to enjoy yourself.'"[101] He found her "very lonely and worried about money. She kept a plate on a table beside the door, and as he was leaving she pointed to it and said, 'People usually put something in that.'"[102] One hopes she found the peace with the Lord that Lewis pointed to throughout those many years of poignant correspondence.

Children

As The Chronicles of Narnia books began appearing annually throughout the 1950s, Lewis started receiving letters from children who were fascinated with the stories. Many of those letters came from America, and he developed, in some cases, a regular correspondence with some who, by the time he died in 1963, were hardly children anymore. His appeal to them may have had its genesis with Narnia, but many went from there into other Lewis works. From the collected letters, it appears the first American child to be honored with a response from Lewis was Hila Newman of New York, eleven years old when she heard back from him about the drawings she had sent of characters from *The Lion, the Witch, and the Wardrobe*. Apparently, she also inquired about whether Aslan is known in this world, so Lewis asked her to consider the following: Did anyone in our world arrive "at the same time as Father Christmas," then sacrificed his life for another, and then came back to life? "Don't you really know His name in this world," he teased. "Think it over and let me know your answer!"[103]

Through Mary Willis Shelburne he became acquainted with the Kilmer family—ten children in all—and to whom he dedicated *The Magician's Nephew*. In their first letter to him, they sent a multitude of drawings related to the Narnia series and *Out of the Silent Planet*. It required a comment on each, to be fair, and his willingness to do so reveals a desire to connect

101. Hooper, "What About Mrs. Boshell?" 36.
102. Hooper, *Collected Letters, Vol. III*, Biographical Appendix, "Mary Willis Shelburne."
103. Letter from Lewis to Hila Newman, 3 June 1953, ibid., 334–35.

with each child personally.[104] When they wrote again (with another batch of pictures), he gave them an update on the publication of *The Magician's Nephew*, along with some interesting tidbits about what they would discover upon reading it: "You must have often wondered how the old Professor ... could have believed all the children told him about Narnia. The reason was that he had been there himself as a little boy. This book tells you how he went there, and ... how he saw Aslan *creating* Narnia, and how the White Witch first got into that world and why there was a lamp-post in the middle of that forest."[105] What literate, inquisitive child would balk at finding out the answers to those mysteries? He wanted to be sure they knew the book he was dedicating to them was well worth reading.

Two of the Kilmer boys—Hugh and Martin—continued a separate correspondence with Lewis. In a 1961 correspondence, as Hugh was leaving childhood behind, they discussed the nature of the resurrected body, a question spurred on by Hugh's reading of Lewis's *Miracles*.[106] In another 1961 letter, they bandied about the issue of how God created all things different and unique.[107] A further indication that this Kilmer son was a deep thinker is that he tackled Lewis's more scholarly work, *An Experiment in Criticism*.[108]

Martin, meanwhile, writing in 1957, sought Lewis's perspective on what Susan's ultimate fate was in the Narnia series. Lewis wanted Martin to know that there is always reason to hope. "There is plenty of time for her to mend, and perhaps she will get to Aslan's country in the end—in her own way."[109] As with Hugh, Martin was branching out into other Lewis works, reading *Perelandra* in 1958, and when he informed Lewis how much he loved it, Lewis confided, "I enjoyed that imaginary world so much myself that I'm glad to find anyone who has been there and liked it as much as I did—just like meeting someone who has been to a place one knows and likes in the real world."[110]

Perhaps one of the most interesting letters Lewis received with respect to children came not from the child himself but from his mother. Philinda Krieg wrote to him on behalf of her son, Laurence, who was about six years old at the time. After reading some of the Narnia books, Laurence was troubled that his love for Aslan might be greater than his love for Jesus. Mrs.

---

104. Letter from Lewis to the Kilmer Children, 24 January 1954, ibid., 414–15.
105. Letter from Lewis to the Kilmer Children, 19 March 1954, ibid., 441–42.
106. Letter from Lewis to Hugh Kilmer, 15 February 1961, ibid., 1239.
107. Letter from Lewis to Hugh Kilmer, 5 April 1961, ibid., 1252.
108. Letter from Lewis to Hugh Kilmer, 26 March 1963, ibid., 1418.
109. Letter from Lewis to Martin Kilmer, 22 January 1957, ibid., 826.
110. Letter from Lewis to Martin Kilmer, 24 April 1958, ibid., 939–40.

Krieg wanted to know how she should talk to Laurence about this. Lewis feelingly obliged with a rather lengthy letter, telling her what to say to her son. He clarified why Lawrence should not be worried. "But Laurence can't *really* love Aslan more than Jesus, even if he feels that's what he is doing. For the things he loves Aslan for doing or saying are simply the things Jesus really did and said. So that when Laurence thinks he is loving Aslan, he is really loving Jesus."

Lewis then gave this advice: "If I were Laurence I'd just say in my prayers something like this: 'Dear God, if the things I've been thinking and feeling about those books are things You don't like and are bad for me, please take away those feelings and thoughts. But if they are not bad, then please stop me from worrying about them.' . . . But it would be kind and Christian-like if he then added, 'And if Mr. Lewis has worried any other children by his books or done them any harm, then please forgive him and help him never to do it again.'"[111]

The American child to whom Lewis wrote the most letters was a young girl named Joan Lancaster, who lived in New York, but whose parents apparently had a vacation home in Sarasota, Florida, from where she wrote some of her letters. The first one arrived in April 1954, and even though Lewis had never heard from her up to this point, he gave her an open invitation to tell him what she thought the last book in the Narnia series ought to be called.[112] When she inquired in her next letter whether there would be any more than seven books, Lewis responded that it was always better to stop when people want more than to go on until they become tired of reading them.[113]

Lancaster seems to have been an artistic child, in love with opera, playing the cello, and seeking to write, in emulation of Lewis. A lot of their correspondence deals with her writing. She would send him the latest attempt, and he would critique it, always being both honest and encouraging as she learned how to develop this talent. The most detailed letter he sent her, in 1956, lays out the basics of good writing that could be applied to anyone, child or adult:

1. Always try to use the language so as to make quite clear what you mean and make sure yr. sentence couldn't mean anything else.
2. Always prefer the plain direct word to the long, vague one. Don't *implement* promises, but *keep* them.

---

111. Letter from Lewis to Philinda Krieg, 6 May 1955, ibid., 602–3.

112. Letter from Lewis to Joan Lancaster, 15 April 1954, ibid., 455. Lewis eventually settled on *The Last Battle* for the title of the final book in the Narnia series.

113. Letter from Lewis to Joan Lancaster, 7 May 1954, ibid., 466–67.

3. Never use abstract nouns when concrete ones will do. If you mean "more people died" don't say "mortality rose."

4. Don't use adjectives which merely tell us how you want us to *feel* about the thing you are describing. . . . Instead of telling us a thing was "terrible," describe it so that we'll be terrified. Don't say it was "delightful": make *us* say "delightful" when we've read the description. . . .

5. Don't use words too big for the subject. Don't say "infinitely" when you mean "very": otherwise you'll have no word left when you want to talk about something *really* infinite.[114]

Lancaster was another one of those child correspondents who grew out of their childhood as they continued to write to Lewis over the years, and the questions became more complex. By December 1962, Lewis, as he contemplated the passage of time, remarked, "Wait till you reach my age and you will find that time doesn't go 'fast' but at space speed!" He also saw great potential in her: "How exciting to be both an opera singer and a cellist. And what a gift it will be for your Press Agent—'It is not commonly known that Miss Joan Lancaster, the world-famous opera singer, could have been a brilliant success in quite another section of the entertainment world.'"[115]

The very last letter exchange, in Lewis's final September, was short and somewhat melancholy, saying merely, "Your letter is full of things that I'd like to reply to properly, but I'm not up to it. Last July I was thought to be dying. I am now an invalid. . . . My brother is away and I have to cope with all the mail. Forgive me."[116]

One would expect C. S. Lewis to ask forgiveness for not being able to write more, but he had no need to ask. For at least eighteen years, he had devoted himself to the labor of communicating God's truths to all who sought him out. So many of those seekers were Americans, and he never turned any of them away.

---

114. Letter from Lewis to Joan Lancaster, 26 June 1956, ibid., 765–66.
115. Letter from Lewis to Joan Lancaster, 29 December 1962, ibid., 1398–99.
116. Letter from Lewis to Joan Lancaster, 7 September 1963, ibid., 1454.

7

The C. S. Lewis Societies

ANOTHER WAY TO GAUGE C. S. Lewis's influence on Americans is to examine the rise of organizations dedicated to him. From a small beginning in 1969, there are now so many societies, study and discussion groups, and institutes devoted to Lewis's life and works that they are nearly impossible to count, not to mention the various Facebook pages for him and other Inklings. This chapter will trace the origin, mission, and development of three of the most prominent Lewis organizations: the New York C. S. Lewis Society; the C. S. Lewis Institute; and the C. S. Lewis Foundation. Together, they are creating a significant Lewis imprint on many Americans.

New York C. S. Lewis Society

American Henry Noel was living in France in 1950. Not only was he not a Christian, he was a convinced agnostic. The school he was enrolled in at the time, in its attempt to teach the best English style, was using as a model Lewis's *The Pilgrim's Regress*. It definitely taught Noel the best English style of writing, but it did far more. Upon his return to America in 1954, he could not get that book out of his mind. "I remembered it and became haunted," he admitted later. "I had to write Geoffrey Bles (the British publisher) to obtain a copy and I bought *Surprised by Joy* merely because I wanted more English of that quality."[1] Those two books were his entrance into the world of C. S. Lewis, as he started buying every Lewis book he could find. The result was a life transformed from agnosticism; he was baptized a Christian in 1963.

---

1. Trexler, "A Brief History," 1.

Noel also was a subscriber to *National Review*, the conservative opinion magazine founded by William F. Buckley. Time and again, he noticed the writers in this magazine would reference Lewis, so he decided to send in a short announcement that appeared in the 23 September 1969 issue, stating, "I invite all those living in or near NYC who are longstanding admirers of Lewis' books, or who, for whatever reason, cherish feelings of affection and gratitude toward his memory, to get in touch with me."[2] He received more than forty inquiries from that announcement, and on 1 November 1969, the first meeting took place. A month later, the assembled individuals made it official by accepting a charter explaining the goals of the Society. That charter reads,

We, the founding members of the New York C. S. Lewis Society, have as our purposes:

- To bring together those in the local area who share for C. S. Lewis, among all authors, a special admiration and affection and an active interest, which have been tried by time, and will persist;
- To meet, and to consider all aspects of the life and work of this rare man, and any matters on which his thought may shed light;
- To assemble and keep a repository of short writings by and about C. S. Lewis, not collected into book form; to help as we may toward an eventual definitive edition of the writings of C. S. Lewis; to encourage scholarship and publication stemming from his writings;
- To establish and maintain contact with others throughout the world who share our active interest in C. S. Lewis;
- To make discreet overtures to persons not familiar with the writings of C. S. Lewis, but who are clearly afoot on their life's pilgrimage and who may have—even unaware—an affinity for the Christian Spirit that he represents, and to whom his writings may prove, as to us, welcome guides.[3]

One of the signers of this charter was James T. Como, whose academic achievements on behalf of Lewis were discussed in an earlier chapter. Another was Eugene McGovern, who contributed one of the essays about Lewis in Como's book, *Remembering C. S. Lewis*. In that essay, McGovern said that he first began reading Lewis in the early 1960s, shortly before Lewis's death.

---

2. Ibid.

3. The New York C. S. Lewis Society Charter, accepted on a motion put to the meeting of 12 December 1969 as amended on 25 May 1970.

"The impression he made was immediate and profound," he wrote, "and it has proved to be lasting." Where did his Lewis adventure begin? "I am one of those who were fascinated by *Screwtape*," he stated, and then "were soon pestering people with quotations from *The Problem of Pain*, and then were pressing *Perelandra* on those who would still patiently hear about the author we had found." He became eager to read anything Lewis had written.

> I have gone on to become one of those readers to whom Lewis's publishers are grateful: readers who have read very little Milton but have read *A Preface to Paradise Lost*; whose knowledge of English literature in the sixteenth century, whether including or excluding drama, is limited to Lewis's *Oxford History* volume; and who will die without having read Spenser, though they have read *The Allegory of Love*.[4]

McGovern speculated on how Lewis, had he been alive, would have responded to the establishment of this Society. "I am sure he would have tried to dissuade us and would have urged us to study instead Scripture, Malory, Hooker, Augustine, Vergil, Dante, Aquinas, and Milton," he mused. "But after we insisted that it was to be his works we would be studying, I think he would be relieved to know that the society receives no support from any source other than its membership." He added, "And I suspect that he would be wryly amused to learn that the details of business are handled for the society by a committee titled the Eldila."[5]

McGovern also commented on the critique that a society like that might be little more than a cult, since the members extended their interest beyond Lewis's writings to the man himself. "To an outsider, even a sympathetic one, there is perhaps something disquieting and even embarrassing about this interest in Lewis the man," he remarked. One might understand admiration for the various styles of writing Lewis engaged in, but why focus on the author? The question he posed was "Can the enthusiasm, once it gives a large place to Lewis himself, avoid becoming narrow, precious, sticky, and cultish?"[6]

Convinced the concern was unfounded, McGovern stated the reasons why it was acceptable to concentrate on Lewis the person and why the Society would never develop into a cult. First, he pointed to how reading Lewis does not narrow one's thinking but expands it. "He is simply the wrong author for someone who wants an uneventful mental life." Those who read Lewis, he insisted, are not allowing their favorite author to do their thinking for them;

---

4. McGovern, "Our Need for Such a Guide," 227–28.
5. Ibid., 228–29. Eldila were angels in Lewis's Space Trilogy.
6. Ibid., 235.

he actually makes them think more deeply, and he noted how often at the meetings the members voiced "firm dissents from some of Lewis's views." And why not be interested in the man behind the words and thoughts that have inspired so many? Would that not be "a perfectly natural and normal outgrowth" of their appreciation for what he had written? "What can be more natural than wanting to know what we can of the man who seems to have dreamed our dreams before us? A nonchalant lack of interest would be an odd response to an opportunity to learn about an author who seems to be at once so profoundly like ourselves and yet so different from anyone we have ever met."[7]

From the very beginning, the New York C. S. Lewis Society published a monthly bulletin that would summarize what had occurred at the previous meeting, offer news of interest to the members, and print essays on topics relating to Lewis. In the last fifteen years, it has been altered into a bi-monthly enterprise "to allow more time to complete the work and more pages to allow for lengthier essays."[8] Only six months after producing the charter, the Society had ninety-seven members spread throughout twenty states and three countries. Today it can point to members in all fifty states and on every inhabited continent (the website humorously exempts the Arctic and Antarctica). Early members included Lewis's own brother, Warnie; his lifelong friend and fellow Inkling, Owen Barfield; Walter Hooper; Clyde Kilby; and Thomas Howard—all individuals who had known Lewis personally. Hooper has spoken at Society meetings, as has Douglas Gresham, Lewis's stepson.

In those first few months, the Society solicited testimonies on how Lewis had affected the lives of those exposed to his writings. One respondent wrote, "You probably know that C. S. Lewis is not fashionable in theology at present, but I think he was something of a prophet and I am sure he will be remembered as one of the finest moral and even systematic theologians of the twentieth century. Certainly he was one of the greatest Christians." By saying that Lewis was not "fashionable," the writer was accurately stating the general consensus of that period, even as Lewis himself believed he would drift into obscurity after his death. The establishment of the Society, along with the efforts of Hooper and Kilby, was crucial to ensuring that did not happen. Another respondent, pleased that Lewis was now getting his due from the Society, nevertheless called attention to the fact that "the honors he is receiving where he is now surpass all human praise." Another thanked Lewis for showing him "a path into a wild, new world." He continued, "I was

---

7. Ibid., 235–36.
8. Trexler, "A Brief History," 2.

(and am) a great science fiction fan. One day I read *The Great Divorce* and really found what I was looking for in science fiction. . . . Long ago I began his theology books and owe most of my Christian growth to the fact that Christ often used him to point the right way for me." Then there was the university professor who shared,

> Like (I suppose) most of C. S. Lewis's readers, I came to him by way of *The Screwtape Letters*, closely followed by *Broadcast Talks* and the three interplanetary novels, and then by everything I could find in our bookstores. I read and reread all of them continually. . . . I have no favorites among Lewis's books; every one of them seems equally great in its own way; they all have the same wonderful quality of insight and the same clear, beautiful style.

He wrote again later to offer an amendment to his previous comments, saying, "I should modify one sentence in . . . my earlier letter to say that my favorite book of CSL's seems always to be the one I happen to be reading at the moment."[9]

The Society's monthly meetings are attended primarily by those in the New York City area, of course, but its influence is more widespread, based on its reputation as the first active organization to promote the works of Lewis and because of the quality of the membership over the years. It can be considered as the "Flagship" for all C. S. Lewis organizations that have followed in its wake.

C. S. Lewis Institute (CSLI)

The C. S. Lewis Institute had an interesting beginning, with a partnership between an academic and a professional golfer. The academic was Dr. James Houston, who was a University Lecturer at Oxford specializing in cultural and historical geography. Since he taught at Oxford from 1947 until 1971, he was a contemporary of Lewis's. Houston was then to become the first Principal of Regent College, a Christian institution established in Vancouver, British Columbia. He served in that role, then as Chancellor, and finally as Professor of Spiritual Theology.[10] The professional golfer was James R. Hiskey. That may seem to be a strange duo, but they came together to found CSLI in 1976. They named it after Lewis because they believed in his approach to the faith: concentrate on the core essentials and connect across

---

9. Author Societies Archive, Box 1, Folder 13—The New York C. S. Lewis Society.
10. http://www.regent-college.edu/faculty/retired/james-houston.

all denominational boundaries. According to the Institute's site, Lewis "was also an outstanding example of a lay person who came to Christ and lived out his faith in a secular calling. As a major figure in 20th-century Christianity, he has been able to communicate his faith in a profound way."[11]

What is the Institute's mission? From the start, the focus has been "to develop disciples who will articulate, defend and live their faith in Christ in personal and public life."[12] The Institute has grown from one site in the Washington, D.C., area, to eleven additional sites. Most of those are in the United States—Annapolis, Atlanta, Central Pennsylvania, Chicago, Cincinnati, Loudoun County (in Virginia, on the outskirts of Washington, D.C.), Northeast Ohio, Seattle, and Virginia Beach—but it also has branches in Belfast, Northern Ireland (the boyhood home of C. S. Lewis) and London.

CSLI is an activist organization, seeking to disciple people "young" in the faith and sending them into the churches to energize them and help keep them on track with the essential message of the Gospel. On one level, CSLI is encouraging churches and other Christian ministries to commit to what it calls a "Decade of Discipleship," for which CSLI will come alongside to provide resources. As the website notes, "We've heard from many pastors, ministry leaders and others that they understand the need for discipleship, but they're not sure where to start. We've identified several books that provide essential information for help to address the discipleship deficit. Each book outlines a different approach, but they all focus on heart and mind discipleship and are excellent resources."[13]

The heart of the Institute, though, is its C. S. Lewis Fellows Program, primarily a year-long discipleship commitment—a second year can be added at the discretion of each site's director—that "focuses on the integration of the heart and mind in an interdenominational setting." Through a combination of teaching sessions, personal mentoring, small group engagement, and Bible study, the goal is "to produce mature believers who can articulate, defend and joyfully live out their faith in every aspect of their life." The groups are organized by age (ranging from twenty-four to fifty-six-plus) and gender. Topics covered include the nature of God, growing in prayer and humility, obedience, apologetics, and what it means, practically, to live out a life of faith as a Christian. There is no set tuition; CSLI simply asks participants to make the Institute "one of the ministries (after the church) that he or she supports on a regular basis." CSLI says that surveys of those who have completed this Fellows Program

11. "About the C. S. Lewis Institute."
12. Ibid.
13. "Decade of Discipleship."

show that 100% increased their involvement in ministry within the family and their neighborhoods, while 88% extended their participation in workplace ministry. Overall, 84% testify that their one-year commitment "transformed or significantly impacted their life."[14]

In addition to the Fellows Program, CSLI holds a number of events/seminars at its various sites where the public can come and hear excellent speakers on subjects such as apologetics or discipleship. It now has a number of online publications that are easily accessed. *Knowing and Doing* is its quarterly teaching magazine that "offers a wide variety of articles from nationally recognized leaders in discipleship, spirituality, theology, apologetics, and cultural analysis." "Reflections" is a one-page message taken directly from the thought of Lewis on some aspect of living the Christian life. "Discipleship As You Go" is a weekly resource in the form of either an article, an audio file, or a video with a new theme each month. And for the children, there is "The Dawn Treader News," that offers "activities and ideas geared to help parents disciple their children from pre-k through teens." A CSLI App provides access to the Institute's resources on any mobile device.[15]

CSLI also has partnerships with other ministries. Ambassadors for Christ (AFC), for instance, an outreach to Chinese intellectuals, is one of those. That ministry says, "The C. S. Lewis Institute has pioneered and demonstrated an unique way to equip the lay leaders today through strategic discipleship curriculums. AFC is inspired by the C. S. Lewis Institute to bring the same spirit and practice to the global Chinese churches." David Chow, President of AFC, adds, "I wish we could offer the Fellows Program everywhere AFC has a presence."[16] Another ministry considered a CSLI partner is Alpha, a course of study for those interested in learning about Christianity. Its website calls it an opportunity to explore life and the Christian faith, in a friendly, open and informal environment.[17] It began in the U.K. but has become worldwide, with more than three million Americans who have participated. "There are now more than 13,000 Alpha courses registered in the USA, which includes every state and spans across 127 denominations."[18] Still another is International Christian Community-Eurasia (ICC-E), which aims to reverse the steady decline of Christian faith in Europe.

Probably the most connected of all the partners is Ravi Zacharias International Ministries (RZIM), which often holds public meetings in

14. "C. S. Lewis Fellows Program."
15. "Publications."
16. "CSLI Partners."
17. www.alpha.org.
18. "CSLI Partners."

conjunction with CSLI. Zacharias is considered by many to be one of the chief Christian apologists of the modern era, following the path that Lewis set forth in the 1940s with his many apologetic works. Zacharias says, "The C. S. Lewis Institute is a great effort to instruct eager minds in probing the depths of moral imagination and spiritual truth." His European Director, Michael Ramsden, affirms, "In all my travels around the world, I have never seen a discipleship program as effective as that at the C. S. Lewis Institute."[19]

Other Christian leaders have voiced similar sentiments with respect to the effectiveness of the CSLI ministry. Alister McGrath, who is not only one of Lewis's key biographers, but also Director of the Oxford Center for Evangelism and Apologetics, calls the Institute "one of the nation's premier catalysts of the Christian mind, offering the churches a rich diet of spiritual and intellectual nourishment. I am thrilled by its vision for the future." The Senior Pastor of Cornerstone Evangelical Free Church in Annandale, Virginia, Dr. Bill Kynes, praises the Fellows Program because it "deepens the faith and commitment of people in the local church, and I found that they come back from their experience . . . more committed to the local church and better equipped to serve." Added to those reflections are the words of Stuart McAlpine, who serves as the Senior Pastor of Christ Our Shepherd Church in Washington, D. C.: "I love the DNA of this ministry that has such a broad appeal to the body of Christ. Not broad in that it waters anything down, but broad in the fact that there is something about the clarity in its presentation of the truth that is so attractive."[20]

CSLI's focus on discipleship across a broad spectrum of Christian denominations, and its aim to develop Christians who can explain and defend their faith in the marketplace is surely a goal C. S. Lewis would have enthusiastically endorsed.

C. S. Lewis Foundation

Stanley Mattson, who holds a history doctorate with an emphasis on intellectual history, has been and is the driving force behind the C. S. Lewis Foundation. Concerned about the relative absence of Christian influence in higher education, he drew together a number of Christian scholars for a retreat in 1972 to discuss what could be done to rectify the situation. At the time, Dr. Mattson was on the faculty of Gordon College, an evangelical institution. The attendees at that retreat agreed to continue to pray and seek

19. Ibid.
20. "Endorsements."

God on how to make the "Christian Mind" more a part of American colleges and universities.

Fourteen years later, Mattson left his teaching post at the University of Redlands in California to begin the fulfillment of that vision, as he launched the C. S. Lewis Foundation for Christian Higher Education. Again, he gathered together a group of Christian scholars to help chart the course for this organization. They ultimately decided to work toward the "establishment of a prototype Christian 'Great Books College,' with a school of visual and performing arts, to be named in honor of C. S. Lewis."[21] Unknown to them at the time, another vital part of this burgeoning ministry was soon to be revealed, as another group, The Kilns Association, was trying to purchase and restore Lewis's Oxford home. By 1988, that group, lacking the financial backing it needed to reach its goal, turned over the responsibility for purchasing the Kilns to the Foundation. They succeeded not only in becoming owners of the home, but also in restoring it completely, a restoration that was finished in 2001. So an American organization inspired by Lewis ended up owning his beloved home in Oxford.

The official mission statement of the C. S. Lewis Foundation reads, "Inspired by the life and legacy of C. S. Lewis, the C. S. Lewis Foundation is dedicated to advancing the renewal of Christian thought and creative expression throughout the world of learning and the culture at large." Enlarging upon that concise statement, the website further says, "Throughout the years, our goal has been singular: to encourage Christian faculty, students, clergy, lay persons, and seekers to actively, openly, and creatively integrate the life of the mind, the life of the imagination, and the life of the spirit in order to live a fully developed and mature life in Christ."[22] The university setting remains the primary focus, as the Foundation notes,

> Students attending secular institutions of higher learning today are appropriately exposed to a wide array of alternative views within the classroom. What is painfully evident, however, is that, with but few notable exceptions, there are virtually no serious, professionally credible, and identifiably Christian intellectuals at the faculty level within the mainstream of American university life today. Most students understandably, if mistakenly, conclude that the Christian faith can't hold its own among serious and intelligent people. The cumulative result, as each

---

21. http://www.cslewis.org/aboutus/history/.
22. http://www.cslewis.org/aboutus/ourmission/.

academic year passes, is a student body that is increasingly devoid of spiritual understanding, vision, and hope.[23]

What this produces is a "secular materialism and moral relativism" that permeates the "entire culture." The professoriate is overwhelmingly non-Christian, and those who are Christian professors "would truly be at risk professionally if they were to dare express opinions that in any way betrayed serious Christian convictions," the website concludes. Then it quotes the words of Lewis from one of his essays, "On the Transmission of Christianity," acknowledging the key role of professors: "The sources of unbelief among young people today do not lie in those young people.... This very obvious fact—that each generation is taught by an earlier generation—must be kept very firmly in mind.... Nothing which was not in the teachers can flow from them into the pupils."[24]

Realizing the state of the professoriate, the Foundation, now with the Kilns as one of its properties, provides an opportunity for faculty to use the home for its Scholars-in-Residence Program, allowing professors who want to take advantage of Oxford's academic resources to live at the Kilns for short- or long-term stays, up to one year. Living, researching, and writing in Lewis's home is an inspiration for many.

Another outreach to Christian scholars is the C. S. Lewis Faculty Forum, which "is dedicated to networking and supporting Christian faculty and administrators in advancing the renewal of Christian thought and creative expression throughout the world of learning." The goals of this particular aspect of the Foundation are clearly articulated. This initiative intends to:

- Facilitate the interaction of college and university faculty, administrators, and trustees of all Christian traditions;
- Celebrate our common commitment to "mere Christianity," the historic faith of Jesus Christ, as expressed in the scriptures of the Old and New Testaments and the ancient creeds;
- Create opportunities for reflection, research, and debate among Christian faculty, as well as between Christian faculty and those of other persuasions, both secular and religious;
- Nurture the development of a consensus concerning the legitimacy of rationally defended, religiously informed thought—whether Christian,

23. Ibid.
24. Ibid.

Jewish, Hindu, Muslim, Buddhist, Native American, or other—within the curricular life of our academic institutions;

- Provide programming, research, teaching and financial resources in support of projects that are relevant to the Forum's mission; and work in cooperation with existing campus ministries.[25]

The Kilns is being put to good use for others besides the scholars who can stay a while and advance their research. Beginning in 2001, once the restoration was completed, Lewis's home has been used for the Summer Seminars ministry, in which up to eight individuals per week have the opportunity to go to the Kilns daily for discussions hosted by one of the scholars in residence.[26]

Every third year, the Foundation sponsors a C. S. Lewis Summer Institute, also known as "Oxbridge," a word that combines the names of the two universities at which Lewis taught. Participants spend time at both universities and hear from renowned Lewis scholars and others who are adept at communicating the "Christian Mind" to the secular world. More than three thousand people have attended since the Institute began in 1988. Subjects of the various Oxbridge gatherings have covered a variety of approaches to Christian thought and culture. The complete list up to this point is as follows:

- 2014: *Reclaiming the Virtues: Human Flourishing in the 21st Century*
- 2011: *Paradigms of Hope: Transcending Chaos & Transforming Culture*
- 2008: *Imago Dei?: The Self and the Search for Meaning*
- 2005: *Making All Things New: The Good, the True, and the Beautiful in the 21st Century*
- 2002: *Time & Eternity*
- 1998: *Loose in the Fire*
- 1994: *Cosmos and Creation: Chance or Dance?*
- 1991: *Muses Unbound: Transfiguring the Imagination*
- 1988: *The Christian and the Contemporary University*

Those are the programs currently active with the Foundation, but more are in preparation. In September 2013, the Foundation purchased an old Victorian home in Northfield, Massachusetts, named Green Pastures, that it plans to use as an American version of the Study Centre at the Kilns. The website says it will be "an embodiment of C. S. Lewis's concept of 'Mere Christianity,' inviting the participation of Christians from all

---

25. http://www.cslewis.org/ourprograms/facultyforum/.
26. http://www.cslewis.org/event/2016-summer-seminars/.

historic communions, and welcoming all in the pursuit of truth, goodness, and beauty." Originally built in 1885, Green Pastures was home to Fleming H. Revell, who not only became famous as a publisher but also was the brother-in-law of Dwight L. Moody. Revell, in turn, sold the house three years later to Daniel B. Towner, a professor of music and writer of some rather well-known hymns, including *Trust and Obey* and *Grace, Greater Than All My Sin*. The home returned to the Moody family (his daughter and, later, his granddaughter), which occupied it until the 1980s. This proposed American Study Center, modeled after the one at the Kilns, is also intended to reach out to the local community through "a lecture series, Great Books seminars, and performing arts concerts."[27]

Mattson's original vision of a Great Books college is now on the drawing board as well. The official name will be C. S. Lewis College, where, according to the Foundation website, "students will learn primarily by engaging faculty and other students in vibrant and collegial analysis and discussion of the Great Books. This will equip students not only with a wide knowledge of a multitude of subjects, but also with the oral and written communication skills to interact meaningfully with the world around them." The site lists the five distinctives of this proposed College:

A Mere Christian Community: This is based on Lewis's concept of drawing together Christians of all denominational backgrounds and theological perspectives. "We will, no doubt, enjoy many fine and spirited theological discussions among ourselves (much as did Jack and his friends), but this enlivening diversity will be lived out in the unity of a shared and loving commitment to Jesus Christ as Lord."

A Great Books Curriculum: The goal is to provide "a close examination of the seminal writings of the greatest thinkers of Western civilization (including several Eastern texts). There will be one course of study at the College, ensuring that all students read the College's entire curriculum of Great Books, ranging from physics to politics to poetry and everything in between."

Discussion-Based Seminars and Tutorials: The lecture method of teaching will not be primary. "This means that students who choose C. S. Lewis College will do so because they desire to assume primary responsibility for their own education. They will be committed to read and carefully study the Great Books and intelligently discuss their significance in seminar dialogue with their fellow students under the guidance and supervision of the faculty."

The Visual and Performing Arts: Since these arts are so central to everyone's lives, the College seeks to establish a school dedicated to the role of the arts in promoting the Christian message to society.

27. http://www.cslewiscollege.org/cslsc-northfield/.

Faculty Governance: All the faculty Fellows of the College will be represented on the Executive Council, in accordance with the tradition of all Oxford colleges. "This will ensure," the Foundation believes, "the primacy and integrity of the College's academic, social, and spiritual mission."[28]

Thomas Howard, an academic who met Lewis and who was profiled in an earlier chapter, commented on the prospects of C. S. Lewis College, proclaiming, "The news of the founding of C. S. Lewis College is very good news indeed, not only for Christendom, but for all of academia, and for Western civilization. The name of C. S. Lewis—the 'Old Western Man'—is a name of good omen for the College." University of Virginia Professor of Economics Kenneth Elzinga notes, "Many who have sought to understand the life and teachings of Jesus have found help in the writings of C. S. Lewis. Now this distinguished scholar can have his influence multiplied even more through a college that bears his name. My desire is that many will be 'surprised by joy' through the influence of C. S. Lewis College." And the pastor of Christ Church in Lewis's hometown of Belfast, Ireland, has praised the effort in these words:

> The Foundation is trying to bring that great academic thinking that you read about, but take the scriptures and ask 'what relevance do they have?' The Foundation sees that Lewis addressed your mind, and they understand what the man was trying to do. This is a brilliant bridge to a rising generation that is skeptical of scripture, the existence of God, the Man hanging on a cross and shedding His blood.... They are building a bridge to those minds through Lewis. I don't know of any other organization that's doing it.[29]

These three seminal organizations—the New York C. S. Lewis Society, the C. S. Lewis Institute, and the C. S. Lewis Foundation—are vibrant testimonies to the impact Lewis has made on many Americans. They do not exist merely to commemorate someone whose influence is relegated to a former time; rather, they see Lewis as a perpetual inspiration for American Christians as they seek to turn back the tide of a rising secularism and the attacks of a culture increasingly hostile to Christian belief and practice.

---

28. http://www.cslewiscollege.org/about-us/distinctives/.
29. http://www.cslewiscollege.org/about-us/endorsements/.

8

The Surveys

SOME ATTEMPTS HAVE BEEN made to accumulate information on just how C. S. Lewis has impacted the lives of Americans. Twice the Marion E. Wade Center at Wheaton College has collected testimonies from individuals who credit Lewis with the vibrancy of their Christian faith. These were unscientific surveys, to be sure, but they did catalog the various reasons why Lewis meant so much to those who responded. The first survey was conducted in 1986, twenty-three years after Lewis's death. An advertisement was placed in a number of Christian publications, asking for people to send their personal testimonies. The exact wording of that advertisement was as follows:

> The Marion E. Wade Collection is seeking evidence of the impact of C. S. Lewis and his writing on people's lives. If you or others whom you know have been markedly influenced by Lewis, will you please write to us and share your reminiscences.[1]

The advertisement spurred dozens of responses, many of them rather lengthy. Dr. Philip Ryken, now President of Wheaton College, in a 1997 article, provided an overview of what those responses indicated. He saw that they could be broken down into categories: those whom Lewis helped lead to salvation; those who use Lewis's works to evangelize others; and those who are grateful to him for solidifying their Christian life and making them into more effective disciples. That last category contained the most responses. As Ryken noted, "The majority of those who responded to the Wade Center query did not write conversion narratives. Instead, men and women from all walks of life wanted to tell how C. S. Lewis had helped them stay

---

1. Ryken, "Winsome Evangelist," 68.

on the pilgrim road."² To those who might then question the usefulness of Lewis's writings, since there were fewer conversion testimonies, Ryken supplied this answer:

> The value of this should not be underestimated. Part of the purpose of apologetics is to shore up the intellectual defenses of Christianity when they start to crumble. This apologetic work is as necessary inside as it is outside the church. Internal evangelism is as valuable as external evangelism. What is the use of rescuing lost sheep if the sheep already in the fold are wandering off, or worse, being pilfered by hungry wolves?³

Ryken drew from another scholar who had investigated Lewis's influence, who said a pattern develops when someone begins to read Lewis: "Into this dark night of the soul swept whatever happened to be the student's first Lewis book. That led inexorably to the others." What other commonality did this scholar see? "And what he or she found there was not so much answers—though they were wonderful beyond all hope—but more, an irrefutable demonstration that at least one Christian mind actually existed."⁴

One of the salvation testimonies that did arrive in that survey spoke of being loaned a copy of *The Screwtape Letters* by a friend. Although intending to read just a few pages at bedtime, the writer found he/she could not put the book down. When in a bookshop shortly afterward, and seeing *The Pilgrim's Regress* on the shelf, and realizing it was authored by Lewis also, the writer felt compelled to buy it and read it as devotedly as *Screwtape*. "The author was my kind of man, educated and critical, and I could not stop reading. Between 3 and 4 Sunday morning I finished the book, and realized that I had become a Christian." The testimony concluded, "For the first time in many years I was free from anxieties and desires.... From that night my life changed.... I owe this change to C. S. Lewis, whose learning was beyond mine and whose direct insight is not confused by complexities."⁵

The survey revealed that using Lewis to evangelize others often took place in the home, as parents sought to raise their children in the faith. When the parents were fascinated by Lewis and thankful for what they had received, they wanted their children to experience the same. One parent wrote, "How could I possibly describe my joy and wonder each time I have read *The Great Divorce*? Any attempt to portray the impact of the

2. Ibid., 69.
3. Ibid., 70.
4 Ibid.
5. C. S. Lewis Testimonies Archive, 1959-1996, Folder 4—Responses from the 1986 Survey (cont.)

breathtaking beauty of *Perelandra* or the sinister terror of *That Hideous Strength* would appear shabby and utterly inadequate," the parent confessed. "Nor is it possible to render all of the shades, hues and colors of emotion and wonder which the Narnian Chronicles evoked in me first, and then in both me and my children as I read these enchanting stories to them."[6] While it may not have been possible to convey everything, the parent at least wanted the children to catch the same vision. Then there was the professor at the University of Arizona who stated, "The writings of C. S. Lewis, perhaps more than any books except the Holy Scriptures, have broken a lot of ice for me as I have read and reread them personally and analyzed and discussed them with my students." What resulted from those discussions? "Several students in my university classes on Lewis have been converted, receiving Jesus Christ as the Savior, as a result of reading and discussing *Mere Christianity*."[7] This response, then, would have to fit into both categories: the evangelical purpose led to specific salvations.

So many testimonies were centered on the efficacy of Lewis's works to strengthen one's Christian life and promote discipleship that only a few can be excerpted here as examples. The examples chosen are those that exhibit perhaps a similarity to Lewis's ability to communicate in words and phrases that capture the mind more readily. One respondent exclaimed,

> The fortress of his writings has bestowed a deep sense of assurance and security in the face of many deadly onslaughts from a tireless enemy. How well I remember the calming effect of *Miracles, Mere Christianity* and even *The Screwtape Letters* as I plowed through my philosophical studies during undergraduate days at the university. In spite of the nearly monolithic worldview of naturalism which disparaged any faith in the supernatural, here was an intelligent, well-educated, extremely articulate writer who really *believed* in the truths of orthodox Christianity. I drank over and over from these chalices of sanity and faith which contained such exquisite elixirs to invigorate a struggling spirit, illumine a dark mind, and refresh a thirsty soul.[8]

Another man testified that by the time he had completed his doctorate and had been overwhelmed with "high powered math and modern physics," he had come to the place where whatever faith he had had was almost completely dissipated. Then came one of those "accidents" in which he just happened to

---

6. C. S. Lewis Testimonies Archive, 1959–1996, Folder 3—Responses from the 1986 Survey.

7. Ibid.

8. Ibid.

come across *The Screwtape Letters*. "My faith came roaring back—adamant, larger than ever it had been. Clean, clear and sweet. I experienced such joy that I almost shouted (very un-Presbyterian)," he confessed. Yet it took him a while to grab another Lewis book; he was concerned that *Screwtape* might have been an anomaly. "Curiously, I fretted that the remarkable author, C. S. Lewis, could not repeat such masterful writing. It was another long stretch of months before I had the fortitude to risk disappointment and try another of his books. It was more sharp joy when I learned he could be trusted to bless the reader with almost all he wrote."[9]

The lengthiest and, arguably, the most original of all the responses on this subject deserves a fuller quote to provide the greater context:

> I think I can truthfully say that C. S. Lewis's writings have had a more profound impact upon me than any other writer. It was not quite a case of love at first sight, though I did enjoy his books from the very beginning; but before long he had completely captivated me; and I found myself devouring everything of his that I could lay my hands on. The wonder of it all was that he somehow managed to capture my mind, my imagination, and my heart all at the same time. So profit was combined with pleasure in a manner and to a degree that I had never known before. It was as if I had suddenly discovered a recipe for liver and spinach that proved to be the tastiest dish at the banquet—or contrariwise that I had just found convincing evidence that ice cream and cookies should be ranked as the number-one health food. Substance wedded to delight! Who could have believed it? Nor has the substance proved passing or trivial; for Lewis gave me a solid, vital, and lasting perspective on the great truths of "mere" Christianity. In particular, he gave me an insight—a living picture—into the meaning of love and personhood (and their opposite) that has proved foundational for much of my understanding of God and man—an understanding that has expanded and deepened with the years.... Over and over again I keep coming back to his books ... and I would be hard put to it to choose a favorite; for each one seems to be a favorite as I reread it. But one which never fails to bring instruction and delight is his "Weight of Glory." Frankly, it is the only thing I have ever read on the Christian hope that so deeply touches my mind and heart. Every time I read it I am amazed afresh at the depth and vitality of the insights there revealed.[10]

9. Ibid.
10. Ibid.

Then in 1996, a second attempt was made to gather more testimonies. This time, with the onset of the Internet age, testimonies were collected via e-mail. The target audience this time was "visitors to one or another C. S. Lewis home page on the Internet" who were asked to tell how Lewis had influenced them either with their conversion or their subsequent Christian walk. "Answers to this question," Ryken explained in his article, "followed a pattern similar to the one that emerged from the earlier survey."[11]

Some salvation stories stood out in this survey, such as the one from a respondent who said a friend gave him *Mere Christianity* to read, and who "encouraged me to use my mighty intellect to overcome the arguments put forth in that book about the nature of the universe." He/she discovered that his/her mighty intellect was not perhaps so mighty after all. "I was stunned. Lewis had taken each of the points I had spent years hanging my hat on, and in his straightforward simple style had made mincemeat of my juvenile 'arguments' against God and Christ and Heaven and whatnot." This respondent came to Christ and credited Lewis with his conversion: "C. S. Lewis . . . spoke to me in what I thought was my strongest area, that of intellect, and with nothing more than common sense knocked me down into humility. . . . I truly believe I owe my salvation to that man."[12] Another reported,

> I would simply like to say that it is because of Lewis that I came to see, as an Atheist, two things: 1. That if I was going to deny God's existence, I had better be prepared to explain why I sometimes wished so desperately that He did [exist]. 2. That if there can be no Absolute Morality, then there can be no Morality, as we understand it, at all. The impact upon me of the realization of these two things cannot be overstated. Lewis, with these and many other thoughts I found in his books, particularly "Mere Christianity," was instrumental in my final acceptance of the Christian explanation to all the heavy questions that plague the minds of men.[13]

A teacher conveyed that The Chronicles of Narnia were so instrumental in her life that she had begun using them in her classroom as an evangelistic tool. "I try to encourage my fourth grade student[s] to feel that same joy each year as I read the entire set aloud. (I work in a Christian school.) It

---

11. Ryken, "Winsome Evangelist," 71.

12. C. S. Lewis Testimonies Archive, 1959–1996, Folder 2—Responses from the 1996 Survey.

13. Ibid.

is exciting to see kids really start to understand the complexities and joys of a life with Christ through the fantasy of a place called Narnia."[14]

Again, as with the 1986 survey, the majority of testimonies concentrated on how Lewis had solidified one's faith and showed the path to discipleship. For one respondent, it was, once again, *Mere Christianity* that made the greatest impact. "For the first time in my life I found solid reasons to bolster my belief," he/she related. "His books have given me a passion for apologetics. They also drove me to major in English Lit/Biblical Studies in College and go on to Seminary. I thank God for writers and thinkers like Lewis. His writings have been and continue to be a major influence in my life."[15] Another came at Lewis in a way most do not, through the literary side first, being enamored with his *A Preface to Paradise Lost*. Lewis's autobiographical *Surprised by Joy* and his *The Four Loves* were foundational for this person: "I kept finding again and again that he was so much like me, only more eloquent. We had endured many of the same struggles and sinned similar sins and still wanted a relationship with Christ. Lewis has not been a solution for my sins—Christ has already taken care of that—but he has been a comfort in my daily struggle to be a better Christian."[16] Then there was this married woman who shared the following:

> I first discovered C. S. Lewis in my early 20's . . . quite by accident. . . . He gave muscle to my faith. So, when the film *Shadowlands* came out in 1993, I insisted that a close group of four friends attend the showing with my husband and me simply because the previews looked great and I already knew the story about Joy. Little could I have anticipated the spark that would be ignited once again by that film. I left the theater with my mind consumed with the glory of this man's life and my eyes filled with tears at the drama of it all. I went home and began re-reading all of his books again, particularly *A Grief Observed*. . . . To this day, I am still consumed with this man and his writings. . . . I know millions of others possess the high regard for Mr. Lewis as I do. He has changed my life forever and my understanding of Christ. I will forever treasure all I can ever learn about Mr. Lewis, because he communicates wisdom and sparks such imagination in me.[17]

Ryken, in his review of these two surveys, found another common thread running throughout the responses. "One striking feature of both the

---

14. Ibid.
15. Ibid.
16. Ibid.
17. Ibid.

1986 and 1996 surveys was the eagerness with which respondents wrote of their hope to meet C. S. Lewis in heaven," he noted. "As they told the stories of their encounters with his writings, they spoke of him with an affection usually reserved for close friends. For C. S. Lewis and his readers, even literary evangelism can become a form of personal, winsome, friendship evangelism."[18]

The 2014 Survey

On a visit to the Wade Center in August 2014, I read through the results from these two surveys and was impressed with the valuable and, in some instances, rather fascinating testimonies. But since nearly two decades had passed since anyone had tried to document such testimonies, I thought the time might be right to do so again. Consequently, in concert with the Wade Center, which posted a notice on its website and on its Facebook page, I collected a new round of personal reflections from Americans on how Lewis's writings had affected their Christian worldview. Whereas the earlier surveys asked only for letters or e-mails with an open-ended request for testimonies, I decided to ask some more specific questions:

- When and how were you introduced to C. S. Lewis?
- Which of his writings have had the greatest impact on your thinking and/or spiritual development?
- Are you now, or have you ever been, involved with a C. S. Lewis society/organization or with some other activity connected with Lewis? Please explain.
- Have you viewed any of the *Shadowlands* productions? If so, what is your opinion of them?
- Have you viewed any of the Narnia productions, whether the ones created for television or the three Narnia films? If so, what is your opinion of them?

Then, at the end of the survey, I also gave an opportunity to add anything else about Lewis and his influence that the respondents wanted to share. In all, the survey received eighty-seven responses, some quite detailed. I've attempted to analyze those responses.

This analysis can in no sense be considered a definitive statement on how Lewis has affected all Americans who have taken the time to read his works. As with the previous two attempts to gather testimonies, it is selective,

18. Ryken, "Winsome Evangelist," 72.

simply because it relies on those who were interested enough to complete the survey. Neither can a survey like this be subject to precise quantitative conclusions. While there will be some statistics involved—particularly in the section dealing with which writings have been most influential to the respondents—most of the analysis will rely on subjective—but reasonable, I trust—evaluations of his impact. The final section, where respondents were free to add whatever they considered significant, will necessarily be limited to the responses that I found to be most valuable as insights into how Lewis has persuaded his readers to take their Christian faith to a higher level.[19]

When and How Were You Introduced to C. S. Lewis?

The responses to this question seemed to fall into four categories, with some overlap, of course. Most were introduced to Lewis's works either on the recommendation of someone, through their family, in a class and/or lecture, or—more surprisingly perhaps than the other three—just by "chance" in a bookstore or library.

Thirteen of the recommendations to read Lewis came from personal friends, with more than half of those coming while in college or from dating a woman who later became one's wife. Is there any significance to the fact that a future wife was the instrument for an introduction to Lewis in some cases but not one of the respondents said a future husband was the key to their first venture into a Lewis book? The numbers are too small for any kind of conclusion that young women have been more responsive to Lewis than young men, but it is worth noting in passing, at least. Some respondents said a respected teacher was the recommender, outside of the classroom. The two most recommended books were *Mere Christianity* and *The Screwtape Letters*, which, unless one begins with the Narnia series as a child, can be considered the gateway, conceivably, into other Lewis works.

It is no surprise that the family is the source for many individuals' first exposure to Lewis, and that the Narnia books would be the vehicle. At least twelve had parents who either gave them a Narnia book or read the books to them. Two others had family members other than parents give them Narnia. When a parent is a teacher, some overlap does occur, as one respondent reported: "I think that my first introduction to C. S. Lewis was when I was in fourth or fifth grade. Since my mom is a teacher, we always had summer reading assignments that we had to complete. One of the required books

---

19. K. Alan Snyder, "Survey: The Influence of C. S. Lewis on American Christians," 2014, C. S. Lewis Testimonies Archive. All facts and quotations for the remainder of this chapter are taken directly from this survey.

she had me read was *The Lion, the Witch, and the Wardrobe*." Another respondent noted, rather amusingly, "My dad read The Chronicles of Narnia all aloud to me before I was three weeks old (literally), I read them all myself before I turned 7, and I have been a bit obsessed with them ever since."

Quite a few—at least ten—were introduced to Narnia by having one of the books, usually *The Lion, the Witch, and the Wardrobe*, read to them in an elementary classroom (not always in a Christian school, either). One respondent, when in ninth grade, read *Miracles* as an extra credit assignment. One woman, who now has her own family, shared how she had both an introduction and a re-introduction: "I was introduced in grade school when I was reading The Chronicles of Narnia. I was 're-introduced' to C. S. Lewis when I began to homeschool my grade school children. We read through The Chronicles of Narnia together. It spurred me to get more of his books."

Seven had a Lewis book as part of a college course: *Mere Christianity* and *The Abolition of Man* were mentioned specifically. One man, who is now a professor of history at a Christian university, also was first drawn to Lewis while in college, but indirectly: "I was introduced to Lewis, his thinking, and his works when I was in college. I was a new Christian and was reading Josh McDowell's *Evidence That Demands a Verdict*. In that book, McDowell references Lewis's 'Lord, Liar, or Lunatic' argument, and I was swept away by the clear, unassailable logic in that argument. So I got a copy of *Mere Christianity* and read it." One respondent was captured by the Lewis mystique when he participated in a study on Lewis by his pastor. Another was part of a youth group where the leader conducted a study on *Mere Christianity*, and another finally decided to read Lewis simply because the pastor kept quoting *The Screwtape Letters* so often.

Fifteen respondents began their C. S. Lewis adventure by coming across the Narnia series in a library or by some other chance encounter. Three picked up their first Lewis book by browsing in a bookstore. One of those purchased *Surprised by Joy* because it was shelved next to the book she had intended to buy. The most likely "first" Lewis book for those who didn't begin with Narnia was either *Mere Christianity* or *The Screwtape Letters*, which, as noted above, was also the case for those who had Lewis recommended by a friend. Probably the most unusual response in this category was the man who discovered Narnia just prior to his wedding, and who then commented, "I first read the 7 Narnia stories while on my honeymoon (!)" The exclamation point is his.

Which of His Writings Have Had the Greatest Impact on Your Thinking and/or Spiritual Development?

In all, twenty of Lewis's writings, counting both books and essays, were mentioned in this category. Respondents were allowed to mention as many books as they wished, since it can be difficult to pick just one that is a favorite. That number—twenty—would have been expanded if I had treated all Narnia and Space Trilogy books (*Out of the Silent Planet*, *Perelandra*, and *That Hideous Strength*) separately, but I chose to handle them as a unity, particularly because they were so often mentioned as a group. The "race," so to speak, to find Lewis's most popular book was a close one. *Mere Christianity* came out on top with thirty-nine separate mentions, The Chronicles of Narnia were a close second with thirty-five, and the Space Trilogy received thirty-two votes. Whenever a respondent mentioned one of the Narnia books separately, the surprise is that *The Last Battle*, not *The Lion, the Witch, and the Wardrobe*, received more votes. For the Space Trilogy, *Perelandra* squeaked by *That Hideous Strength* by one vote, twelve to eleven.

Fourth in popularity was *The Screwtape Letters* with twenty-three tallies, followed by *The Great Divorce*, which earned nineteen. Another possibly unexpected result is that Lewis's novel *Till We Have Faces* came in sixth, with thirteen respondents claiming it as one of their favorites. That would have pleased Lewis considerably since, in his lifetime, it was not as well received as he hoped it would be; he often mentions in his letters that it was his favorite, yet his biggest failure. That assessment, over time, is not shared by many who have endorsed it enthusiastically. *The Problem of Pain* and perhaps Lewis's most famous sermon, "The Weight of Glory," took the next two places. After that, there are a number of works clustered together in a tie vote—*Miracles*, *The Abolition of Man*, *The Four Loves*, and *A Grief Observed*.

What can be said about these results? Apparently, the apologetics presented in *Mere Christianity* continue to attract people. They are drawn to Lewis's logical reasoning and his reasonable explanations for the truth of the Christian faith. After that, they appreciate his ability to bring the faith alive in the imagination through his novels—Narnia and the Space Trilogy—and also by imaginative approaches to conveying Christian beliefs—*The Screwtape Letters* and *The Great Divorce*. Those are the top five.

Are You Now, or Have You Ever Been, Involved with a C. S. Lewis Society/Organization or with Some Other Activity Connected with Lewis? Please Explain.

This section of the survey showcased just how organizations with some connection to C. S. Lewis have proliferated in America. Starting with just one in 1969, The New York C. S. Lewis Society (two of the respondents currently are connected with this group), such societies are now found in many states. Respondents noted their participation in societies located in the greater southern California area, Washington, D.C., Seattle (at which one of the respondents presented a paper), Portland (Oregon), and Pittsburgh. Others have taken part in societies outside the United States, in Toronto and, for one respondent, at Lewis's own Oxford. Universities in America also have C. S. Lewis societies; one, in particular, was noted at Southern Wesleyan University in South Carolina. A Socratic Club at Duke University was modeled after Lewis's club of the same name at Oxford. One respondent was a member of that club prior to its dissolution in 2009.

Others have been involved in organizations that are not necessarily Lewis-centric but have him as one component of their interest: a local Inklings group, in one instance, and the Mythopoeic Society for another. One respondent said, "I have started 3 Lewis Societies and visited/spoken at others in the US and UK." Four respondents have, at one time or another, worked at the Wade Center, which has only deepened their appreciation for all things Lewis. As one of those respondents remarked, "In my years as a student at Wheaton College I worked as a student employee for two years at the Wade Center as a book processor. I learned about and handled many Lewis books, letters, and artifacts at that time." Another recounts a connection with the C. S. Lewis Foundation in California, which now owns Lewis's home, the Kilns: "I visited the Kilns this past February where I met the director of the C. S. Lewis Foundation. It was wonderful to have tea with her, have a tour, walk the grounds, and walk to his old church and gravesite."

The arrival of the Internet—which was not a factor in the 1986 survey and only in its infant stages in 1996 for the second survey—was mentioned quite often as a way in which these Lewis fans have participated in activities. Six noted their membership in a Facebook page devoted to Lewis, three specifically mentioned working in connection with "NarniaWeb," and one is a participant in the "Into the Wardrobe" website. Another stated, "I am an administrator on narnia.wikia.com, an online encyclopedia about the Chronicles."

Overall, thirty-nine of the eighty-seven respondents have had some connection with a Lewis organization, a percentage that probably will only increase in the coming years as more Internet possibilities for participation increase.

Have You Viewed Any of the Shadowlands Productions? If So, What Is Your Opinion of Them?

In asking this question, I knew most people would be familiar with the big-budget Hollywood version starring Anthony Hopkins (Lewis) and Debra Winger (Joy) that came out in 1993. Not as many, I was sure, would be cognizant of the earlier BBC production from 1985 that aired on both CBS and PBS, with Joss Ackland as Lewis and Claire Bloom as Joy. Yet that BBC offering won more than a dozen prestigious awards, including the International Emmy for Best Drama and two British Academy Awards. My hope was to get comments that might compare the two, and I did get some, although the majority of respondents were, as I expected, more aware of the 1993 version. I'll begin with comments on the Hopkins-Winger movie exclusively, then move on to those that compare the two versions.

Some respondents were very pleased with the Hollywood production. As one enthused, "Beautiful story. I saw the Winger/Hopkins movie. . . . I laughed, I cried, I wept when they couldn't. From the leads to the housekeeper, beautiful casting and wonderful execution." Another explained, "I have only seen part of the Anthony Hopkins film version, but I enjoyed it. I appreciated being able to visualize Lewis as a person rather than a picture." One respondent liked it enough to keep it on the shelf: "Thought Hopkins and Winger were brilliant in the 1993 movie. Purchased the DVD and re-watch occasionally." Then there was the respondent who linked enjoyment of the film to one of Lewis's books: "I found [the] film starring Anthony Hopkins very meaningful in its own right and useful to more fully understanding *A Grief Observed*."

Others, though, thought the Hopkins-Winger version was deficient, particularly in its portrayal of Lewis's faith and the kind of man he was. As one noted, "It is a good movie, but it is absolutely false in its pale and timid portrayal of Lewis's robust personality." Another cast aspersions on the director's decision on how to portray Lewis: "Richard Attenborough's film. Serious falsification of Lewis. Simplification and belittling, as if he was a pompous idiot until Joy showed up." More than one thought Winger did an exceptional job depicting Joy, but their enthusiasm was tempered by the Lewis persona as shown in the film: "While a good movie on its own (I thought Debra Winger nailed what I think Joy was like), there was much left out, especially in relation to Lewis's faith. This was a disappointment." Others did their best to try to appreciate the good while recognizing the shortcomings. Here are two examples: "It missed much of what makes Lewis so impacting but was entertaining and enlightening into his everyday life"; "It was OK. He didn't seem like C. S. Lewis . . . not jovial enough." The reviews are mixed; this might be the best representation of those who saw the problems but still thought the movie was worthwhile:

> I was very moved by both the film (Hopkins version) and the stage version. I've always heard that Hopkins was a poor representation of Lewis and that Debra Winger did a better job portraying Joy. I think, after studying Lewis a lot more, that although not all the facts are correct, the adaptations still do capture a great spirit of the true story and are wonderful for others to watch and ponder the issues they present.

Those who saw both adaptations seemed clearly to come out in favor of the 1985 BBC TV movie. One respondent definitely preferred Ackland's Lewis to Hopkins's version, while simultaneously praising the production values of the latter: "Joss Ackland has made the best Lewis so far. The Anthony Hopkins *Shadowlands* was the best film overall, best cinematography." Another who preferred Ackland to Hopkins still had kind words for Winger's portrayal: "I think the actor portraying Lewis in the BBC version was great. I think the actress in the Hollywood version who portrayed Joy was great. I did not care for Anthony Hopkins, felt like he didn't even try to portray Lewis—just a stereotype of an English professor." This comment from another respondent was similar: "The first, BBC, version is infinitely superior in almost every regard. Closer to the facts, and more true to the spiritual journey. The only superiority of the later theatrical film is Debra Winger's performance as Joy." One summarized what seems to be the main complaint for those who were less than thrilled with Hollywood's offering: "The one with Anthony Hopkins had good acting, good production values, but the script was horrible. The one with Joss Ackland was much better."

In order to represent fairly the consensus of the survey respondents to the two films, one would have to say that, in general, for those who saw both, they acknowledged the excellent production values of Hollywood's 1993 version, but were far more enamored with the depiction of Lewis in the BBC version, which they felt was closer to the reality of who the man was.

Have You Viewed Any of the Narnia Productions, Whether the Ones Created for Television or the Three Narnia Films? If So, What Is Your Opinion of Them?

This question had the same problem as the previous one, in that not everyone would be familiar with earlier Narnia productions. Most were obviously more attuned to the more recent Hollywood movies. Yet there were some respondents with knowledge of previous attempts to make Narnia come alive on screen.

The least-known version would have to be the 1979 animated television program of *The Lion, the Witch, and the Wardrobe*. The producer for that program was Caroline Rakestraw, who founded the Episcopal Radio-TV Foundation. Rakestraw had been the driving force behind convincing Lewis, in 1958, to record sessions for the *Episcopal Radio Hour*, broadcasts that then became the basis for *The Four Loves*.

Then, from 1988–1990, the BBC produced a children's miniseries on Narnia that featured *The Lion, the Witch, and the Wardrobe*, *Prince Caspian*, *The Voyage of the Dawn Treader*, and *The Silver Chair*. The series was nominated for fourteen awards, including "Outstanding Children's Program."

As with the two versions of *Shadowlands*, I was interested in any comparisons the respondents could make among the three very different portrayals of Narnia. While comments on the latest three movies naturally dominated, there were some who could make the comparisons. I'll begin, though, as I did in the last section, by focusing on the positive reactions to the Hollywood films, then showcase the negative responses, followed by comparisons with the earlier versions.

Some respondents were fulsome in their praise of the recent movies, such as the one who commented simply, "I love them. Excellent films and all seem to follow the book fairly closely." Added to that was another's perspective: "I thought these films portrayed Lewis's books very well. They made Lewis's characters come to life." And a third contributed, "I believe they are a creative representation of the Biblical narrative that can penetrate hearts and souls." All of these responses concentrated on the substance of the films and a sense of satisfaction that they conveyed the essence of what Lewis sought to communicate. Another thought the quality of the production highlighted Lewis's themes: "Amazing! I love the graphics, the film quality supported the story line and made it so real to me."

Others, while supportive of the movies, noted some concerns about alterations of the message and about parts that were omitted and/or the addition of extra material that Lewis himself had not introduced. For instance, one respondent commented, "I thought the movies were well done, and while there were either parts from the book left out or elements added to the story, I thought the allegory was still very clearly presented. Aslan and his nature in particular were portrayed really well." A slightly more critical pose came through in this evaluation: "I have seen all three Narnia theatrical films. I enjoyed all three and thought they were generally well done. I was a little disappointed that they 'watered down' the Christian elements a bit, but I still thought they were good films and largely faithful to Lewis's ideas and vision." A third statement in this category seemed to suggest that there are natural limitations whenever one tries to convert a book into a film: "I appreciated how they brought the Narnia books to the big screen and made them understandable and attractive for a wider audience. I don't believe that the movies could ever have quite the depth of the books but I did appreciate the translation of some elements to visual art." Similar in tone was this remark: "I have viewed the first two Narnia films. I enjoyed them, but felt that the content of the Narnia stories is better communicated in book form. Film diminishes the charm of Lewis's authorial voice." Perhaps the judgment that best captures the mixed emotions of some Lewis adherents about the films is this one:

> I felt the recent ones visually captured things better and were successful at recapturing the wonder inspired by reading the books. But *The Lion, the Witch, and the Wardrobe* shortened the resurrection sequence, taking away some of the importance of the moment, which was disappointing. *Prince Caspian* departed from the book too much. *Voyage of the Dawn Treader* also departed from the book, but I felt the buildup of the dark island and the defeat of it was true to the book and in line with the allegory nature of the series.

Despite those positive and semi-positive reviews, comments decrying the loss of Lewis's vision and disappointment with some of the decisions on how to communicate the message of the books on screen were more numerous. Here are the most representative samples in this grouping:

> Disappointing. I liked the first movie, and liked the third with reservations. I refused to watch the second because of Susan being in the battle. Frankly, I think the producers sold out.

> I have seen all three films based on The Chronicles of Narnia. I think they are well done cinematically, although some scenes hint at a low budget and inexperienced actors. They maintain the integrity of Lewis's characters and stories in name and outline, but the deviations therefrom are numerous and sometimes so great as to ruin almost entirely the theological, personal, and

practical insights and applications made available in the books. I am glad they exist . . . because they get the word out, as it were, about the books, but I am concerned that the films, being somewhat shallow and noncommittal, will turn people away from what would likely be a rich and edifying literary experience. I have always thought that they could not be presented without our modern CG, but even then I felt that they could not convey the strength of the books.

I watched The Chronicles of Narnia films. I think they were good, but commercialized. I think that C. S. Lewis has saturated the market, which is good, but I believe people begin to miss the depth that he provided. Also, the struggle that C. S. Lewis had with the Christian faith. I believe that the popularity of these movies has brought popularity to C. S. Lewis, but I hope that people explore more of his works and begin to wrestle with the different thoughts and ideas that he presented.

I have been SO upset about the ways in which the movies, especially *The Voyage of the Dawn Treader*, diverged from the book. The book is my favorite of the series, as it is many others. The movie just took liberties that were "unforgivable." *Wardrobe* was good, and *Caspian* was a "B" also because of things like having the White Witch show up.

Not impressed. They lack the depth and, really, the real sadness of the books which then leads to real joy.

I was greatly disappointed with both *Prince Caspian* and *Voyage of the Dawn Treader*. These are great epics in the mind of the children and young adults who read them, but the movies left much to be desired. Besides straying from the books a great deal, they were not entirely well done. *Dawn Treader* was most guilty of this.

A few of the respondents remembered either the animated version or the BBC productions. They were not shy about making comparisons between those and the films. Generally, they believed the BBC attempt was much truer to the original stories than were the later movies. Typical of this attitude was the comment, "The BBC versions are delightful. The new films are tiresome: too much hype and drama, not enough heart." Another offered a harsher assessment, though the critique went both ways: "BBC—pretty good, cheesy, though, the SFX [special effects] are. At least they stuck to the books mostly, unlike the 3 Disney films, the first of which was not so bad, but the later films were simply disasters." Still another found one positive in the films, while nevertheless showing a preference for the BBC version: "The cinematography of the newer films far surpasses the older BBC version, but the BBC is far truer to Lewis." Sounding a similar note, this respondent opined, "The BBC series, albeit dated with the special effects, was *far* superior (imo) to the newer films. The BBC was much more faithful to the books and, to me, that is crucial. I cringe at some of the changes made to the new *PC* [*Prince Caspian*] and *VotDT* [*Voyage of the Dawn Treader*]."

Two respondents took more time dissecting their reactions to all three versions. The extra thought they put into their analyses deserves more attention, so I will give them their due. The first analysis begins, "I have seen all of the Narnia films that are currently available on DVD. The animated *LWW* was one I didn't care very much for, but that was due mostly to the style of the animation. The BBC productions I have always loved since seeing them completely." His analysis then becomes more specific as to why the BBC productions are dearer to him: "Even though the production value is far smaller than the Walden films, I still find things in the BBC versions that are definitive for me, such as Tom Baker's Puddleglum and the care the writers took to use dialogue directly from the book."

When he turns to the Hollywood films, they come in for a more searing review:

> The Walden films are more problematic for me. I love the more realistic appearance that Narnia and its inhabitants have. I dislike, with increasing force as the films have gone on, the disregard for the books that become more apparent in the later films. *LWW* is nearly perfect for my tastes, with only a few things bothering me now as I rewatch it (such as the emphasis on the Pevensies' importance vs. Aslan's). *PC*, while a good film, does not strike me as the best adaptation they could have made. It diverges from the plot and themes of the book in ways that were unnecessary to make it a good film.

He saves his most scathing comments, however, for the adaptation of *The Voyage of the Dawn Treader*: "*VDT*, with the exception of the casting of Will Poulter as Eustace, is nigh on anathema in our household. The green mist, seven swords, and complete mangling of the adventure and Eustace's and Reep's encounters with Aslan make me sick to the point that I can only watch the very beginning and very ending of the film, with perhaps the better Eustace/Reep moments in between."

The other in-depth scrutiny offers the most commentary on all three, beginning with the 1979 animated version:

> The animated one has a special place in my heart as it was the first one I saw, even before reading the books. I still think it has the best death scene of Aslan due to the poignancy and sadness of the scene and the way it captures the numinous quality of the death. All *Nature* reacts when the animated Aslan dies, making the audience and characters pause in a moment of realization for the magnitude of the act.

Remarking on both the animated *Lion, Witch, and Wardrobe* and the BBC productions, she acknowledges the critique some have of both, but feels she can overlook the deficiencies because they are outweighed by the positives: "I know the animation and the BBC version special effects are seen as 'hokey' by today's audiences, but I truly feel they captured the spirit of the books far better than the other more recent adaptations." Turning to the BBC productions specifically, she points to their strengths: "I appreciate the BBC versions for their authenticity and understanding not only the spirit of the books, but also the 'Britishness' of the characters and the story line. They are more straightforward adaptations, not a lot of frills or path-forging creativity, but have proved very enjoyable on the whole for me to watch over the years."

The Hollywood attempts do not fare nearly as well, although she does attempt to be charitable in her critique:

> I felt very disconnected from the Disney/Walden Media death scene (and movie as a whole) and felt the newer live action films lacked the understanding of the spiritual undertones of the works and Aslan's character. . . . Disney/Walden's *LWW* was the strongest of the recent films. Most people I've talked to felt that *Prince Caspian* was a huge letdown and *Voyage* could not make up the difference. The screenwriters did not seem to understand the necessary components for maintaining a believable fantasy world either. Adding things like magic swords and green mist with no explanation for them or basis in the world tore apart the cords that made the world function. The scenery and costuming were beautiful, though.

How to summarize what these C. S. Lewis adherents felt about all the attempts at putting Lewis in the visual arts is not easy. Their views are divergent, yet there are some common threads. First, most do seem to appreciate the attempts overall, even when they have concerns about accuracy. Second, for those who have seen the animated and BBC versions, appreciation for their faithfulness to the heart and soul of the stories is nearly universal. Third, of the three Hollywood films, *The Lion, the Witch, and the Wardrobe* comes across as the best. Fourth, there is a strong sense of disappointment in Hollywood's renditions of *Prince Caspian* and *The Voyage of the Dawn Treader*. Fifth, although there is criticism of deviations in the Hollywood scripts and depictions, nearly all agree the special effects are superior.

Other Details about Your Lewis Experience That You Would Like to Share

The survey ended with an invitation for respondents to say anything else they felt was significant about their C. S. Lewis experience. Nearly all did write something more, so I have had to choose what I consider to be either the most representative samples of those comments or ones that are unique enough to warrant attention.

A number of respondents credit Lewis with halting their slide into unbelief while in college. "Lewis sustained me through years of doubting my faith in college," wrote one. "I'm not exaggerating to say that Lewis re-evangelized me when I might have otherwise abandoned my childhood faith." "Lewis, along with Francis Schaeffer," opined another, "helped me to remain orthodox while most of my college friends have fallen by the wayside. My first published novel . . . is in part a tribute to *That Hideous Strength*." Still another remembered,

> When I was an arrogant college student who believed only weak and/or stupid people believed in Christ, Lewis showed me beyond question that faith could make sense even to an intellectual. He awakened my spiritual imagination with his fiction and persuaded my reason with his nonfiction. He also gave me a grounding in traditional Christianity that facilitated my later conversion to Orthodoxy.

A respondent who is currently working through a doctoral degree had this to say about how Lewis provides help: "Lewis is frequently on the tip of my tongue—his characters remain alive in my heart as friends and relatives—his lessons often spring to mind. As a doctoral student in theology, I often find connections to Puddleglum or Eustace at the heart of theological arguments." And those who have moved on into their careers, such as this respondent, can also point to Lewis as an inspiration: "I have always appreciated Lewis's clear, precise, and elegant writing style. As an academic researcher, I have tried to emulate his style in my professional writing." Another provided a more in-depth scrutiny of how Lewis dealt with the intellect:

Lewis's works exemplify what I consider a Holy Spirit baptized intellect. Knowledge on holy fire. His ability to frame the issues in a succinct way and then address them with such extremely critical thinking skills provides a wonderful exemplar for Christians all over the world on how to not only be people of faith, but also engage our intellect (verbal and writing skills) to provide a "defense for the hope that is within us." His work, *Mere Christianity*, remains one of my favorite recommendations for intellectual unbelievers who are serious about weighing through claims of Christian faith. I believe many will either embrace Christ for the first time or reinforce their beliefs in Him through its reading.

"Since my study of C. S. Lewis, I have not been able to talk about anything else," enthused one respondent. "It is as though I am on fire after having been asleep." Beyond the purely intellectual appeal, Lewis and his writings also have impacted the emotions and encouraged Christians in their various struggles. "I am working through some very difficult personal and family issues at this point in my life, and Lewis's Space Trilogy has Ransom, its protagonist, facing challenges that are shockingly relatable, in spite of their obvious differences in nature," related another respondent. "I have no Unman to fight off, for example, but the nearly overwhelming burden of evil is clear and present. God has used these books in particular, as well as all of Lewis's work in general, to improve my life and my understanding of His holy nature." One woman was willing to share her personal struggles and how staying in touch with Lewis made a huge difference in her life:

> When I walked away from my Christian faith during my twenties and early thirties, Lewis was one of the few Christian authors I still trusted and could stand to read. I was grieving, angry, and depressed, and when I reread The Chronicles of Narnia, the hope that shone through them was almost painful. Emotionally, it was as though a frozen and numb part of me began to regain feeling. Some years later, a passage from *The Screwtape Letters* was instrumental in helping me realize that I'd been angry at the church when, in fact, the church had been my truest friends and best support through very dark days.

Another had the privilege of spending some time at Lewis's home, the Kilns, and came away humbled by the experience. He and his wife sometimes read Lewis aloud to one another in the evenings. "I've never read a story, book, or essay by him I did not enjoy. Even his literary criticism is wonderful!" One sentence from another respondent speaks of how Lewis has made God more real to him: "I find very moving the endings of *Perelandra, Voyage of the Dawn Treader, The Last Battle,* and *The Great Divorce*; where the veil is briefly pulled back and God's reality shines in."

Narnia, naturally, has impacted those who were first introduced to Lewis as children. One comment might express how many children have felt after reading those books: "As a kid when I was sick I used to pray, 'God, I don't care if I die as long as you take me to Narnia.'" There was one respondent, though, who went into greater detail on how Narnia affected, and continues to affect, her. She had much more to say than what is quoted here, but this selection adequately reflects her views:

> Perhaps the most thrilling liberation of being a child in Narnia is Lewis's assertion that children can understand complex things. The problem with most children's TV shows, children's books, children's anything is that they work too hard to suit children. Books that oversimplify ideas so children can understand them teach children to think simplistically. All sorts of ideas from Lewis's non-fiction work and from classical philosophers appear somewhere in Narnia. I discovered Aristotelian logic from Professor Kirke, Plato's Theory of Forms in Aslan's country, and the fallacious nonsense of an ad hoc rescue from Narnian dwarves. I love Narnia not only because I find things to ponder in it, but because it taught me how to ponder. C. S. Lewis created a complex world, and it taught me to think complex thoughts. I am content in Narnia not because I am comfortable, but because I am uncomfortable. It stretches me—my leadership, my character, and my understanding. It acknowledges not that I am a grown-up, but that I am a person, and therefore capable of maturity regardless of my age.

While that excerpt from a more lengthy comment focused entirely on Narnia, another respondent sought to explore the wider scope of Lewis's writings:

> C. S. Lewis manages to express in many unique and wonderful ways ideas about Christianity that are difficult to describe. Narnia tells of a lion whom you fear, but is good—we should fear God, but love God. *Screwtape* shows how devious and unrelenting (even in the face of conversion of the subject) Satan can be in the temptations of a person/Christian. In *Mere Christianity, Surprised by Joy,* "The Weight of Glory," etc., Lewis expresses truths about Christianity in practical and meaningful ways that are easy to understand and remember. I love the variety of his writings.

Yet it is not only the writings of C. S. Lewis that have captured the hearts of many; it is also the man himself. As one wrote, "We've all heard the question of what single person, living or dead, we would most like to meet. I can name dozens of intriguing figures I would love to meet, but none so much as Lewis." Another expressed the identical sentiment, but in a different way, when she shared this hope: "I long to go with others on a walking tour in heaven with Jack (as he used to do with Warnie and others) and have a good lengthy chat with this man who for years now has seemed like a good, dear friend."

Conclusion

This survey focused on Americans only and made no attempt to compare Lewis's influence with a modern British readership. Alister McGrath's comment that Americans have appreciated Lewis more than their British counterparts may still hold true, but perhaps there is a glimmer of hope. The inclusion of a Lewis memorial in Poets Corner in Westminster Cathedral, placed there in November 2013 to commemorate his death fifty years earlier, may be a sign that more Britons are becoming aware of his significance. One would hope that his native nation would awaken more to his contributions.

Regardless, for those who completed this survey, there is no doubt that C. S. Lewis remains a source of spiritual strength and intellectual rigor for many American Christians. He has kept many from losing their faith while in college; his books continue to sell briskly more than half a century after he penned his last one; he has inspired children with his Narnia tales and introduced them to Christ in the form of a beloved lion; societies are springing up throughout the land devoted to the study of Lewis; and major Hollywood movies have attempted to put his vision and message into the mainstream of American entertainment. C. S. Lewis appears to be in America to stay.

9

Conclusion: The C. S. Lewis Impact on America

THIS VOLUME BEGAN WITH some scrutiny of C. S. Lewis's attitude toward Americans, showing that whatever false impressions and/or biases he may have exhibited about America and Americans lessened over time as he dealt more directly with individual Americans. It continued with an examination of how American Chad Walsh was converted largely through Lewis's writings, and how he wrote the first book to evaluate Lewis and his approach to the Christian faith. Then Joy Davidman Gresham entered the picture, another American—Jewish, atheist, and communist—who also credited Lewis with her Christian commitment. The added feature, of course, is that she became his wife. Lewis's relationship with her was deep and fulfilling.

Lewis then, in the last year of his life, become good friends with Walter Hooper, an American whose greatest joy in life was to meet Lewis face-to-face and delve into his mind. That relationship burgeoned into an invitation from Lewis for Hooper to be his secretary, a goal cut short by Lewis's death. Yet Hooper remained in Britain and became the editor of Lewis's works and a trustee of his estate. The next chapter highlighted a number of friendships Lewis developed with American academics, Clyde Kilby and Sheldon Vanauken being the most prominent. It also covered the panoply of scholars who never met him personally but who are heavily indebted to his works and the pervasiveness of Lewis's influence among the American clergy and others who work in Christian ministry, not the least example of which was Charles Colson, founder of Prison Fellowship. Chapter six was a detailed look at some of Lewis's regular American correspondents: how he devoted himself to answering them all, no matter how trivial the subject; how he counseled them in their personal problems; how he discussed significant topics, whether theological, literary, or governmental.

After all those chapters that dealt with Lewis's personal relationships and correspondences, the book turned to the key C. S. Lewis organizations in America and their missions. These organizations have been inspired by Lewis to promote his works and his ideas, to create ministries that develop mature disciples of Christ, and even to dream of establishing a C. S. Lewis College. One of them went so far as to purchase the Kilns, turning it into a study center for American scholars. Finally, this examination of Lewis's impact on America focused on three surveys that elicited responses from individuals who trace either their salvation or their substantial growth in the faith to the influence of Lewis. The latest survey not only sought testimonies, but it also asked further probing questions about how people were first introduced to Lewis, which of his writings were of the greatest importance to them, to what extent they are involved in a Lewis organization, and their opinions on the cinematic attempts to portray Lewis himself and The Chronicles of Narnia.

Taken together, all the information shared thus far in this book indicates Lewis has exerted a formidable sway over the nature of American Christianity, particularly the evangelical variety, of the twentieth century, an influence that now extends into the twenty-first and seems unlikely to stop anytime soon. As historian Mark Noll has noted as just one example, the July–August 2012 issue of *Touchstone: A Journal of Mere Christianity*, cited Lewis twenty-two times in its various articles, yet not one of those articles was about him specifically.[1] He sometimes appears to be omnipresent. How do we account for this in America precisely?

What Has Been Lewis's Impact on America and Why Is He So Popular? Chad Walsh's Analysis

A few Lewis scholars have attempted to offer reasons for Lewis's American popularity, beginning with his close friend, Chad Walsh. His reflections and views on this topic might be dated now, since they were penned in 1976, but they are still important as a snapshot of what an admirer of Lewis believed slightly more than a decade after his death. Walsh began his thoughts with a concern that the job of assessing Lewis's impact on America might be too great a task for a single individual. He joked that he probably should follow the "good American fashion" in which one approaches "one of the

---

1. Noll, "C. S. Lewis in America, 1932–1945."

great philanthropic organizations and ask for an adequate grant and a staff of social scientists to accomplish the field work" of sending out questionnaires and dispatching "a crew of interviewers to question a sufficient cross-section of the population." He concluded, though, that "short of a grand scale sociological enterprise of this kind," he would have to settle for his "own personal impressions based on hit-or-miss witness" for the twenty years between the publication of *The Screwtape Letters* in its 1943 American edition and Lewis's death. His first personal impression in his article is the declaration that "during those two decades I am convinced that he had an impact on American religious thinking and indeed on the American religious imagination which has been very rarely, if ever, equaled by any other modern writer."[2]

As noted in the first chapter, Walsh dates the onset of fascination with Lewis on the American side of the Atlantic with the success of *Screwtape*: "The combination of urbanity, wit, imagination and uncompromising orthodoxy caught the imagination of many reviewers and a large reading public." It was so different from other religious works of the era that many Americans found they now had "a religious book, indeed a specifically Christian book, written with such sophistication and elegance that one need not apologize for leaving it out on the coffee table."[3]

What other factors did Walsh point to as reasons for Lewis's popularity? He thought perhaps Lewis's status as an "amateur" might have helped. What he meant by that is Lewis was not a clergyman, yet wrote on religious topics. Of course, that was a critical accusation against Lewis at Oxford, that he was out of his field writing about such issues as the problem of pain and miracles. For Americans, though, this was a plus. They had a tendency to view theologians "as being up in the clouds and not saying anything too relevant to the earth as it actually exists," Walsh theorized. Lewis had solid academic credentials "in a field which most people might not understand but at least vaguely respected," and with this as a basis, "he was able to venture forth into theology and gain a more respectful hearing with many readers than would have been possible if he had been a seminary professor." The reading public knew his livelihood did not depend on his religious beliefs the way a clergyman's did, so they "were willing to listen to him."[4]

Walsh also attempted some analysis of Lewis's readership. What types of people were attracted to him? He supposed most were "high-brow and middle-brow," yet he suspected that the audience also included "people of

2. Walsh, "Impact on America," 106.
3. Ibid., 109.
4. Ibid., 110.

quite humble educational and intellectual backgrounds" who "found much meat in his writing." Those with a literary tendency would "intuitively" recognize Lewis "as one of themselves—not only because of his professional area of specialization, but because of the civilized way he wrote."[5] Walsh himself was a literature professor, so he naturally would see the connection there. He also had been a religious skeptic until Lewis turned his thinking around, and he saw skeptics as another segment to whom Lewis would appeal. "America now has a fair number of second and third generation agnostics," Walsh commented. "What these various readers had in common was a desire for a religious faith which would have its roots sunk deep in the main Christian tradition but which would not do violence to their intellects and knowledge. They wanted 'orthodoxy,' not 'an obscurantist fundamentalism.' They found what they were looking for in Lewis," he affirmed.[6]

Walsh also looked at the era in which Lewis became well known and decided he had been "lucky in his timing." The Second World War, with its suffering and death, opened people up more to religious themes. The decade and a half from that war until about 1960 saw an increase in active church involvement in America. That interest was reflected in the publishing trade. "Soon many publishing houses that had brought out only an occasional religious book were setting up special departments. Religion was in the air." Writing from his perspective in 1976, Walsh concluded, "At any rate, religion was in the public eye to a greater extent than it had been previously and more than it is today." This interest in religion "coincided with the time when the enthusiasm for C. S. Lewis was most evident in America."[7]

Interestingly, Walsh also felt that Lewis was generally appreciated by most of the professional theologians in America.

> Though many of them must have felt that he stated things too simply and almost too clearly they were glad to have such a gifted ally in the war against secularist thought. His works were particularly popular with clergy who were on the intellectual firing line—for example, college and university chaplains. It sometimes seemed that they bought his books by the gross in order to give them to eager young intellectuals who were disturbed by religious questions.[8]

Walsh then turned to the America of his day, in 1976, and analyzed what had changed. As a college professor himself, he had firsthand

---

5. Ibid., 110–11.
6. Ibid., 111.
7. Ibid. 112–13.
8. Ibid., 113.

knowledge of the campus atmosphere. What he saw was that students talked less about religion than before. They were not much concerned with what was true or false theologically; if they thought of religion at all, it was only to wonder how it was any longer relevant. Social unrest and politics dominated this new era. Walsh's analysis continued,

> The most profound expression of religious feeling among young people in America today is probably membership in the Peace Corps or participation in inter-racial activities and demonstrations. It is action rather than talk and theorizing. To such young persons Lewis seems much too theoretical and abstract. They find in his books very little having to do with political and social questions and it is these dilemmas that dominate the thought and feeling of ... young people in America today.... The intellectual climate in America is increasingly dominated by a kind of diffused existentialism. It is not that most people, whether university students or not, have read the works of the existentialists, but rather that an existentialist stance has somehow come into being. Lewis's schematic works do not fit well with the existentialists' toe-hold in the universe.[9]

Walsh cannot be faulted for not seeing the future, but it was almost at the exact time he was writing this essay that a Lewis revival was underway. The mid- to late-1970s saw an upsurge in evangelicalism's fascination with Lewis. Walsh also made a prediction about the staying power of Lewis's works that has turned out to be only half accurate. He did not believe that Lewis's apologetic offerings, including his *Mere Christianity*, would remain popular. Yet, as noted in chapter one, *Christianity Today* declared it to be the most influential Christian book of the twentieth century.[10] Walsh was more on target, though, with his prediction about Lewis's imaginative books: Narnia, *Screwtape*, *The Great Divorce*, and the Space Trilogy. He felt they would "live on with full force and become a permanent part of the literary and religious heritage.... In these books where his imagination has full scope he presents the Christian faith in a more eloquent and probing way than ever his more straightforward books of apologetics could. These books are not for a day but for a very long time to come."[11]

Another prescient comment he made at the end of this essay had to do with the lack of knowledge that existed in 1976 concerning all those letters Lewis wrote to Americans. "Only after as many of his letters as possible

---

9. Ibid., 115.
10. Marsden, "*Mere Christianity* and American Culture."
11. Walsh, "Impact on America," 116.

have been collected will it be possible to know how many Americans corresponded with him occasionally or on a more-or-less regular basis," Walsh noted. "Any consideration of his impact on America must take these letters into account."[12] That is exactly what this current study has done.

What Has Been Lewis's Impact on America and Why Is He So Popular? Philip Ryken's Analysis

Speaking to the Oxford University C. S. Lewis Society in 1995, Philip Ryken gave what might be the most detailed attempt to explain Lewis's popularity in America. He pinpointed a number of characteristics of Lewis's life and works that he thought might "account for his stature among American evangelicals." The first one he identified was simply that Lewis was British. As he put it,

> Lewis evokes for Americans all the sophistication and quaintness of England. To read Lewis is to enter a world where school children wait on railway platforms at the end of their holidays or crawl from attic to attic in London rowhouses. It is a world where people use torches instead of flashlights and listen to the wireless rather than the radio. It is a world where, wonder of wonders, Turkish Delight is available in all the shops!

And to top it off, Lewis taught at Oxford, which for many Americans, "is the quintessence of England."[13]

A second reason noted by Ryken is a bit more complicated. He thought evangelicals' attraction to Lewis could have something to do with their love of allegory, i.e., their love of a tale "in which central characters and episodes display direct correspondence with theological truths." The complication is that, except for *The Pilgrim's Regress*, Lewis didn't consider his works to be allegorical. Nevertheless, because his fiction is "saturated with doctrinal themes," evangelicals can relate to them. "And to Lewis's claim that 'any amount of theology can be smuggled into people's minds under cover of romance without their knowing it,' the evangelical utters a heartfelt, 'Amen.'"[14]

A third link between Lewis and evangelicals, according to Ryken, is his deep belief in a conversion experience, as indicated by Lewis's own life as he altered his belief from atheism to orthodox Christianity. "American evangelicals," Ryken argued, "are not surprised by *Surprised by Joy*." Ryken agreed that, as Lewis himself said, most of his works were evangelistic in

---

12. Ibid.
13. Ryken, "Patron Saint," 70.
14. Ibid., 71–72.

nature. Yet "much of his apologetic work has an off-hand style about it, as if to say: 'Look here, Christianity seem ever so reasonable to me, and here's why, but you can take it or leave it.' His apologetic method sometimes lacks the 'You must be born again' asseveration of Jesus in the Gospels."[15] However, his own conversion settles the matter for most evangelicals. This meshes with another factor—Lewis's clear writing on the need for a close fellowship with God, which is the essence of the evangelicals' concept of a "personal relationship" with Christ. Lewis wrote often of the need for a daily time of prayer and Bible reading, an emphasis entirely in line with evangelical teaching.

A final aspect of Lewis's popularity with Americans, Ryken felt, has been The Chronicles of Narnia. "It seems unlikely that the Narnia Chronicles will fall out of favour," Ryken predicted, "at least while the West remains literate. C. S. Lewis is the patron saint of American evangelicalism because he is *fun for the whole family*." Ryken provided a personal testimony at this point: "I first encountered *The Lion, the Witch and the Wardrobe* before I was able to read it myself. Even before that time, I heard the name of C. S. Lewis uttered in reverential tones. If he was not a family member, he was at least someone we knew well."[16] Ryken's father taught at Wheaton, and that afforded the son the opportunity to see firsthand many Lewis artifacts, including Lewis's drawings of his Boxen stories from his childhood. Yet there was one artifact that dwarfed all others:

> More impressive than Lewis's juvenilia was the richly carved and ornamented wardrobe which then guarded the entrance to the English Department. It was, of course, *the* wardrobe which had belonged to Lewis's grandfather and had been shipped from Belfast for reassembly. Westmont College in California rescued a second wardrobe from the Kilns, Lewis's home near Oxford. At Wheaton we have always recognized the Westmont wardrobe as an impostor, although some insist that the Westmont wardrobe more closely matches the description in *The Lion, the Witch and the Wardrobe*. In any case, that Lewis's personal effects can arouse such an argument demonstrates that he has become the patron saint of American evangelicalism. Few things convey legitimacy upon a potential saint as effectively as disputed relics.[17]

Ryken concluded with one more possibility for Lewis's fame in America: in short, he said "there are many Lewises to love." What he meant is

---

15. Ibid., 73.
16. Ibid., 75.
17. Ibid., 76.

that evangelicals have a lot to choose from among Lewis's writings. If one doesn't have a hankering for apologetics precisely, he can turn to the imaginative works. That works in the opposite direction, too, of course. There is a breadth to Lewis that allows evangelicals to pick and choose. And, as noted previously, there is Lewis's omnipresent quality:

> One can scarcely read a magazine or listen to a sermon without hearing a quotation from C. S. Lewis. What evangelical has not heard Lewis's account of his conversion, or his "further up, further in" description of heaven in *The Last Battle*, or the "liar, lunatic or Lord" trilemma from *Mere Christianity*, or any number of other well-known quotations from his writings? Already in the 1970s, Michael J. Christensen observed that "it is quite fashionable these days to quote Lewis on any number of theological subjects as an authority approaching that of a church father." The Lewis quotation is the religious equivalent of the political sound byte, and every bit as American.[18]

What Has Been Lewis's Impact on America and Why Is He So Popular? Alister McGrath's Analysis

As mentioned in the preface to this book, the genesis of this study came from a comment by Alister McGrath in his biography of Lewis when he stated rather categorically, "Lewis has always been appreciated more in the United States than in England."[19] While he did not follow up with a full explanation of that statement, he did devote a few pages to the subject. In his overview, he showed how American evangelicals shifted from a fundamentalism that promoted "cultural disengagement and isolationism" to a more active engagement with the "mainstream American culture," a shift helped along by the influence of Billy Graham and Carl F. H. Henry. "This new form of American evangelicalism," McGrath opined, "was a strongly populist movement, capturing the hearts and wills of many. But many noted that it had yet to engage the mind, or see the importance of connecting with the intellectual subculture."[20] That is where Lewis came in.

Another British evangelical, John R. W. Stott, entered the fray with a well-received book, *Basic Christianity*, which appeared in 1958. McGrath considers it "a masterpiece of reasoned argument," and it dovetailed nicely

---

18. Ibid., 77.
19. McGrath, *C. S. Lewis, A Life*, 369.
20. Ibid., 372.

with American evangelicals' greater discovery of Lewis, which McGrath dates as starting in the mid-1970s.[21] This study already has documented that Lewis began receiving a flood of mail from Americans from the mid-1940s until his death in 1963, so it would be misleading to say that evangelicals did not read Lewis or know about him earlier, but his mass appeal, according to McGrath, began at this later date. If he had lived into the 1970s, letters from Americans would have overwhelmed him even more. Another spur to Lewis's popularity among evangelicals was the testimony of Charles Colson in his book *Born Again*, which, as explained in an earlier chapter, gave credit to Lewis for his conversion.

Stott's apologetics and Lewis's differed in approach. Stott's assumed some Biblical knowledge already present in his readers; Lewis's did not, as he wrote to an audience he presumed needed some general principles and observations based on "shared human experience." That meant Lewis's works were more useful as evangelistic tools to speak to the atheist/agnostic portion of the population. One Christian ministry more attuned to reaching out to intellectuals who did not have a Biblical basis was InterVarsity Christian Fellowship, which became a mainstay on many university campuses. InterVarsity used Lewis materials extensively. McGrath declared,

> As American evangelicals read Lewis, they encountered a vision of the Christian faith that they found to be intellectually robust, imaginatively compelling, and ethically fertile. Those who initially valued Lewis for his rational defence of the Christian faith now found themselves appreciating his appeal to the imagination and emotions. Lewis's multilayered conception of Christianity enabled evangelicals to realise that they could enrich their faith without diluting it, and engage secular culture in ways other than through reasoned argument.[22]

When the philosophical trends eventually led to postmodernism, Lewis became even more attractive, according to McGrath. The rigid rationalism of someone like Stott faded during this time, and the narrative and imaginative mode of Lewis's thinking became more prominent. As American evangelicals began to turn to the arts to make their case, Lewis was their guide. McGrath believes that Lewis "has been instrumental in changing the cultural outlook of American evangelicalism." No longer were evangelicals as suspicious of conveying their message through literature, films, and the other arts. "Evangelical admiration for Lewis may have begun with respect

---

21. Ibid.
22. Ibid., 373–74.

for his ideas; it soon developed into a respect for the modes and manners in which Lewis expressed those ideas."[23]

McGrath's conclusion is partly based on his own personal experience teaching some American evangelical university students.

> Since 1985, I have taught at summer schools in Oxford attended by large numbers of young American evangelicals. Lewis has been a topic of conversation throughout that entire period. At the time of writing, there is not the slightest sign of any loss of interest. On the basis of those extended conversations over a quarter of a century, I have come to my own conclusion about why Lewis appeals so powerfully to a rising evangelical generation in the United States: Lewis is seen to enrich and extend faith, without diluting it. In other words, evangelicals tend to see Lewis as a catalyst, who opens up a deeper vision of the Christian faith, engaging the mind, the feelings, and the imagination, without challenging fundamental distinctives. . . . For many young evangelicals, reading Lewis gives added depth and power to their evangelical commitments.[24]

What Has Been Lewis's Impact on America and Why Is He So Popular? A Wheaton Seminar's Analysis

On 1 November 2013, Wheaton College assembled a panel of Lewis experts to deal specifically with the topic of Lewis's impact on America. This special event was the C. S. Lewis and American Culture Seminar, with two American historians, Mark Noll and George Marsden, an American professor of English, Alan Jacobs, and a professor of divinity from the University of St. Andrews in Scotland, Trevor Hart. Each presented a paper on some aspect of Lewis's influence and popularity in America, and all then participated in question-and-answer sessions with the audience.

Mark Noll led off the seminar with his topic, "C. S. Lewis in America, 1932–1945," uncovering the early years of Lewis's contacts with Americans and how they received him. He showed how the first acknowledgements of Lewis came from Catholic sources and a few academics who read *The Pilgrim's Regress* and *The Allegory of Love*. When mainline Protestantism began commenting on his works, the reviews were mixed, and more critical than those from Catholic reviewers. What seemed to surprise Noll the most,

---

23. Ibid., 374.
24. Ibid., 375.

though, was how Lewis was picked up by mainstream media publications of the era, such as *Time* magazine, revealing, even as Chad Walsh noted in his analysis of Lewis's influence, a strong interest in Christianity in postwar America that allowed the Christian faith and authors who devoted their writing to it to be considered part of mainstream culture at that time.[25]

Marsden followed Noll with "*Mere Christianity* and American Culture," an examination of the continuing impact of that book on Americans' thinking. He noted that its popularity took off after Lewis's death, spurred on by Clyde Kilby's *The Christian World of C. S. Lewis*, which was published in 1964. Marsden then gave his reasons for why *Mere Christianity* was, as he put it, "such a breath of fresh air" to American Christians. His first reason is that Lewis always looks to the timeless truths as opposed to ideas that are culturally bound. He was grounded in history, whereas many American Christians looked to the Bible, but then had a tendency to skip over the next nineteen centuries. They were not historically connected, Marsden argued, and would therefore come up with innovations at times that might not have any foundation in Christian history. Lewis provided the background they needed.

A second reason is that Lewis's point of contact with his audience was always "perennial human nature." His immersion in literature helped him see the commonality of humanity and actually helped him relate better to everyone. He was the opposite of the stereotype of the ivory tower academic, a false image that led many to critique the *Shadowlands* film. Marsden commented that this is why, when asked to do the BBC broadcasts in World War II, he knew where to start, where his audience was in their thinking.

The third reason Marsden gives for the popularity of *Mere Christianity* is the clarity of language Lewis used, along with his effective use of imagination, metaphor, and analogy. Some have mistakenly dismissed Lewis as a rational apologist, Marsden said. While there are certainly rational arguments put forth in the book, even in that apologetic manual Lewis appealed to the imagination equally.

Fourth, Marsden believed that the subject itself—mere Christianity—had an innate appeal. Lewis avoided all controversies among Christians on specific doctrines and focused entirely on what all Christians believe, and have believed throughout history. What stands out, though, is that his treatment did not devolve into a "lowest-common-denominator Christianity." Rather, he presents Christianity as a substantial and powerful force. As to why the book continues to sell, Marsden concluded that the appeal is even wider today due to the current era being more post-denominational.

25. Noll, "C. S. Lewis in America, 1932–1945."

Finally, Marsden pointed out that the Christianity Lewis offered the reader was not one of cheap grace. Readers instead find themselves drawn into a Christianity that is demanding upon them personally, losing one's self-centeredness and becoming more Christlike. The call to discipleship is attractive.[26]

In the panel discussion that occurred later, Marsden gave his assent to one of the reasons offered by Ryken for Lewis's appeal—that Americans give more weight to British thought, to some extent, simply because of the accent. Although Americans did not hear Lewis speak, there was a bent toward respecting anyone who was a smart Christian, especially if "Oxford" or "Cambridge" were attached.[27]

Alan Jacobs, who followed after Marsden, gave his testimony of discovering Lewis as a nineteen-year-old Alabama boy who walked into a Christian bookstore in the 1970s and bought *Mere Christianity*, the volume that propelled him forward into his Christian life and into everything that has happened to him since. Jacobs opined that Americans' ignorance of Lewis's background might be one key to his acceptance. Americans, Jacobs said, have no idea what it means to be an ordinary layman in the Church of England. Since Lewis did not fit into the typical landscape of American religious life, they had to evaluate him purely on the basis of what he had to offer. If they had been familiar with the Church of England they might have had some baggage of their own to discard before listening to what he had to say; since they had no such baggage, and were free of the subsequent bias that some Englishmen would have, they were more open to his writings.

With respect to those writings, Jacobs added that even though Americans are not as familiar with Lewis's academic works, his breadth of knowledge comes across in his popular works also. So he is not merely perceived as brainy or smart only in a narrow sense, such as in theology, but also in the wider sense. The reader feels good about Lewis's broad base of knowledge, which lends itself to his persuasiveness.[28]

Trevor Hart's presentation, "C. S. Lewis and America From the Other Side of the Pond," opened with a number of Lewis's imaginative responses to letters from Americans, and also included some of his critiques of America (refer back to chapter one). In attempting to answer the question as to why he was so accepted by Americans, Hart offered a list in no particular order of significance:

- His lucidity as a writer;

26. Marsden, "*Mere Christianity* and American Culture."
27. Panel discussion in connection with Jacobs, "Response to Noll and Marsden."
28. Ibid.

- His wit and intellect;
- His ability to aim at the weakest points in an opponent's armor;
- His unashamed love for the wisdom of the past rather than jumping on every passing intellectual bandwagon;
- His eye for the identifiably human—that which pops up in all of humanity; he has the sense of the "transhistorical," that which applies to everyone's personal experience, such as pain, sin, and death;
- His air of culture and sophistication;
- His attempt to heal the rift between imagination and reason.

In response to a question about why the British are not as enamored with Lewis as Americans, Hart thought that one reason may be that the British, and the Christians in Britain specifically, do not buy books with the same regularity as Americans do. Christian bookstores do not flourish there like they do in America. He also pointed to a distinction in perception: Americans like the "air" of the Oxford-Cambridge feel, whereas the British do not have quite the same respect or awe for that heritage. They are too close to it; perhaps distance gives it more of a "flavor" or "fascination."[29]

What Has Been Lewis's Impact on America and Why Is He So Popular? A Personal Analysis

There is value in every proposition offered by the analysts noted above. I could repeat everything they said and add a simple "amen." Instead, I will try to draw out of their responses what I consider to be the most important factors for the phenomenon of Lewis's popularity and for his impact on America.

I do think there is validity in the idea that Britishness has an inherent appeal to a large number of Americans, including American evangelicals. American culture seems to have a fascination with an image of what it means to be British. A royal couple has a royal baby and a significant segment of the population on this side of the Atlantic hangs on every news bulletin. What will they name this child? When can we see him/her? There is a subgroup of Americans who are enamored with Sherlock Holmes and anything that smacks of British mysteries, and how can one account for the avid following of a series such as *Downton Abbey* unless there is a reservoir of special feeling for the Britain of yesteryear? One might be led to wonder,

29. Hart, "Other Side of the Pond."

at times, whether the Declaration of Independence ever was penned and a war fought over that issue.

So, yes, there is a natural attraction for many to an image of Britain that plays in their minds. And yes, C. S. Lewis fits into that image for many Christians. I will admit to being drawn to the British accent and the spires of Oxford and Cambridge. There is an "otherness" about it for Americans that can be fascinating. Further, Lewis's connection to those universities adds to that image because he was an intellectual who commanded respect for his wide learning. American Christians, whether of wide learning themselves or not, find that appealing. I have heard recordings of Lewis's voice—the ones he did for the Episcopal Radio-TV ministry—that are rather mesmerizing. He comes across with a rich, full brogue that captivates while delivering real substance.

That is the second factor. Substance. No matter how British one may be, and regardless of the appeal of that Britishness, for Christians that can never be enough. There must be something communicated that is worth reading and learning. What American Christians, especially evangelicals, want to see is fidelity to Scripture—faithfulness to the truth. They witness that in Lewis. While there are quibbles over his view of Scripture—how he handles the inerrancy issue, for instance—it is clear that he believes Scripture is the only genuine authority to follow for the Christian life. His apologetic works are foundational; that is why they are used so often to reach out to the agnostics and atheists. Confidence that Lewis is grounded in the Word is essential to American evangelicals. They have that confidence.

Then there is his style of writing. It has all the features that Trevor Hart listed above: he is lucid and witty; he aims for the weakest point in another's argument and hits his target; he writes with an eye for history and with an ability to empathize with his readers; he easily combines rational thought with vivid imagination. There is a reason why C. S. Lewis quotes abound on the Internet—he is just so quotable. The key is to authenticate those quotes since there is a tendency to attribute something to Lewis he never said. Yet even all those misattributions attest to the desire to emulate his pithiness.

Additionally, as some of the analysts mentioned, his fiction works, especially The Chronicles of Narnia, have stood the test of time. Each emerging generation, particularly in American evangelical households, is reared on a lion named Aslan, a world of talking animals interacting with humans from our earth, and examples of courage and faithfulness to the truth. As each generation matures, *Out of the Silent Planet*, *Perelandra*, *That Hideous Strength*, *The Screwtape Letters*, and *The Great Divorce* are added to their enjoyment and instruction. None of these books have ever gone out of print, and they are unlikely ever to do so.

CONCLUSION: THE C. S. LEWIS IMPACT ON AMERICA

There is another factor with respect to Lewis's favorable reception in America that none of the analysts mentioned, but which deserves some comment. America, despite the loosening of ties to Christian faith, is still the home of a more vibrant and public Christian orthodoxy, evangelical and otherwise, than is Britain. In 2013, only 10 percent of the British population were church members. Of course, being a member of a church is not the same as being a committed Christian who attends regularly and devotes himself/herself to Christian service. That percentage is significantly lower than mere membership rolls indicate. The only reason the membership rate is as high as 10 percent, according to a recent study, is that there has been a mass migration from Eastern Europe and Africa into Britain lately, bringing with it resurgent numbers for the Catholic Church via Polish immigrants and a rising number of Pentecostal churches stemming from the African immigrants.[30] Statistics on American church attendance are controversial at present, with some polls indicating up to 37 percent regular attendance, while other studies show only about 20 percent.[31] Most agree, though, that the evangelical segment of the American churches has done much better than mainline denominations, which are losing members at a rapid rate as they increasingly depart from traditional Biblical doctrines. Regardless of which statistic is correct with regard to overall attendance, it is still clear that there is a larger portion of the American population connected to orthodox Christianity than in Britain. That, in itself, provides Lewis's works with a broader and a far more interested and motivated audience.

For all those reasons, and undoubtedly more, Lewis has developed a true fan following in America. This book has shown his many interactions with Americans of his day. He became good friends with many of them, whether in person or via mail. His correspondence is overflowing with responses to Americans on the full panoply of issues, and he was quite willing to share the progress of his personal life and faith with them as well. He married an American. The man he thought would serve best as his personal secretary was an American. Thousands of Americans he never communicated with or met, both during his lifetime and after, have testified to their lives being changed by his words. Societies bearing his name have cropped up all over the United States. One institute has developed a discipleship program inspired by him. An American foundation named after him bought his home in Oxford and uses it as a study center. That same foundation is now working to establish a college named after him. While it is impossible

30. Gledhill, "Church Attendance Has Been Propped Up by Immigrants, Says Study."
31. Shattuck, "7 Startling Facts: An Up Close Look at Church Attendance in America."

to quantify his impact on America and Americans, the documentary evidence is plentiful that American Christians look to him in a way that is unique among all the Christian writers and teachers, both past and present, available to them as mentors.

In one of Lewis's essays, "Is Theology Poetry?" we see a shining example of all the features of his writing that appeal, not only to Americans, but to all who thrill at hearing words of truth communicated elegantly. In this essay, he says,

> The Pagan stories are all about somebody dying and rising, either every year, or else nobody knows where and nobody knows when. The Christian story is about a historical personage, whose execution can be dated pretty accurately, under a named Roman magistrate, and with whom the society that He founded is in a continuous relation down to the present day. It is not the difference between falsehood and truth. It is the difference between a real event on the one hand and dim dreams or premonitions of that same event on the other.[32]

That essay then concludes with the words that can be found on Lewis's commemorative stone in Westminster Abbey's Poets Corner: "I believe in Christianity as I believe that the Sun has risen, not only because I see it, but because by it I see everything else."[33]

Through C. S. Lewis, a multitude of Americans have learned to believe in Christianity because they have seen it come to life in his writings, and by those writings he has shown them how to see everything through the lens of the Christian faith. That is his legacy. That is what a man who never saw America has given to Americans—an illumined Christianity that lights up all of life.

---

32. Lewis, "Is Theology Poetry?" 128–29.
33. Ibid., 140.

Bibliography

"About the C. S. Lewis Institute." http://www.cslewisinstitute.org.
"About Philip Yancey." Official Philip Yancey website. http://philipyancey.com/about.
Aitken, Jonathan. *Charles W. Colson: A Life Redeemed.* Colorado Springs, CO: Waterbrook, 2005.
Alan Mason Chesney Medical Archives of the Johns Hopkins Medical Institutions. http://www.medicalarchives.jhmi.edu/papers/firor.html.
Alcorn, Randy. "About Randy," EPM: Eternal Perspective Ministries, http://www.epm.org/about-randy/.
———. "C. S. Lewis on Heaven and the New Earth: God's Eternal Remedy to the Problem of Evil and Suffering." In *The Romantic Rationalist: God, Life, and Imagination in the Work of C. S. Lewis*, edited by John Piper and David Mathis, 105–29. Wheaton, IL: Crossway, 2014.
———. "Learning to Love God While Fearing Him." In *Mere Christians: Inspiring Stories of Encounters with C. S. Lewis*, edited by Mary Anne Phemister and Andrew Lazo, 40–42. Grand Rapids, MI: Baker Books, 2009.
Author Societies Archive, Box 1, Folder 13—The New York C. S. Lewis Society, The Marion E. Wade Center. Wheaton College, Wheaton, IL.
Bayley, Peter. "From Master to Colleague." In *Remembering C. S. Lewis: Recollections of Those Who Knew Him*, edited by James T. Como, 164–76. San Francisco: Ignatius, 2005.
Brady, Charles A. "C. S. Lewis II," *America* 71 (10 June 1944); reprinted in *The New York C. S. Lewis Society Bulletin #26* (December 1971).
———. "Finding God in Narnia," *America* (27 October 1956); reprinted in *The New York C. S. Lewis Society Bulletin #30* (April 1972).
———. "Introduction to Lewis," *America* 71 (27 May 1944); reprinted in *The New York C. S. Lewis Society Bulletin #25* (November 1971).
Chad Walsh Papers. The Marion E. Wade Center. Wheaton College, Wheaton, IL
Colson, Charles. *Born Again.* Old Tappan, NJ: Chosen, 1976.
———. *God and Government: An Insider's View on the Boundaries between Faith & Politics.* Grand Rapids, MI: Zondervan, 2007.
——— and Nancy Pearcey. *How Now Shall We Live?* Wheaton, IL: Tyndale House, 1999.
——— with Ellen Santilli Vaughn. *The Body.* Dallas, TX: Word, 1992.

Como, James T. "An *Apologia* on the Way." In *Mere Christians: Inspiring Stories of Encounters with C. S. Lewis*, edited by Mary Anne Phemister and Andrew Lazo, 85–88. Grand Rapids, MI: Baker Books, 2009.

———. *Branches of Heaven: The Geniuses of C. S. Lewis*. Dallas, TX; Spence, 1998.

———, ed. *Remembering C. S. Lewis: Recollections of Those Who Knew Him*. San Francisco: Ignatius, 2005.

C. S. Lewis Foundation. www.cslewis.org.

C. S. Lewis Letter Collection, The Marion E. Wade Center, Wheaton College. Wheaton, IL.

C. S. Lewis Institute. www.cslewisinstitute.org.

"C. S. Lewis: Mere Christian." Official Philip Yancey website. http://philipyancey.com/c-s-lewis-mere-christian.

C. S. Lewis Testimonies Archive, 1959–1996. The Marion E. Wade Center, Wheaton College. Wheaton, IL.

Davidman, Joy. "The Longest Way Round. In *These Found the Way: Thirteen Converts to Protestant Christianity*, edited by David Welsey Soper, 13-26. Philadelphia: Westminster, 1951.

Dorsett, Lyle W. *And God Came In: The Extraordinary Story of Joy Davidman*. Peabody, MA: Hendrickson, 2009.

———. *Seeking the Secret Place: The Spiritual Formation of C. S. Lewis*. Grand Rapids, MI: Brazos, 2004.

———. "The Writing of C. S. Lewis Has Changed My Life." In *Mere Christians: Inspiring Stories of Encounters with C. S. Lewis*, edited by Mary Anne Phemister and Andrew Lazo, 95–96. Grand Rapids, MI: Baker Books, 2009.

Downing, David C. "When the Science Is Fiction but the Faith Is Real." In *Mere Christians: Inspiring Stories of Encounters with C. S. Lewis*, edited by Mary Anne Phemister and Andrew Lazo, 97–102. Grand Rapids, MI: Baker Books, 2009.

Gledhill, Ruth. "Church Attendance Has Been Propped Up by Immigrants, Says Study." *The Guardian*, 3 June 2014. http://www.theguardian.com/world/2014/jun/03/churchattendance-propped-immigrants-study.

Hart, Trevor. "C. S. Lewis and America From the Other Side of the Pond." *C. S. Lewis and American Culture Seminar*. Wheaton College, 1 November 2013 (MP3 audio).

Hooper, Walter, ed. *The Collected Letters of C. S. Lewis, 3 Vols*. San Francisco: HarperCollins, 2007.

———. "Editing Lewis."

———. E-mail to K. Alan Snyder, 24 October 2014.

———. "Introduction." *The Weight of Glory*. San Francisco: HarperCollins, 2001.

———. "My Original Encounter with C. S. Lewis." In *Mere Christians: Inspiring Stories of Encounters with C. S. Lewis*, edited by Mary Anne Phemister and Andrew Lazo, 139–42. Grand Rapids, MI: Baker Books, 2009.

———. "Personal Testimony." Originally titled "Rockingham CC."

———, ed. *Present Concerns: Essays by C. S. Lewis*. New York: Harcourt Brace Jovanovich, 1986.

———, ed. *They Stand Together: The Letters of C. S. Lewis to Arthur Greeves, 1914–1963*. New York: Macmillan, 1979.

———. "What About Mrs. Boshell?" In *C. S. Lewis Remembered: Collected Reflections of Students, Friends, & Colleagues*, edited by Harry Lee Poe and Rebecca Whitten Poe, 36–51. Grand Rapids, MI: Zondervan, 2006.

Howard, Thomas. "We All Have the Same Difficulty." In *Mere Christians: Inspiring Stories of Encounters with C. S. Lewis*, edited by Mary Anne Phemister and Andrew Lazo, 143–45. Grand Rapids, MI: Baker Books, 2009.
http://www.pumphreyfuneralhome.com/obituary/Vera-Marie-Gebbert/Washington-DC/1461076.
http://www.regent-college.edu/faculty/retired/james-houston.
Jacobs, Alan. *The Narnian: The Life and Imagination of C. S. Lewis*. San Francisco: HarperCollins, 2005.
Kilby, Clyde S. "C. S. Lewis: Everyman's Theologian." *Christianity Today*, 3 January 1964.
———. "An Interpretation of *Till We Have Faces*," 1968–1969. Submitted by Carol Wald Saia, a former student of Kilby's.
———, ed. *Letters to an American Lady*. Grand Rapids, MI: William B. Eerdmans, 1967.
———. "A Visit with C. S. Lewis," *Kodon* VIII (December 1953) 11, 28, 30.
King, Don W., ed. *Out of My Bone: The Letters of Joy Davidman*. Grand Rapids, MI: Wm. B. Eerdmans, 2009.
———. "A Writer We Can Read for the Rest of Our Lives." In *Mere Christians: Inspiring Stories of Encounters with C. S. Lewis*, edited by Mary Anne Phemister and Andrew Lazo, 159–61. Grand Rapids, MI: Baker Books, 2009.
Kirkus Review, 18 January 1956. https://www.kirkusreviews.com/book-reviews/chad-walsh/behold-the-glory/.
Lewis, C. S. "Foreword." In Joy Davidman, *Smoke on the Mountain: An Interpretation of the Ten Commandments*. Philadelphia: Westminster, 1954.
McGovern, Eugene. "Our Need for Such a Guide." In *Remembering C. S. Lewis: Recollections of Those Who Knew Him*, edited by James T. Como, 227–38. San Francisco: Ignatius, 2005.
McGrath, Alister. *C. S. Lewis, A Life: Eccentric Genius, Reluctant Prophet*. Colorado Springs, CO: Tyndale House, 2013.
Marsden, George. "*Mere Christianity* and American Culture." *C. S. Lewis and American Culture Seminar*. Wheaton College, 1 November 2013 (MP3 audio).
Martindale, Wayne. "The Great Divorce: Journey to Heaven and Hell." In *C. S. Lewis: Life, Works, and Legacy, Vol. 3*, edited by Bruce L. Edwards, 133–52. Santa Barbara, CA: Praeger, 2007.
New York C. S. Lewis Society. www.nyclssociety.com.
New York C. S. Lewis Society Charter, 25 May 1970.
The New York C. S. Lewis Society Bulletin #7 (May 1970).
Noll, Mark A. "C. S. Lewis in America, 1932–1945." *C. S. Lewis and American Culture Seminar*. Wheaton College, 1 November 2013 (MP3 audio).
Obituary. "Chad Walsh, Teacher and Writer of Poetry and Prose." *New York Times*, 19 January 1991. http://www.nytimes.com/1991/01/19/obituaries/chad-walsh-teacher-and-writer-of-poetry-and-prose.html.
Patterson, W. Brown. "C. S. Lewis: Personal Reflections." In *C. S. Lewis Remembered: Collected Reflections of Students, Friends, & Colleagues*, edited by Harry Lee Poe and Rebecca Whitten Poe, 89–97. Grand Rapids, MI: Zondervan, 2006.
Phemister, Mary Anne. "A Mind Sharp as a Scalpel." In *Mere Christians: Inspiring Stories of Encounters with C. S. Lewis*, edited by Mary Anne Phemister and Andrew Lazo, 156–58. Grand Rapids, MI: Baker Books, 2009.

Ryken, Philip G. "C. S. Lewis as the Patron Saint of American Evangelicalism." In *Beyond Aslan: Essays on C. S. Lewis*, edited by Burton K. Janes, 60–82. Bridge-Logos, 2006.

———. "Winsome Evangelist: The Influence of C. S. Lewis." In *C. S. Lewis: Lightbearer in the Shadowlands*, edited by Angus J. L. Menuge, 55–78. Crossway, 1997.

Sayer, George. *Jack: C. S. Lewis and His Times*. San Francisco: Harper & Row, 1988.

Shattuck, Kelly. "7 Startling Facts: An Up Close Look at Church Attendance in America." *Church Leaders*, n.d. http://www.churchleaders.com/pastors/pastor-articles/139575-7-startling-facts-an-up-close-look-at-church-attendance-in-america.html.

Snyder, K. Alan. "Survey: The Influence of C. S. Lewis on American Christians," 2014. C. S. Lewis Testimonies Archive. The Marion E. Wade Center, Wheaton College. Wheaton, IL.

Starr, Nathan Comfort. "Good Cheer and Sustenance." In *Remembering C. S. Lewis: Recollections of Those Who Knew Him*, edited by James T. Como, 219–26. San Francisco: Ignatius, 2005.

"Symposium on Religion and Culture in Elizabethan England." The University of the South, 27 February 2015. http://theology.sewanee.edu/news/event/symposium-on-religion-and-culture-in-elizabethan-england.

Trexler, Robert. "A Brief History of the New York C. S. Lewis Society." A talk given at Taylor University's C. S. Lewis & Friends Symposium, June 2014. In *The New York C. S. Lewis Society Bulletin* #464 (November/December 2014).

Vanauken, Sheldon. *A Severe Mercy*. San Francisco: Harper & Row, 1977.

Wacker, Grant. *America's Pastor: Billy Graham and the Shaping of a Nation*. Cambridge, MA: The Belknap Press of Harvard University Press, 2014.

Walsh, Chad. *C. S. Lewis: Apostle to the Skeptics*. Macmillan, 1949.

———. "Impact on America." In *Light on C. S. Lewis*, edited by Jocelyn Gibb, 106–16. Harcourt Brace Jovanovich, 1976.

———. "Several Roads Lead to Jerusalem." In *These Found the Way: Thirteen Converts to Protestant Christianity*, edited by David Soper, 117–28. Philadelphia: Westminster, 1951.

Woodcock, Sue. "Clyde Kilby: Friend and Curator of the Oxford Christians." *Wheaton Alumni* (July/August 1977) 23.

Yancey, Philip. "Shadow Mentor." In *Mere Christians: Inspiring Stories of Encounters with C. S. Lewis*, edited by Mary Anne Phemister and Andrew Lazo, 211–14. Grand Rapids, MI: Baker Books, 2009.

Index

A

A Grief Observed, 47, 156, 160, 162
A Naked Tree: Love Sonnets to C. S. Lewis and Other Poems, 95
A Preface to Paradise Lost, 140, 156
A Severe Mercy, vi, 72, 79, 108
A Travel Guide to Heaven, 92
Abolition of Man, The, xi, 5, 77, 79, 84, 86, 106, 118, 159, 160
Ackland, Joss, 162, 163
Acland Nursing Home, 54–56
Adelmann, Father Frederick Joseph, 7
Adler, Mortimer, 76
Africa, 187
Agnosticism, 16, 17, 67, 90, 138, 181, 186
Albert C. Outler Prize in Ecumenical History, 83
Alcorn, Randy, 92, 98–100
Allegory of Love, The, 3, 83, 140, 182
Allen, Belle, 13, 119, 120, 122
Allen, Edward, 9–11, 13, 119–22
Alpha, 144
Ambassadors for Christ, 144
America, 5, 64
American Freeman, The, 21
American Library Association, 94
American Society of Church History, 83
An Experiment in Criticism, 89, 135
And God Came In, 91
Anderson, Hans Christian, 65
Anya, 28

Apologetics, xv, 15, 23, 25, 76, 89, 126, 143–45, 152, 156, 160, 177–81, 183, 186
Apostle to the Skeptics, 21, 22, 24, 31
Aquinas, Thomas, 140
Aristotle, 171
Arnold, Benedict, 55
Aslan, 65, 99, 135, 165, 167, 168, 171, 186
Atheism, 16–18, 27–32, 37, 47, 58, 79, 155, 173, 181, 186
Atlantic Monthly, The, 19
Atlee, Clement, 118
Atomic Bomb, 120, 127
Attenborough, Richard, 162
Augustine, 18, 140

B

Baker, Tom, 167
Barfield, Owen, 60, 61, 79, 141
Basic Christianity, 180
Bayley, Peter, 40
BBC, 6, 73, 162–64, 166, 168, 183
Beeson Divinity School at Samford University, 91
Behold the Glory, 23
Beloit College, xv, 4, 16
Benét, Stephen Vincent, 11
Benét, William Rose, 31
Beyond the Shadowlands: C. S. Lewis on Heaven and Hell, 93

Bide, Peter, 44
Birth Control, 34
Bles, Geoffrey, 138
Bloom, Claire, 162
Bob Jones University, 50
Bodleian Library, 61, 74, 78, 80
Body, The, 105
Born Again, 101, 181
Boston College, 7
Boucher, Anthony, 10
Boxen, 179
Boyer, William, 129
Bradbury, Ray, 10
Brady, Charles, 5, 10, 64–66, 79
BreakPoint, 105
British Museum, 80
Broadcast Talks, 142
Broken Pattern, 129
Brown University, 100
Bryn Mawr College, 4
Buckley, William F., 139
Buddhism, 147
Bush, Douglas, 23

C

C. S. Lewis at the Breakfast Table, 90
C. S. Lewis College, 149, 150, 174
C. S. Lewis Faculty Forum, 147
C. S. Lewis Fellows Program, 143–45
C. S. Lewis Foundation, xiii, xvi, 138, 145–50, 161
C. S. Lewis Institute, xvi, 138, 142–45, 150
C. S. Lewis Summer Institute (Oxbridge), 148
C. S. Lewis, Poet: The Legacy of His Poetic Impulse, 95
C. S. Lewis: A Companion and Guide, 62
C. S. Lewis: Letters to Children, 91
Cambridge University, 7, 15, 23, 36, 38, 39, 46, 57, 71, 74, 85, 107, 115, 133, 184–86
Campus Life, 96
Cancer, xv, 42, 45–47, 102, 117
Canisius College, 5, 64
Capitalism, 28

Carroll, Lewis, 65
Case for Faith, The, 92
CBS, 162
Chambers, Whittaker, 128
Cherwell River, 83
Chesterton, G. K., 65, 68, 74, 79, 90
Christensen, Michael, 180
Christian Book of the Year Award, 96
Christian Century, The, 76
Christian Scholar's Review, 95
Christian World of C. S. Lewis, The, 15, 73, 78, 183
Christianity Today, 15, 76–78, 96, 177
Church, Anglican, 4, 33, 41, 43, 44, 50, 54, 184
Church, Catholic, 4, 5, 7, 25, 87, 106, 131, 182, 187
Church, Episcopal, 100, 103, 122, 125, 131
Church, Presbyterian, 5, 110, 154
Churchill, Winston, 9
Cold War, 121
Colgate University, 79
Collected Poems of C. S. Lewis, The: A Critical Edition, 95
Colson, Charles, xvi, 61, 100–108, 173, 181
Communism, xv, 28, 29, 31, 47, 62, 121, 127, 128, 173
Communist Party, 28, 29, 41
Como, James, 1, 88–90, 139
Congregation of the Sisters of the Holy Redeemer, 125
Conscience, 105, 120
Conversion, 1, 3, 16, 27, 29, 33, 34, 64, 68, 69, 85, 90, 96, 102, 105, 109, 127, 151, 152, 155, 169, 173, 178, 180, 181

D

Dante, 140
Davidman, Jeannette Spivack, 26, 28, 37
Davidman, Joseph Isaac, 26, 27, 37
Davidman, Joy. *See* Lewis, Joy

Death, ix, x, xv, 7, 18, 25, 47, 59, 60, 62, 69–72, 77, 78, 84, 86, 108, 112, 117, 119, 122, 132, 133, 139, 141, 168, 173, 175, 181, 183, 185
Declaration of Independence, 186
DeStefano, Anthony, 92
Dickens, Charles, 2
Discarded Image, The, 106
Discipleship, 143–45, 151, 153, 174, 184
Disney, 97, 166, 168
Divorce, 35, 36, 39–41, 98, 114, 116, 117
Dorsett, Lyle, 41, 44, 90, 91, 122
Downing, David, 93, 94
Downton Abbey, 185
Duke University, 161
Dymer, 10

E

Eastern Europe, 187
Economics, 117, 120
Economy, 12
Education, 17, 36, 41, 46, 64, 79, 85, 112, 114, 118, 145–47, 149
Eldredge, John, 92
Elizabethtown College, 94
Elliot, Elisabeth, 86
Elliot, Jim, 86
Ellsberg, Daniel, 101
Elzinga, Kenneth, 150
Episcopal Radio Hour, 164
Episcopal Radio-TV Foundation, 24, 46, 164, 186
Episcopal Theological School, 85
Eternal Perspective Ministries, 98
Evangelical Christian Publishers Association, 94, 96
Evangelicals, xi, xv–xvii, 4, 15, 73, 86, 87, 93, 96, 145, 153, 174, 177–82, 185, 186
Evangelism, 152, 155, 157, 169, 178, 181
Everlasting Man, The, 68
Evidence That Demands a Verdict, 159
Evil, 17, 87, 104, 112
Existentialism, 177

F

Farrer, Austin, 60
Farrer, Katherine, 60
Fascism, 28
Firor, Warfield, ix, x, 7, 8, 10–12, 109–13, 119
Forgiveness, 132
Four Loves, The, 24, 46, 100, 108, 156, 160, 164
France, 1, 138
Freud, Sigmund, 27
Ft. Benning, 86
Ft. Bragg, 50

G

Gebbert, Charles, 113, 116, 118
Gebbert, Karl, 113, 117
Gebbert, Vera, 9, 11–13, 113–20, 122, *See also* Mathews, Vera
Germany, 17, 121
Gibb, Jock, 61
God and Government, 106
God in the Dock, 61, 106
Goelz, Genia, 122, 124
Gold Medallion Book Award, 94
Gordon College, 87, 145
Gospels, 18, 34, 179
Graham, Billy, xii, 15, 91, 107, 180
Great Depression, 28
Great Divorce, The, xi, 5, 29, 32, 91–93, 115, 141, 152, 160, 171, 177, 186
Greece, 47, 84
Green Pastures, 148
Greeves, Arthur, 2
Gresham, David, 29, 33, 36, 41, 42, 44, 116
Gresham, Douglas, 29, 36, 41, 42, 44, 57, 59, 91, 116, 141
Gresham, Joy. *See* Lewis, Joy
Gresham, William Lindsay (Bill), 29, 33, 35, 36, 38–40, 42, 44, 45
Griffiths, Dom Bede, 11

H

Hanegraaf, Hank, 92
HarperCollins, 62
Hart, Trevor, 9, 182, 184, 186
Harvard University, 4, 79, 100
Harwood, Cecil, 60
Havard, Robert (Humphrey), 53
Hawthorne, Nathaniel, 2, 10
Heaven, xi, 91–93, 98, 155, 180
Heaven by Alcorn, 92
Heaven by Tada, 92
Heine, Heinrich, 21
Hell, xi, 55, 93, 95
Henry, Carl, 15, 180
Hinduism, 67, 147
His, 5
Hiskey, James, 142
Hitler, Adolf, 11, 17, 67, 68
Hobbit, The, 86
Hollywood, 162–64, 167–69, 172
Holmes, Sherlock, 185
Holy Spirit, 68, 170
Holy Trinity Church, 58
Hooker, Richard, 140
Hooper, Walter, xii, xiii, xvi, 14, 48–63, 78, 80, 81, 88–90, 108, 109, 134, 141, 173
Hopkins, Anthony, 162, 163
Horse and His Boy, The, 36
Houston, James, 142
How Now Shall We Live?, 106
Howard, Thomas, 86, 87, 141, 150
Huckleberry Finn, 10
Humanitarian Theory of Punishment, The, 106
Huxley, Aldous, 21

I

Images of Salvation in the Fiction of C. S. Lewis, 74
Imagination, 19, 85, 94, 99, 146, 154, 160, 169, 175, 177, 180–84, 186
Ingersoll, Robert, 16, 21
Inklings, 5, 52, 53, 80, 87, 90, 108, 110, 111, 113, 161

International Arthurian Society, 81
International Christian Community-Eurasia, 144
InterVarsity Christian Fellowship, 5, 181
Into the Region of Awe, 94
Into the Wardrobe, 94
Ireland, 14, 45
Belfast, 2, 143, 150, 179
Iron Curtain, 61, 118
Is Theology Poetry?, 188
Islam, 147
Israel, 74

J

Jacobs, Alan, 1, 182, 184
Japan, 14, 120
Jerusalem, 75
Jesuits, 5, 7, 64
Jesus Christ, 18, 27, 30–34, 49, 56, 58, 65, 68, 76, 86, 91, 96, 98, 100, 102–5, 107, 132, 135, 142, 143, 147, 149, 150, 153, 155, 156, 169, 172, 179
Jesus I Never Knew, The, 96
Jewish-Jews, xv, 17, 26–28, 30, 31, 47, 74, 147, 173
John Brown's Body, 11
John Paul II, 62
Johns Hopkins, ix, 110
Jones, Bob, 50
Journalism, 5, 10, 28, 53, 58, 75
Jungle Books, 65

K

Kalmbach, Herb, 105
Kantzer, Kenneth, 86
Kennedy, John F., x, 59
Kilby, Clyde, xvi, 7, 15, 73–80, 88–91, 108, 129, 141, 173, 183
Kilmer, Hugh, 135
Kilmer, Joyce, 129
Kilmer, Kenton, 129
Kilmer, Martin, 135
Kilns, xvi, 35, 36, 42, 44, 51, 53, 54, 56, 57, 60, 73, 82, 86, 116, 117, 146–49, 161, 170, 174, 179

Kilns Association, 146
King Arthur Today: The Arthurian Legend in English and American Literature, 1901-1953, 79
King James VI and I and the Reunion of Christendom, 83
King, Don, 94, 95
Kipling, Rudyard, 65
Kirkus Review, 23
Knowing and Doing, 144
Krieg, Laurence, 135
Krieg, Philinda, 135
Kynes, Bill, 145

L

Lancaster, Joan, 136, 137
Last Battle, The, 160, 171, 180
Lenin, Vladimir, 31
Letter to a Comrade, 28
Letters to an American Lady, 129
Letters to Malcolm Chiefly on Prayer, 61, 125
Letters to Young Churches, 49
Lewis, Albert, 1, 2, 118
Lewis, C. S.
   America, Attitude toward, xv, 1–3, 8–10, 12, 14, 53, 173
   America, Invitations to Visit, ix, 6–8, 12, 23, 24, 75, 110, 111, 123
   American Academics, Relationships with
      Brady, Charles, 5, 10, 66, 79
      Hooper, Walter, xii, xvi, 14, 48, 50–59, 63, 81, 108, 173
      Howard, Thomas, 86–88
      Kilby, Clyde, xvi, 7, 15, 74–77, 79, 90, 108, 173
      Madeleva, Sister, 6, 10
      More, Paul Elmer, 4, 10
      Patterson, William Brown, 83–85
      Starr, Nathan Comfort, 10, 12, 79–81
      Vanauken, Sheldon, xvi, 66–73, 79, 108, 173
   Walsh, Chad, xv, 19–21, 23–25, 31, 35, 40, 42, 43, 47, 81, 108, 173, 174
   Young, Karl, 6, 10
   American Literature, Views on, 2, 10, 11
   American Politics and Government, Views on, 11, 127
   British Politics and Government, Views on, 10, 12, 13, 21, 113, 118, 120, 121, 127, 128
   Death, Attitude toward, ix, x, 47, 58, 69, 71, 112, 119, 124, 132, 133
   Education, Views on, 46, 81, 112, 118
   Gifts from Americans, 9, 10, 13, 110, 111, 114, 119
   Health Concerns, 7, 47, 54–56, 82, 116, 123, 128, 132
   Humility of, 21, 50, 57, 70, 75, 87, 89, 114
   Money, Attitude toward, 55, 59, 107, 116, 129, 131
   Prayer, Views on, 125
   Writings
      A Grief Observed, 47, 156, 160, 162
      A Preface to Paradise Lost, 140, 156
      Abolition of Man, The, xi, 5, 77, 79, 84, 86, 106, 118, 159, 160
      Allegory of Love, The, 3, 83, 140, 182
      An Experiment in Criticism, 89, 135
      Broadcast Talks, 142
      Chronicles of Narnia, The, x, xvi, 6, 46, 65, 66, 85, 87, 96, 97, 99, 109, 134, 135, 153, 155, 157–60, 164, 165, 167, 170, 171, 174, 177, 179, 186
      Horse and His Boy, The, 36
      Last Battle, The, 35, 160, 171, 180
      Lion, the Witch, and the Wardrobe, The, 60, 94, 99, 115, 134, 159, 160, 164–68, 179
      Magician's Nephew, The, 129, 134
      Prince Caspian, 99, 164–68
      Silver Chair, The, 99, 164

Lewis, C. S. (*cont.*)
    Voyage of the Dawn Treader, The, 164–68, 171
    Discarded Image, The, 106
    Dymer, 10
    Four Loves, The, 24, 46, 100, 108, 156, 160, 164
    God in the Dock, 61, 106
    Great Divorce, The, xi, 5, 29, 32, 91, 115, 141, 152, 160, 171, 177, 186
    Humanitarian Theory of Punishment, The, 106
    Introduction to Letters to Young Churches, 49
    Is Theology Poetry?, 188
    Letters to an American Lady, 129
    Letters to Malcolm Chiefly on Prayer, 61, 125
    Mere Christianity, xvi, 6, 15, 73, 86, 90, 96, 97, 102, 103, 105, 106, 109, 153, 155, 156, 158–60, 170, 171, 177, 180, 183, 184
    Ministering Angels, 11
    Miracles, xi, 49, 50, 74, 86, 106, 135, 153, 159, 160
    On the Transmission of Christianity, 147
    Out of the Silent Planet, xi, 3, 10, 99, 134, 160, 186
    Oxford History of English Literature, The, 7, 35, 113, 115, 140
    Perelandra, xi, 8, 10, 18, 19, 54, 89, 93, 94, 99, 135, 140, 153, 160, 171, 186
    Pilgrim's Regress, The, 3, 4, 27, 94, 122, 138, 152, 178, 182
    Preface to Smoke on the Mountain, 38
    Problem of Pain, The, xi, 3, 74, 97, 99, 127, 140, 160
    Screwtape Letters, The, xi, 3–5, 29, 55, 65, 66, 75, 79, 86, 90, 95, 106, 115, 118, 128, 140, 142, 152–54, 158–60, 170, 171, 175, 186
    Screwtape Proposes a Toast, 46
    Shoddy Lands, The, 11
    Spirits in Bondage, 10
    Surprised by Joy, 36, 39, 60, 90, 123, 130, 138, 156, 159, 171, 178
    That Hideous Strength, xi, 10, 19, 31, 66, 99, 114, 130, 153, 160, 169, 186
    Till We Have Faces, 40, 46, 75, 76, 87, 130, 160
    Weight of Glory, The, 63, 154, 160, 171
Lewis, Joy, x, xv, 3, 7, 24–47, 53, 60, 73, 81, 82, 91, 95, 108, 116, 118, 122, 123, 132, 173
Lewis, Warren (Warnie), 2, 6, 35, 36, 60, 61, 78, 90, 109, 117, 121, 137, 141, 172
Lion, the Witch, and the Wardrobe, The, 60, 94, 99, 115, 134, 159, 160, 164–68, 179
Looking for the King: An Inklings Novel, 94
Lord of the Rings, The, 53, 86
Lowell, James Russell, 3, 10
Lucado, Max, 92
Lynchburg College, 70

M

MacDonald, George, 65, 77, 79, 94
Madeleva, Sister, 6, 10
Magdalen College, 20, 37, 39, 69, 80, 82, 111
Magician's Nephew, The, 129, 134
Malory, Thomas, 140
Marion E. Wade Center, xii, xiii, 91, 151, 157, 161
Marriage, xv, 7, 12, 29, 33, 35, 36, 41, 42, 44–47, 71, 72, 98, 116, 124, 173, 187
Marsden, George, 15, 182–84
Martin Chuzzlewit, 2
Martindale, Wayne, 91, 92
Marx, Karl, 28
Marxism, 28, 31, 32

INDEX

Mathews, Vera, ix, x, 9, 113, *See also* Gebbert, Vera
Mattson, Stanley, 145, 149
McAlpine, Stuart, 145
McDowell, Josh, 159
McGovern, Eugene, 139, 140
McGrath, Alister, xi, 145, 172, 180–82
Mead, Marjorie Lamp, 91
Mencken, H. L., 17
Mere Christianity, xvi, 6, 15, 73, 74, 86, 90, 96, 97, 102, 103, 105, 106, 109, 153–56, 158–60, 170, 171, 177, 180, 183, 184
Merton, Thomas, 4
Milton Society of America, 23
Milton, John, 140
Ministering Angels, 11
Miracles, xi, 49, 50, 74, 86, 106, 135, 153, 159, 160
Montreat College, 94
Moody, Dwight L., 149
Moore, Janie King, x, 6, 7, 123
More, Paul Elmer, 4, 10
Most Reluctant Convert, The: C. S. Lewis's Journey to Faith,, 94
Mother Teresa, 107
Mythopoeic Society, 94, 161

N

Narnia, x, xvi, 6, 24, 35, 36, 46, 65, 66, 85, 87, 95–97, 99, 109, 134, 135, 153, 155, 157–61, 164–67, 170–72, 174, 177, 179, 186
Narnia and Beyond: A Guide to the Fiction of C. S. Lewis, 87
Narnian, The: The Life and Imagination of C. S. Lewis, 1
National Institute of Arts and Letters, 28
National Review, 88, 139
Navigators, 93
New Masses, 28
New York C. S. Lewis Society, xvi, 87, 89, 138–42, 150, 161
New York Times, 4, 16, 101
New York Times Book Review, 31
New York University, 73

Newman, Hila, 134
Nixon, Richard, xvi, 101, 105
Noel, Henry, 138, 139
Noll, Mark, 4, 174, 182
Notre Dame University, 6
Novels of Charles Williams, The, 87

O

Obedience, 126, 143
On the Transmission of Christianity, 147
Orthodoxy, 90
Out of My Bone, 95
Out of the Silent Planet, xi, 3, 10, 99, 134, 160, 186
Oxford, xvi, 13, 23, 37, 48, 51, 69, 80, 82, 89, 111, 114, 146, 187
Oxford Center for Evangelism and Apologetics, 145
Oxford History of English Literature, The, ix, 7, 35, 113, 115, 140
Oxford University, ix, x, xvi, 2, 6, 10, 14, 20, 21, 23, 31, 36, 37, 64, 66, 67, 69, 70, 73–75, 78–80, 83, 85, 123, 132, 142, 150, 161, 175, 178, 179, 182, 184–86
Oxford University C. S. Lewis Society, 178

P

Patterson, William Brown, 83–85
Paul, Apostle, 132
PBS, 162
Pentagon Papers, 101
Pentecostals, 187
Perelandra, xi, 8, 10, 18, 19, 54, 89, 93, 94, 99, 135, 140, 153, 160, 171, 186
Personal Heresy, The, 4
Phantastes, 32, 94
Phillips, J. B., 49
Phillips, Tom, 102–5
Piccadilly Hotel, 37
Pierce, Renée, 33, 35, 40
Pilgrim's Regress, The, 3, 4, 27, 94, 122, 138, 152, 178, 182

Pittenger, Norman, 76, 77
Planets in Peril: A Critical Study of C. S. Lewis's Ransom Trilogy, 94
Plato, 171
Poetry, 4, 6, 10, 11, 22, 23, 27, 28, 31, 34, 50, 80, 129, 149, 188
Poetry Society of Virginia, 129
Poets Corner, 172, 188
Poland, 17, 61, 62, 187
Politics, 11, 85, 114, 127, 149, 174, 177
   American Government, 11
   British Government, 10, 12, 21, 113, 117, 121
   Conservatism, 11, 12
   Democracy, 127, 128
   Democrats, 11
   Freedom-Liberty, 11, 12
   Labour Party, 12, 110, 113, 118, 120, 121, 128
   Social Democrats, 28
   Socialism, 9, 11–13, 28
Porter, Kenneth, 33, 34
Postmodernism, 181
Poulter, Will, 167
Prayer, 103, 123, 125, 126, 136, 143, 179
Prejudice, 1, 3, 10, 14
Presbyterian Guardian, 4
Pride, 97, 100, 102, 104, 105
Prince Caspian, 99, 164–68
Prison Fellowship, xvi, 61, 105–7, 173
Problem of Pain, The, xi, 3, 74, 97, 99, 127, 140, 160
Protestants, 4, 106, 182
Psychiatry, 87
Purdue University, xi
Purgatory, 87

Q

Quotable Lewis, The, 92

R

Radcliffe College, 79
Rakestraw, Caroline, 164
Ramsden, Michael, 145
Ransom, Elwin, 18, 94, 170

Rationing, ix, 9, 12, 110, 119, 121
Ravi Zacharias International Ministries, 144
Raytheon Corporation, 102
Regent College, 142
Remembering C. S. Lewis: Recollections of Those Who Knew Him, 1, 90, 139
Renaissance, 74, 83, 85
Restrepo, Father George, 7
Resurrection, 33, 50, 71, 72, 92, 119, 132, 135
Revell, Fleming H., 148
Rhodes Scholarship, 83
Rollins College, 79, 81
Root, Jerry, 92
Rough Years, The, 24
Russell Loines Memorial Fund Award, 28
Russia-Soviet Union, 11, 121, 127
Ryken, Philip, 151, 152, 155, 156, 178, 179, 184

S

Sacred Romance, The, 92
Saturday Review, 5
Sayer, George, 3, 60
Sayers, Dorothy, 79
Schaeffer, Francis, 169
Schmidt, Laura, xiii
Scholars-in-Residence Program, 147
Science Fiction, x, xi, 10, 19, 69, 85, 98, 99, 142
Scientology, 33
Scotland, 9, 182
Screwtape, 55
Screwtape Letters, The, xi, 3–5, 29, 55, 65, 66, 75, 79, 86, 90, 95, 106, 115, 118, 128, 140, 142, 152–54, 158–60, 170, 171, 175, 177, 186
Screwtape Proposes a Toast, 46
Seeking the Secret Place: The Spiritual Formation of C. S. Lewis, 91
Shadowlands, 62, 156, 157, 162, 164, 183
Shakespeare, 84
Shelburne, Jacob, 129
Shelburne, Mary Willis, 12, 14, 45, 129–34

INDEX

Shoddy Lands, The, 11
Silver Chair, The, 99, 164
Smoke on the Mountain, 33, 35, 38
Society for the Prevention of Progress, The, 5
Socratic Club, 161
Solzhenitsyn, Alexander, 107
Sophocles, 84
Southeastern University, xiii
Southern Wesleyan University, 161
Spanish Civil War, 29
Spenser, Edmund, 35, 140
Spirits in Bondage, 10
St. John's University, 79, 87
St. Mary's College, 6
Stalin, Josef, 67, 68, 121
Starr, Nathan Comfort, 10, 12, 79–82, 90
Starr, Nina, 81, 82
Statue of Liberty, 12
Stott, John R. W., 180, 181
Strobel, Lee, 92
Suffering, 127, 132
Suicide, 72
Summer Seminars, 148
Sunday Telegraph, 58
Surprised by Joy, 36, 39, 60, 90, 123, 130, 138, 156, 159, 171, 178
Swift, Jonathan, 14

T

Tada, Joni Eareckson, 92
Tao, 77
Taylor, Elizabeth, 53
Templeton Prize, 107
That Hideous Strength, xi, 10, 19, 31, 67, 99, 114, 130, 153, 160, 169, 186
The Magazine of Fantasy and Science Fiction, 11
Theology, 66, 76, 84, 93, 114, 122, 125, 127, 141, 144, 169, 174–78, 180, 184
Through Gates of Splendor, 86
Till We Have Faces, 40, 46, 75, 76, 87, 130, 160
Tillyard, E. M. W., 4
Time, 5, 6, 128, 130, 183

Tolkien, J. R. R., 79, 80, 82, 86, 87, 94, 120
Tom Sawyer, 10
Touchstone: A Journal of Mere Christianity, 174
Towner, Daniel, 149
Truman, Harry, 11
Twain, Mark, 10

U

Ukraine, 28
University of Arizona, 153
University of Arkansas, 73
University of Denver, 90, 91
University of Florida, 79
University of Kentucky, 48, 59
University of Minnesota, 73
University of North Carolina, 48
University of Redlands, 146
University of St. Andrews, 9, 182
University of the South, 83
University of Virginia, 17, 150

V

Van Deusen, Mary, 13, 122–28
Van Deusen, Van, 122
Vanauken, Jean (Davy), 66, 68–73, 108
Vanauken, Sheldon, vi, xvi, 66–73, 79, 80, 108, 173
Venus, 18
Vergil, 140
Voyage of the Dawn Treader, The, 164–68, 171

W

Walden, 167, 168
Walsh, Chad, xv, 4, 16–25, 31, 32, 34, 35, 38, 40, 42, 43, 45, 47, 51, 54, 56, 64, 78, 80, 81, 93, 108, 123, 173–78, 183
Walsh, Eva, 20, 34, 35, 42, 43, 45
War Poems of the United Nations, 28
Watergate Scandal, xvi, 101, 102

Weight of Glory, The, 63, 154, 160, 171
Welbon, Henry, 4
Wells, H. G., 65
Western Star, 11
Westminster Abbey, 188
Westminster Cathedral, 172
Westminster Theological Journal, 5
Westmont College, 93, 94, 179
What's So Amazing About Grace, 96
Wheaton College, xii, xiii, xvi, 7, 9, 15, 73, 76–79, 86, 89, 91, 108, 129, 151, 161, 179, 182
When Christ Comes, 92
Why I Believe in Narnia: 33 Reviews and Essays on the Life and Work of C. S. Lewis, 90
Wilberforce Forum, 105
Wilberforce, William, 105
William Perkins and the Making of a Protestant England, 83
Williams College, 79
Williams, Charles, 33, 34, 79, 82, 94, 115
Williams, Michal, 34
Wilson, Woodrow, 2
Winger, Debra, 162, 163

Wirt, Sherwood, 15
Witness, 128
Woodstock College, 7
World War I, 2, 6, 79
World War II, 2, 9, 10, 22, 79, 176, 183
Worship, x, 111, 113, 125

Y

Yale University, 6
Yale Younger Poet Competition, 28
Yancey, Philip, 96, 97
Yarros, Victor, 21
Yet One More Spring: A Critical Study of Joy Davidman, 95
York College of the City University of New York, 90
Young, Karl, 6, 10

Z

Zacharias, Ravi, 144
Zen Buddhism, 33

www.ingramcontent.com/pod-product-compliance
Lightning Source LLC
Chambersburg PA
CBHW070321230426
43663CB00011B/2184